Proxy Wars, Po[...]
Legacy of Arming Future Adversaries

Weapons of Misfortune

JOSH LUBERISSE

WEAPONS OF MISFORTUNE

Proxy Wars, Power Vacuums, and the U.S. Legacy of Arming Future Adversaries

Josh Luberisse

Fortis Novum Mundum

Copyright © 2024 Fortis Novum Mundum

All rights reserved

The characters and events portrayed in this book are fictitious. Any similarity to real persons, living or dead, is coincidental and not intended by the author.

While every precaution has been taken in the preparation of this book, the publisher assumes no responsibility for errors or omissions, or for damages resulting from the use of the information contained herein.

THE AUTHOR(S) AND PUBLISHER(S) EXPRESSLY DISCLAIM ANY AND ALL LIABILITY FOR ACTIONS TAKEN BASED ON THE CONTENT OF THIS WORK. READERS ASSUME ALL RISKS FOR ANY SUCH ACTIONS.

No part of this book may be reproduced, or stored in a retrieval system, or transmitted in any form or by any means, electronic, mechanical, photocopying, recording, or otherwise, without express written permission of the publisher.

The authors, publishers, and contributors to this book will not be held liable for any damage or harm caused by the misuse of the information contained within. All readers are advised and expected to use this information responsibly, ethically, and legally.

By reading and using the information in this book, you acknowledge and agree to these conditions. If you cannot agree to these conditions, please refrain from using this book and its content.

Cover design by: Fortis Novum Mundum

"You can't keep snakes in your backyard and expect them only to bite your neighbors. You know, eventually those snakes are going to turn on whoever has them in the backyard."

HILLARY RODHAM CLINTON, FORMER U.S. SECRETARY OF STATE

"America exists today to make war. How else do we interpret 19 straight years of war and no end in sight? It's part of who we are. It's part of what the American Empire is. We are going to cheat and steal to do whatever it is we have to do to continue this war complex. That's the truth of it. And that's the agony of it."

COL. LAWRENCE WILKERSON, US ARMY (RET.), CHIEF OF STAFF TO FORMER U.S. SECRETARY OF STATE COLIN POWELL

"And it's no secret to you that the thinkers and perceptive ones from among the Americans warned Bush before the war and told him: "All that you want for securing America and removing the weapons of mass destruction - assuming they exist - is available to you, and the nations of the world are with you in the inspections, and it is in the interest of America that it not be thrust into an unjustified war with an unknown outcome."

OSAMA BIN LADEN, FOUNDER OF AL-QAEDA

"We came, we saw, he died."

HILLARY RODHAM CLINTON, FORMER U.S. SECRETARY OF STATE

CONTENTS

Title Page

Copyright

Epigraph

Epigraph

Epigraph

Epigraph

Table of Contents

Preface

Introduction   1

Part I: The Iranian Catalyst   8

Chapter 1 - The 1953 Iranian Coup D'état: Operation Ajax and the Fall of Mosaddeq   9

Chapter 2 - The Shah's Regime: Modernization and Repression   14

Chapter 3 - The 1979 Iranian Revolution: Fall of the Shah and the Rise of Khomeini   21

Part II: The Cold War Battlegrounds   55

Chapter 4 - Operation Cyclone: Arming the Mujahideen in Afghanistan   56

Chapter 5 - The Soviet Withdrawal and the Power Vacuum in Afghanistan   69

Chapter 6 - Proxy Wars in Africa: Angola, Mozambique,   80

and the Legacy of U.S. Support for Insurgents

Part III: Post-9/11 Era: The War on Terror	99
Chapter 7 - Revisiting Afghanistan: Operation Enduring Freedom and the Fall of the Taliban	100
Chapter 8 - Operation Iraqi Freedom: The Fall of Saddam Hussein and the Rise of ISIS	126
Chapter 9 -. Syria: Civil War and Proxy Conflict	152
Part IV: The Middle East in Chaos	187
Chapter 10 - The Libyan Crisis: Gaddafi's Ouster and the Chaos Left Behind	188
Chapter 11 - Yemen: The Forgotten Proxy War	205
Chapter 12 - Rise of Iran as a Regional Power	233
Part V: Global Consequences	247
Chapter 13 - Expansion of The War on Terror: U.S. Intervention in Somalia, Niger, and Beyond	248
Chapter 14 - Role of Russia and China: New Power Players in the Middle East	267
Chapter 15 -. Reflections on U.S. Foreign Policy: Lessons Learned and the Path Forward	292
Appendices	313
Chronology of U.S. Interventions in the Middle East	315
Key Players in Proxy Wars: A Reference Guide	325
Glossary of Terms	331
Bibliography	339
About The Author	343
Books By This Author	345
Books In This Series	375

TABLE OF CONTENTS

Preface

Introduction

Part I: The Iranian Catalyst

Chapter 1 - The 1953 Iranian Coup D'état: Operation Ajax and the Fall of Mosaddeq

Chapter 2 - The Shah's Regime: Modernization and Repression

Chapter 3 - The 1979 Iranian Revolution: Fall of the Shah and the Rise of Khomeini

Part II: The Cold War Battlegrounds

Chapter 4 - Operation Cyclone: Arming the Mujahideen in Afghanistan

Chapter 5 - The Soviet Withdrawal and the Power Vacuum in Afghanistan

Chapter 6 - Proxy Wars in Africa: Angola, Mozambique, and the Legacy of U.S. Support for Insurgents

Part III: Post-9/11 Era: The War on Terror

Chapter 7 - Revisiting Afghanistan: Operation Enduring Freedom and the Fall of the Taliban

Chapter 8 - Operation Iraqi Freedom: The Fall of Saddam Hussein and the Rise of ISIS

Chapter 9 -. Syria: Civil War and Proxy Conflict

Part IV: The Middle East in Chaos

Chapter 10 - The Libyan Crisis: Gaddafi's Ouster and the Chaos Left Behind

Chapter 11 - Yemen: The Forgotten Proxy War

Chapter 12 - Rise of Iran as a Regional Power

Part V: Global Consequences

Chapter 13 - Expansion of The War on Terror: U.S. Intervention in Somalia, Niger, and Beyond

Chapter 14 - Role of Russia and China: New Power Players in the Middle East

Chapter 15 -. Reflections on U.S. Foreign Policy: Lessons Learned and the Path Forward

Chronology of U.S. Interventions in the Middle East

Key Players in Proxy Wars: A Reference Guide

Glossary of Terms

Bibliography

PREFACE

My personal favorite perk of studying history is the ability it offers to peer into the decisions of the past and compare the expectations of those making these decisions with the reality they ultimately produced. The choices made by leaders, particularly in the realm of foreign policy, are often driven by a mix of strategic goals, ideological beliefs, and immediate pressures. Yet, when looking back, it is clear that the outcomes of these decisions frequently diverge—sometimes dramatically—from the intended objectives. Nowhere is this more evident than in U.S. interventions in the **Middle East** over the past several decades.

The United States, in its quest to secure its interests, has repeatedly intervened in the affairs of other nations, often with the goal of protecting **national security**, promoting **democracy**, or maintaining **geopolitical dominance**. However, many of these interventions have led to unintended consequences, exacerbating instability rather than fostering the peace and prosperity that were promised. From the **1953 coup in Iran** to the **invasion of Iraq** in 2003, the patterns of U.S. foreign policy reveal recurring mistakes: **short-term victories** gained at the cost of **long-term stability**.

This book is an exploration of those decisions and their outcomes. It seeks to understand the deeper, more complex forces at play behind U.S. interventions in the Middle East, showing how many of these actions—whether motivated by ideological zeal, geopolitical rivalry, or economic interests—have failed to account for the broader historical context in which they occurred. By examining key case studies, this book illustrates the extent to which the U.S. has repeatedly underestimated the importance of understanding local dynamics, cultural nuances, and the long-standing political grievances of the nations it has sought to influence.

Take, for example, the **overthrow of Mohammad Mosaddegh** in Iran. The U.S. believed that by toppling a democratically elected leader and reinstating the **Shah**, it could secure a reliable ally in the Cold War. In the short term, the coup achieved its goal, but the longer-term consequences were disastrous. The U.S. failed to anticipate how the 1953 coup would contribute to the rise of **anti-Western sentiment** and **Islamic fundamentalism**, culminating in the **1979 Iranian Revolution** that brought **Ayatollah Khomeini** to power. What was meant to secure a pro-Western government in Iran instead created a theocratic regime that remains one of America's staunchest adversaries.

Similarly, the U.S. invasion of Iraq in **2003** was predicated on the belief that removing **Saddam Hussein** would lead to the establishment of democracy and a more stable Middle East. Yet, the decision to dismantle Iraq's military and political infrastructure created a **power vacuum** that led to a protracted civil war, the rise of **ISIS**, and ongoing regional instability. The U.S., once again, misjudged the complexities of Iraq's sectarian divisions and the broader regional implications of its intervention. The war may have removed a brutal dictator, but it also unleashed a wave of violence and chaos that continues to affect the region to this day.

These interventions—and others like them—highlight the core problem that has plagued U.S. foreign policy for decades: the failure to take a **long-term view**. Time and again, American policymakers have prioritized **immediate tactical victories** over the more difficult task of building sustainable political, economic, and social structures that can support long-term peace. The result has been a series of interventions that have temporarily succeeded in achieving their initial objectives but have ultimately left the region in greater disarray.

What becomes clear, as one examines the historical record, is that the **recurring flaws** in U.S. strategy stem from a fundamental misunderstanding of the **historical context** and **local dynamics** of the nations where the U.S. has chosen to intervene. From the **mujahideen** in Afghanistan, whom the U.S. armed and supported during the Soviet-Afghan War, to the **Libyan rebels** who received U.S. backing to overthrow **Muammar Gaddafi**, America's reliance on proxy forces has often backfired, as these groups have either turned against the U.S. or contributed to further destabilization.

The U.S. has also repeatedly miscalculated the implications of removing entrenched regimes without providing a clear vision for the future. This failure to anticipate the complexities of **nation-building** has resulted in prolonged conflict and the rise of extremist groups, as seen in Iraq, Libya, and **Syria**. In each case, the U.S. has been unable to create the stable, democratic governments it promised, leaving these countries in a state of chaos and uncertainty.

The reflections of former military officials and foreign policy experts reveal just how deep-seated these strategic flaws have been. **General David Petraeus**, **John Nagl**, and **Andrew Bacevich**, among others, have spoken at length about the U.S.'s over-reliance on military solutions and the lack of comprehensive strategies for political and economic stabilization. Their insights offer valuable lessons for future U.S. engagement, lessons that point to the need for a more **holistic** and **long-term** approach to foreign policy.

The time has come for the U.S. to rethink its approach to the Middle East—and to the broader global order. Military interventions may achieve short-term objectives, but they cannot replace the hard work of diplomacy, governance reform, and economic development. Moving forward, U.S. foreign policy must focus on **diplomatic engagement**, **multilateral cooperation**, and **addressing the root causes of conflict**, rather than relying on the quick fix of military force.

This book aims to offer not just a critique of past U.S. interventions but also a roadmap for the future. By drawing on the lessons of history and the voices of those who have experienced the consequences of U.S. foreign policy firsthand, it seeks to provide a more nuanced and sustainable vision for American engagement in the Middle East and beyond. The failures of the past need not define the future. By learning from its mistakes, the U.S. can craft a foreign policy that is both effective and responsible, one that promotes peace, stability, and respect for the sovereignty of nations.

As we look ahead, it is clear that the challenges of the **21st century** will require a different kind of leadership from the U.S. If America is to maintain its influence on the global stage, it must move beyond the **short-termism** that has characterized its interventions for so long. It must invest in **understanding**, **diplomacy**, and **long-term planning**, recognizing that the most enduring victories are those won not on the battlefield, but in the careful cultivation of relationships, institutions, and trust. This book is a step in that direction, an attempt to grapple with the past in order to chart a more thoughtful path forward. I hope you enjoy it.

INTRODUCTION
Unintended Consequences of U.S. Interventions

History has an unsettling way of revealing the stark contrast between expectation and reality. When we look back at key moments in history, it is easy to see how decision-makers, often with the best of intentions, find their choices leading to outcomes far beyond what they envisioned. Such has been the case with U.S. foreign policy, particularly in the Middle East, where the drive to contain perceived threats and secure allies has often led to the empowerment of forces that later become hostile.

The U.S. intervention in Iran in 1953 offers one of the earliest and clearest examples of this pattern. The CIA's orchestration of the coup that overthrew Prime Minister Mohammad Mosaddeq was driven by Cold War calculations and a desire to secure Western control over Iranian oil. The hope was to create a stable, pro-Western regime that would serve as a bulwark against Soviet influence. In reality, the coup planted the seeds of the Iranian Revolution and the eventual rise of the Islamic Republic—an enduring adversary of the United States.

As time progressed, this method of arming and supporting local forces to achieve short-term geopolitical goals has become a recurring feature of U.S. foreign policy. From Afghanistan to Libya, the U.S. has often pursued tactical alliances, only to watch those alliances unravel, leaving power vacuums that extremist forces quickly fill. The unintended consequence is a region not only less stable but also more antagonistic to U.S. interests.

In this manuscript, we will explore how this policy of arming local forces has played out in key regions, creating a legacy of hostility. From the mujahideen in Afghanistan, who were armed and trained to fight the Soviets only to later become the backbone of al-Qaeda, to the Libyan rebels whose support turned into chaos after Gaddafi's fall, U.S. interventions have consistently sown instability. Power vacuums filled by extremist groups or authoritarian regimes, hostile to the very nations that once empowered them, serve as a grim reminder of the long-term consequences of short-term decisions.

When the U.S. orchestrated the coup against Iran's popular Prime Minister Mohammad Mosaddeq in 1953, it was operating under the assumption that a Western-friendly, autocratic regime would stabilize the region and safeguard American interests. The Iranian people, meanwhile, had embraced democracy in the hopes of escaping poverty and securing greater autonomy from foreign influence, particularly over their prized oil resources. What followed was not a triumph of Western influence, but the beginning of an enduring conflict between Iran and the U.S., culminating in the 1979 revolution and the establishment of the Islamic Republic.

The Shah, who came to power in the wake of the coup, was seen as a puppet of the West, and his modernization efforts —backed by American arms and economic support—failed to resolve the deep economic disparities within the country. By the late 1970s, inflation, shortages, and inequality had left the Iranian economy in tatters, despite the Shah's efforts to modernize Iran through a Westernized, secular vision. Meanwhile, the Shah's political repression, carried out through his secret police (SAVAK), further alienated the Iranian public, setting the stage for Ayatollah Khomeini's return and the rise of an anti-Western regime that endures to this day.

What the U.S. intervention in Iran illustrates is the unintended domino effect that a singular action can have over decades. By empowering an autocratic leader like the Shah, the U.S. inadvertently fueled the forces of religious nationalism, creating a powerful ideological movement that saw the West not as a liberator but as an oppressor. The 1979 Iranian Revolution was a direct response to this perception, and it created a regime that continues to challenge U.S. interests and Western hegemony in the region.

This pattern would repeat itself across various parts of the Middle East and beyond, each time with new local actors, different historical circumstances, but ultimately the same result—a vacuum of power filled by hostile forces. Whether it was the mujahideen in Afghanistan, the rebels in Libya, or insurgent groups in Iraq, the U.S. found itself arming future adversaries in the hope of achieving immediate geopolitical goals.

However, these short-term tactical decisions often failed to consider the underlying complexities of the societies involved. In many cases, U.S. interventions upended fragile political ecosystems, further destabilizing countries rather than creating the intended security. The alliances formed in the heat of conflict, based on mutual short-term interests, seldom accounted for what would happen once the U.S. stepped back. These dynamics often left the people of these regions suffering the most, grappling with prolonged instability, extremism, and foreign meddling.

As we explore the historical context of these interventions, this book aims to uncover how the U.S.'s reliance on proxy forces not only undermined its long-term strategic interests but also created a series of adversarial relationships that continue to shape global geopolitics today. From the rise of al-Qaeda in Afghanistan to the chaos in post-Gaddafi Libya, these unintended consequences paint a sobering picture of the cost of foreign intervention.

The Domino Effect: From Iran to Afghanistan and Beyond

The coup against Mosaddeq in 1953 set a precedent for how the U.S. would approach foreign policy in the Middle East and beyond. By prioritizing short-term strategic interests—whether securing access to resources or containing Soviet influence—the U.S. repeatedly backed authoritarian regimes and insurgent forces without fully accounting for the long-term consequences. This strategy would play out again with even more dramatic consequences in Afghanistan during the Soviet-Afghan War of the 1980s.

In the late 1970s, the Soviet Union invaded Afghanistan, prompting the U.S. to view the conflict through the same Cold War lens that had shaped its intervention in Iran. In response, the U.S. launched Operation Cyclone, a covert CIA program that funneled billions of dollars in arms, training, and financial support to the Afghan mujahideen through Pakistan's Inter-Services Intelligence (ISI). The goal was to bleed the Soviet Union dry by bogging it down in a costly and protracted conflict—a strategy that succeeded in weakening the Soviet regime.

But as history would soon show, the forces armed and trained by the U.S. did not simply fade away once the Soviets withdrew. Among the mujahideen leaders supported by the U.S. was Gulbuddin Hekmatyar, who received hundreds of millions in aid and developed strong connections with emerging Islamist figures like Osama bin Laden. These networks, funded in part by Saudi and American resources, laid the foundation for the creation of al-Qaeda.

By the early 1990s, Afghanistan was left in chaos as the U.S. shifted its attention elsewhere. The very groups the

U.S. had supported, now left unchecked, began to turn their focus toward establishing Islamic governance and combating perceived Western imperialism. Osama bin Laden, once seen as a useful ally in the Cold War, soon became the mastermind behind the most devastating terrorist attack in American history—September 11, 2001. What began as a Cold War proxy conflict had transformed into a global war on terror, a direct consequence of U.S. miscalculations in arming and empowering local forces.

Libya: A Cautionary Tale of Intervention

The U.S. intervention in Libya during the Arab Spring in 2011 provides another stark example of how short-term tactical victories can lead to long-term strategic vulnerabilities. As protests against Colonel Muammar Gaddafi escalated, the U.S. and its NATO allies saw an opportunity to support the Libyan rebels and remove a long-standing dictator. Backed by U.S. airstrikes and military aid, the rebels overthrew Gaddafi, and the intervention was initially hailed as a success.

However, the removal of Gaddafi left a power vacuum that was quickly filled by competing militias and extremist groups. Without a stable government to replace Gaddafi's regime, Libya descended into chaos, with various factions vying for control of the country's resources and territory. Among these factions were Islamist groups such as Ansar al-Sharia, which would go on to carry out the deadly attack on the U.S. consulate in Benghazi in 2012. The same rebels once armed by the U.S. and NATO were now a threat to American lives and interests.

The chaos in Libya has since expanded beyond its borders, fueling instability across North Africa and the Sahel region. Weapons from Gaddafi's stockpiles, looted during the uprising, have found their way into the hands of militant groups across the region, including al-Qaeda in the Islamic

Maghreb (AQIM) and the Islamic State. The intervention that was meant to secure stability and promote democracy instead unleashed a wave of violence and extremism that continues to destabilize the region.

The Syrian Civil War: Another Proxy Conflict Gone Awry

The Syrian civil war, which erupted in 2011 as part of the broader Arab Spring, became yet another theater for U.S. proxy warfare. In its effort to oust President Bashar al-Assad, the U.S. provided arms and training to various Syrian rebel groups, hoping to cultivate a pro-Western alternative to Assad's regime. However, much like in Afghanistan and Libya, these efforts backfired.

Many of the U.S.-supported groups were either too weak to challenge Assad or ended up collaborating with extremist factions such as the al-Nusra Front, al-Qaeda's Syrian affiliate. As the war dragged on, the lines between "moderate" rebels and extremists became increasingly blurred. U.S.-supplied weapons and resources often ended up in the hands of jihadist groups, fueling the rise of ISIS and prolonging the conflict.

The failure of U.S. policy in Syria can also be seen in the rise of Iranian influence in the region. While the U.S. was focused on arming rebel forces, Iran—through its proxy Hezbollah—stepped in to support Assad, solidifying its foothold in the Levant. Russia, too, became involved, using Syria as a battleground to challenge U.S. influence in the Middle East. What began as an attempt to remove a dictator has evolved into a complex proxy war involving multiple regional and global powers, with no end in sight.

Legacy of Proxy Wars and Power Vacuums

The pattern is unmistakable. Time and again, U.S. foreign policy has relied on arming local forces to achieve immediate tactical objectives, often without fully considering the long-term consequences. These interventions frequently create power vacuums that are filled by extremist groups or authoritarian regimes hostile to the U.S. and its allies. The arming of the mujahideen in Afghanistan led to the rise of al-Qaeda. The removal of Gaddafi in Libya unleashed chaos across North Africa. And the arming of Syrian rebels contributed to the rise of ISIS and the deepening of Iranian and Russian influence in the region.

Even beyond the Middle East, this pattern can be seen in other U.S. interventions. The arming of anti-communist forces in Central America during the Cold War, for instance, contributed to decades of violence and instability that continue to affect the region today. In Africa, U.S. support for anti-Soviet rebel groups in Angola and Mozambique left behind a legacy of conflict and devastation.

The lesson is clear: while proxy warfare may seem like a low-risk strategy in the short term, the long-term consequences can be far more damaging. By empowering local forces without fully understanding their motivations or long-term goals, the U.S. has often sown the seeds of future conflict, creating adversaries out of former allies.

PART I: THE IRANIAN CATALYST

CHAPTER 1 - THE 1953 IRANIAN COUP D'ÉTAT: OPERATION AJAX AND THE FALL OF MOSADDEQ

a. Pre-1953 Conditions

In the years leading up to the 1953 coup, Iran was a country at the crossroads of economic ambition, political reform, and increasing foreign influence. Iran had a rich history and a strong sense of nationalism, but it was also beset by deep socio-economic inequalities, autocratic governance, and foreign meddling in its internal affairs. Central to this turmoil was the issue of oil—a resource that had become both a blessing and a curse for the country.

The Anglo-Iranian Oil Company (AIOC), which had a virtual monopoly over Iran's oil industry, became a focal point of growing resentment. Established in the early 20th century as a British entity, AIOC controlled Iran's most valuable asset, reaping enormous profits while leaving the Iranian people and government with a disproportionately small share of the revenues. Despite the vast wealth generated by its oil, Iran remained largely impoverished, and the ruling elite's close ties to Western powers fueled public dissatisfaction.

By the late 1940s, the situation had reached a tipping point. Nationalist fervor was growing, and there was increasing pressure to take back control of the nation's resources. Mohammad Mosaddeq, a popular and charismatic figure, emerged as the leader of this movement. His platform of nationalizing Iran's oil industry resonated with a broad swath of the population, from intellectuals and middle-class reformers to the working poor. In 1951, Mosaddeq was appointed Prime Minister, and shortly thereafter, he nationalized the AIOC, a bold move that significantly escalated tensions between Iran and the West.

Mosaddeq's government represented a significant departure from the autocratic tendencies of previous Iranian rulers. He sought to implement democratic reforms, reduce the power of the monarchy, and redistribute the wealth generated by oil to benefit the Iranian people. But his nationalization of the oil industry set him on a collision course with Britain and the United States, both of which had strategic and economic interests in maintaining control over Iran's oil reserves.

b. The 1953 Coup (Operation Ajax)

With the Cold War in full swing, Western powers saw Mosaddeq's rise as a threat not just to their economic interests but to the geopolitical balance in the region. For Britain, the loss of control over Iranian oil was a direct financial blow, while the U.S. feared that the instability in Iran could lead to a communist takeover, aligning the country with the Soviet Union. The nationalization of the oil industry and the growing influence of leftist parties within Iran's political landscape heightened these concerns.

In response, the British government, in collaboration with the U.S., devised a plan to overthrow Mosaddeq and restore control over Iran's oil. This operation, codenamed **Operation Ajax**, would become the first covert operation by the CIA to overthrow a foreign government. The motivations behind this intervention were twofold: to regain control over Iranian oil and to prevent what the U.S. perceived as the spread of communism in the region.

Working closely with British intelligence (MI6), the CIA orchestrated a detailed plan to destabilize Mosaddeq's government. The operation was spearheaded by Kermit Roosevelt Jr., a CIA officer, and relied on a combination of propaganda, political manipulation, and direct bribery of key military and political figures within Iran. A key tactic involved leveraging the influence of the Shah, who had become increasingly marginalized under Mosaddeq's rule. Though reluctant at first, the Shah was eventually persuaded to sign a royal decree dismissing Mosaddeq and appointing General Fazlollah Zahedi as the new Prime Minister.

The coup unfolded in August 1953. The first phase of the operation, which involved a failed attempt to arrest Mosaddeq and install Zahedi, briefly plunged the country into chaos. Mosaddeq initially survived the coup attempt, rallying popular support and turning the military against the plotters. However, the CIA and MI6 quickly regrouped, deploying more aggressive tactics. They orchestrated mass protests, spreading anti-Mosaddeq propaganda and using paid mobs to create the impression of widespread public dissatisfaction with the Prime Minister. Military units loyal to the Shah eventually succeeded in toppling Mosaddeq's government, and Mosaddeq himself was arrested.

The Immediate Aftermath

With Mosaddeq removed from power, the Shah returned to Iran from his brief exile, consolidating his rule with the backing of the U.S. and Britain. The coup had effectively restored the monarchy's power, but at the cost of Iran's fledgling democracy. The Shah's regime, while initially supported by much of the West, quickly became increasingly autocratic. With U.S. support, the Shah's government embarked on a modernization program, focusing on economic reforms and infrastructure development. However, political dissent was harshly suppressed.

The coup also marked a turning point in Iran's relations with the West. The re-establishment of foreign control over Iran's oil, now shared between U.S. and British companies, and the Shah's increasingly repressive policies planted the seeds of resentment that would explode into revolution in 1979. For the U.S., the coup was seen as a Cold War success, a strategic victory that secured a vital ally in the region. But in the long term, Operation Ajax would come to symbolize the dangers of foreign intervention, its legacy shaping Iranian attitudes toward the West for decades to come.

The consequences of Operation Ajax extended far beyond the immediate removal of Mosaddeq. It set a dangerous precedent for U.S. foreign policy, demonstrating that covert operations could be used to control the internal affairs of other nations to achieve strategic goals. However, it also showcased the limitations of such interventions. By backing an authoritarian regime, the U.S. not only undermined Iran's democratic aspirations but also alienated a generation of Iranians who had hoped for greater political freedoms.

For the Iranian people, the coup was a devastating blow to their national sovereignty and a clear example of foreign exploitation. The popular support that had initially rallied around Mosaddeq's calls for oil nationalization did not dissipate with his ouster; instead, it simmered beneath the surface, manifesting in growing resentment toward both the Shah and his Western backers. The coup also marked the beginning of a deep distrust of the West, particularly the United States, which Iranians came to see as an imperial force more concerned with its geopolitical interests than with supporting genuine democratic movements.

The ramifications of the coup rippled across the Middle East. Other nationalist leaders, such as Egypt's Gamal Abdel Nasser, observed the dangers of aligning too closely with Western powers or pursuing policies that would threaten Western economic interests. For the U.S., Operation Ajax served as a template for future covert actions during the Cold War, but it also revealed the inherent risks of manipulating foreign governments—risks that would eventually come to haunt American policymakers in the decades that followed.

CHAPTER 2 - THE SHAH'S REGIME: MODERNIZATION AND REPRESSION

a. Modernization and Westernization Efforts

The Shah's return to power following the 1953 coup heralded a new chapter in Iran's modern history, one defined by rapid modernization, economic transformation, and political repression. Buoyed by the support of the United States, Mohammad Reza Shah embarked on an ambitious program of reforms aimed at transforming Iran into a modern, secular, and industrialized nation that would serve as a beacon of Western values in the Middle East. These reforms, collectively known as the **White Revolution**, represented the Shah's vision for Iran as a regional powerhouse—one that was both economically self-sufficient and closely aligned with Western interests.

At the core of the Shah's modernization efforts was his desire to consolidate power while also satisfying Western expectations of progress and development. The White Revolution, launched in 1963, introduced a series of sweeping changes to Iran's land ownership system, industrial policies, and social structure. Key components of the White Revolution included land reforms that aimed to redistribute land from large landowners to tenant farmers, a move intended to weaken the political power of the landed elite while fostering a new class of loyal rural supporters.

Alongside land reform, the Shah sought to expand Iran's industrial base, leveraging the country's oil wealth to fund massive infrastructure projects and industrial ventures. The growth of the oil sector was central to this strategy, with revenues from petroleum exports providing the financial resources needed to modernize Iran's urban centers and industrialize its economy. New factories, highways, and dams sprung up across the country, symbolizing the Shah's drive to bring Iran into the ranks of the world's advanced economies.

Social reforms were another hallmark of the White Revolution. The Shah, seeking to emulate the West, pursued policies designed to Westernize Iranian society. Women were granted the right to vote and participate in political life, and education was expanded, with efforts to secularize the curriculum and diminish the influence of the clergy in public life. In the Shah's vision, Iran was to be a modern, cosmopolitan nation, free from the constraints of religious conservatism and aligned with Western ideals of progress.

However, these modernization efforts were not without significant opposition. The land reforms, while intended to benefit rural farmers, often failed to deliver on their promises, leaving many landless and embittered. Industrial growth concentrated wealth in the hands of a small elite, exacerbating economic inequalities and fueling discontent among the working class. Furthermore, the Shah's efforts to secularize and Westernize Iranian society alienated the country's conservative religious establishment, which saw his policies as an affront to Islamic values and traditions.

The Role of SAVAK in Suppressing Dissent

As opposition to the Shah's modernization policies grew, so

too did the regime's reliance on authoritarian measures to maintain control. Central to this effort was **SAVAK**, the Shah's secret police, which became one of the most feared and reviled institutions in Iran. Established with the help of the CIA and Israel's Mossad in the aftermath of the 1953 coup, SAVAK was tasked with rooting out political dissent, monitoring opposition movements, and ensuring that the Shah's rule remained unchallenged.

SAVAK's methods were brutal and uncompromising. The organization engaged in widespread surveillance, censorship, and intimidation, targeting anyone perceived as a threat to the Shah's regime. Political opponents, journalists, intellectuals, and religious leaders were routinely arrested, tortured, and in many cases, executed without trial. The mere mention of SAVAK was enough to instill fear among ordinary Iranians, who knew that any expression of dissent, no matter how mild, could result in imprisonment or worse.

Despite its brutality, SAVAK's actions were tolerated, and even supported, by the United States, which viewed the Shah as a critical ally in the fight against communism. For Washington, Iran's stability under the Shah was paramount, and SAVAK's role in suppressing leftist movements and curbing the influence of the Tudeh Party (Iran's communist party) was seen as essential to maintaining Iran's strategic alignment with the West. However, SAVAK's heavy-handed tactics only deepened popular resentment of the Shah's regime, further eroding its legitimacy and sowing the seeds of revolution.

As the Shah continued to push forward with his modernization agenda, his reliance on repression to maintain order became increasingly untenable. While his reforms transformed Iran into a more modern state, they also alienated broad swaths of the population, from rural farmers and the urban poor to religious leaders and political dissidents. By the late 1970s, this simmering discontent would boil over, leading to the collapse of the Shah's regime and the rise of the Islamic Republic—a direct consequence of the very policies the Shah had hoped would cement his rule.

b. Economic and Social Impact

The Shah's efforts to rapidly modernize Iran, encapsulated in his White Revolution, led to profound economic and social consequences that transformed the country. While the Shah's vision was to create a prosperous, Westernized nation, the unintended side effects of these reforms contributed to deepening inequality, the displacement of rural populations, and a growing cultural divide between secular elites and the traditional religious classes.

Consequences of Rapid Modernization: Urbanization, Rural Displacement, and Economic Disparities

One of the cornerstones of the Shah's modernization efforts was his plan to redistribute land in rural areas. Under the White Revolution, the Shah sought to break the power of the large landowners who had traditionally dominated Iran's rural economy by redistributing their land to tenant farmers. This was intended not only to weaken the influence of the rural aristocracy but also to transform the agricultural sector and create a more prosperous class of small landholders loyal to the monarchy.

However, in practice, these land reforms were only partially successful. Many tenant farmers were left with plots of land that were too small to be economically viable, forcing them to abandon agriculture and move to the rapidly growing urban centers in search of work. The influx of displaced rural workers into cities like Tehran, Isfahan, and Shiraz led to massive urbanization, overwhelming the cities' infrastructure and creating sprawling slums on the outskirts of these metropolitan areas.

Urbanization brought with it new economic opportunities, particularly in the industrial and service sectors, but it also exacerbated existing inequalities. While a small segment of the population—mainly the Shah's loyal supporters and Western-educated elites—reaped the benefits of industrialization and economic growth, the vast majority of Iranians saw little improvement in their living standards. The growing disparity between the rich and the poor, combined with the visible contrast between the luxurious lifestyles of the urban elite and the harsh conditions of the urban poor, stoked popular resentment against the regime.

Iran's burgeoning oil wealth played a central role in this dynamic. The Shah's government relied heavily on oil revenues to fund its modernization projects, but the distribution of this wealth was highly unequal. Much of the oil income was funneled into large infrastructure projects, military spending, and the import of luxury goods for the wealthy, while ordinary Iranians saw little of this wealth trickle down to their daily lives. The disconnect between the promises of modernization and the reality of economic hardship for many Iranians only deepened the sense of alienation felt by those left behind by the Shah's reforms.

Impact on Traditional Structures and the Rise of Secular Elites vs. Conservative Clerical Opposition

As Iran modernized, the social fabric of the country began to unravel, particularly in the divide between the secular elites who benefited from the Shah's policies and the conservative religious classes who saw these reforms as an existential threat to their traditional way of life. The Shah's aggressive push to Westernize Iranian society, coupled with his attempts to marginalize the clergy, fueled a cultural and ideological battle that would come to define the political landscape of Iran in the decades that followed.

The secular elites, many of whom had been educated

in Western universities and held key positions in the government, military, and business sectors, were the primary beneficiaries of the Shah's modernization policies. They embraced the Shah's vision of a modern, cosmopolitan Iran, aligning themselves with Western cultural and political values. This group became increasingly influential in the cities, forming a new ruling class that enjoyed the privileges of modernity and economic progress.

In stark contrast, the traditional religious classes, led by conservative clerics, saw the Shah's policies as an attack on Iran's Islamic identity and a betrayal of the country's cultural heritage. For centuries, the Shia clergy had held significant social and political influence in Iran, serving as both religious leaders and guardians of traditional values. The Shah's secularization efforts—such as granting women the right to vote, reforming family laws, and reducing the role of religious education—directly challenged the authority of the clergy, who viewed these changes as part of a broader attempt to undermine Islam in Iranian society.

The Shah's decision to strip the clergy of their traditional privileges, combined with his close ties to the United States and his embrace of Western cultural norms, intensified the opposition from religious leaders. Chief among these was Ayatollah Ruhollah Khomeini, who emerged as the most vocal critic of the Shah's regime. Khomeini condemned the Shah's reforms as un-Islamic and accused him of selling out Iran to foreign interests, particularly the United States and Israel.

The growing divide between the secular elites and the conservative religious classes was exacerbated by the Shah's increasingly authoritarian rule. While the secular elites enjoyed the benefits of modernization and social progress, the religious classes, along with many rural and urban poor, felt marginalized and alienated. The traditional social structures that had once provided a sense of stability and continuity were eroding, replaced by a society that was increasingly polarized between those who embraced Westernization and those who clung to traditional Islamic values.

This polarization would ultimately play a decisive role in the Shah's downfall. The cultural and ideological conflict between the secular elites and the religious conservatives provided fertile ground for the revolutionary fervor that would sweep through Iran in the late 1970s. The very reforms that the Shah had hoped would modernize and strengthen Iran instead contributed to the growing opposition that would culminate in the 1979 revolution and the establishment of the Islamic Republic.

CHAPTER 3 - THE 1979 IRANIAN REVOLUTION: FALL OF THE SHAH AND THE RISE OF KHOMEINI

Rise of Anti-Western Sentiment

By the late 1970s, Iran was a nation on the brink of revolution. While the Shah's ambitious modernization policies had transformed the country's infrastructure and economy, they had also deepened economic inequalities and alienated vast segments of the population. Most crucially, the Shah's close ties to Western powers, particularly the United States and Israel, fostered a rising wave of anti-Western sentiment that permeated both religious and nationalist opposition movements.

At the forefront of this opposition was a man whose influence would not only reshape Iran but also alter the geopolitical landscape of the Middle East for decades to come: Ayatollah Ruhollah Khomeini. Khomeini's ideology, grounded in both religious fervor and political pragmatism, would come to embody the growing frustration with the Shah's regime and the broader rejection of Western dominance in Iranian affairs.

a. Religious and Political Opposition

The role of religious leaders in Iran's political landscape cannot be overstated. The Shia clergy had long served as a moral authority in Iran, providing spiritual guidance and exerting significant influence over the country's political and social structures. However, the Shah's secularization efforts, coupled with his perceived subservience to Western interests, pushed the clergy into open opposition.

Chief among the clerical opposition was Ayatollah Khomeini, whose critique of the Shah's regime was both religious and political. Khomeini's opposition to the Shah had its roots in the 1960s, when he had publicly condemned the White Revolution as an attack on Islam and an effort to undermine the role of the clergy in Iranian society. For Khomeini, the Shah's policies represented not just a betrayal of Iran's Islamic heritage but also a capitulation to foreign—specifically Western—interests.

Khomeini's rhetoric was steeped in a profound critique of Western imperialism. He argued that the Shah's modernization efforts were merely a façade for Western exploitation, with Iran's oil resources being siphoned off by foreign powers while the Iranian people suffered. Khomeini framed his opposition to the Shah within a broader struggle between Islam and Western imperialism, positioning himself as the defender of Iran's Islamic values against the corrupting influence of the West.

One of Khomeini's central themes was the idea of *gharbzadegi*, or "Westoxification," which described the cultural and moral decay brought about by the Shah's embrace of Western ideals. According to Khomeini, the Shah's desire to transform Iran into a secular, Western-style state had eroded the country's Islamic identity and made it subservient to foreign powers. His message resonated deeply with large segments of the Iranian population who were disillusioned with the rapid pace of change, the increasing gap between the wealthy elite and the poor, and the loss of cultural and religious traditions.

Khomeini's religious opposition was further fueled by his denunciation of the Shah's close ties with Israel, a state that was deeply unpopular among Iran's Muslim population due to the ongoing Israeli-Palestinian conflict. Khomeini portrayed the Shah's alignment with Israel as part of a broader Zionist and imperialist conspiracy to undermine the Islamic world. This framing of the Shah's foreign alliances as a betrayal of Islam served to further galvanize religious opposition to his regime.

While Khomeini's opposition was grounded in religious ideology, it also had a powerful political dimension. He saw the Shah's regime as fundamentally illegitimate, not only because of its secularism but also because of the Shah's autocratic style of governance, which left little room for political pluralism or democratic expression. Khomeini's vision for Iran was not just a return to Islamic governance but also a rejection of Western-style democracy, which he viewed as corrupt and incompatible with Islamic values.

As Khomeini's influence grew, so too did his following. His messages, smuggled into Iran from exile in the form of cassette tapes, pamphlets, and letters, reached millions of Iranians who were increasingly disillusioned with the Shah's rule. Khomeini's ability to frame the struggle against the Shah as both a religious duty and a nationalistic endeavor was key to uniting disparate opposition groups—from religious conservatives to secular leftists—under the common cause of overthrowing the regime.

How the Shah's Close Ties with the U.S. and Israel Fueled Opposition

The Shah's alignment with Western powers, particularly the

United States and Israel, was a major source of resentment among both religious and secular opposition groups. Since the 1953 coup that had restored him to power, the Shah had enjoyed the unwavering support of the U.S., which viewed him as a crucial ally in the Cold War struggle against Soviet influence in the Middle East. Over the years, the Shah had received billions of dollars in military aid and economic assistance from the U.S., making Iran one of the most heavily armed nations in the region.

However, this close relationship with the U.S. came at a steep political cost. For many Iranians, the Shah's ties to the U.S. symbolized Iran's subservience to foreign powers, reinforcing the perception that the Shah was little more than a puppet of American interests. The visible presence of American advisors, military personnel, and corporations in Iran further fueled this resentment, with critics arguing that the Shah had sold out Iran's sovereignty in exchange for Western support.

The Shah's relationship with Israel was equally contentious. Despite the fact that most of the Muslim world had severed ties with Israel following the 1948 Arab-Israeli War, the Shah maintained a covert but close alliance with the Israeli government. This alliance, which included intelligence sharing and military cooperation, was seen by many Iranians as an affront to the Islamic world's solidarity with the Palestinian cause. Khomeini seized on this issue, accusing the Shah of betraying Islam by aligning himself with Israel and its Western allies.

The 1973 oil embargo, led by Arab members of the Organization of Petroleum Exporting Countries (OPEC) in response to U.S. support for Israel during the Yom Kippur War, further inflamed anti-Western sentiment in Iran. While the embargo temporarily increased Iran's oil revenues, the Shah's decision to continue his close cooperation with the U.S. and Israel during this period only deepened public anger. For many Iranians, the Shah's foreign policy choices were a clear indication that he prioritized Western interests over the needs and aspirations of his own people.

By the late 1970s, the combination of economic mismanagement, political repression, and the Shah's overt alliance with Western powers had created a perfect storm of opposition. Religious leaders, leftist intellectuals, students, and working-class Iranians all rallied behind the banner of anti-imperialism and anti-Western sentiment. Khomeini's ability to articulate this discontent in both religious and nationalistic terms made him the unifying figurehead of the revolutionary movement.

As protests against the Shah's regime escalated, the rhetoric of anti-Westernism became increasingly central to the revolutionary discourse. Demonstrators frequently chanted slogans such as "Death to America" and "Death to Israel," reflecting the widespread belief that the Shah's downfall was not just a domestic issue but part of a larger struggle against foreign domination. The revolution that would eventually topple the Shah was, in many ways, a rejection of both his autocratic rule and the broader influence of the West in Iran's political and economic affairs.

b. Key Incidents and Public Perception

While Ayatollah Khomeini's ideological opposition to the Shah was crucial in galvanizing the anti-Western movement, a series of key incidents further fueled the growing sentiment against both the Shah and his Western allies. These moments crystallized the discontent simmering under the surface of Iranian society, transforming it into a full-blown revolutionary movement. At the same time, public intellectuals, students, and leftist thinkers played an instrumental role in shaping how these incidents were perceived by the public and amplified anti-Western rhetoric.

The 1963 Demonstrations and the Role of Khomeini

One of the most pivotal events in the rise of anti-Western sentiment was the **June 1963 demonstrations**, also known as the **15 Khordad Uprising**. These protests erupted in response to the Shah's modernization efforts under the White Revolution, which included land reforms and granting women the right to vote. While these reforms were intended to modernize and secularize Iran, they were viewed by many, particularly religious conservatives, as an assault on Islamic values and a capitulation to Western ideologies.

Ayatollah Khomeini, who had become one of the Shah's most vocal critics by this point, publicly condemned these reforms as anti-Islamic and part of a larger plot by foreign powers—especially the United States and Israel—to dominate Iran. Khomeini's opposition was not limited to the White Revolution itself; he also fiercely criticized the Shah's perceived subservience to the U.S., framing it as a betrayal of Iran's independence and Islamic identity.

Khomeini's fiery speeches against the Shah, particularly a notable sermon delivered on **June 3, 1963**, accused the Shah of "destroying Islam" under the orders of foreign powers. His rhetoric struck a chord with many Iranians who were already resentful of the Shah's increasingly authoritarian rule and his close ties with the West. Shortly after this sermon, the government arrested Khomeini, sparking massive demonstrations in Tehran and other cities. The 1963 uprising was brutally suppressed by the Shah's security forces, resulting in the deaths of hundreds of protestors.

While the uprising was quelled, its significance in shaping public perception of the Shah and his Western allies was profound. Khomeini's arrest only amplified his status as a symbol of resistance, and the violent response to the protests deepened popular resentment. The 1963 demonstrations marked a turning point, where opposition to the Shah became more organized and widespread, and the link between anti-regime sentiment and anti-Western sentiment became solidified.

The 1978 Cinema Rex Fire and Public Backlash

Another key incident that exacerbated public hostility toward the Shah's regime and its Western connections was the **Cinema Rex fire** in **August 1978**. In the city of Abadan, a popular movie theater, Cinema Rex, was set ablaze during a screening, resulting in the deaths of over 400 people. It was one of the deadliest acts of arson in modern history, and its impact on the Iranian revolution was significant.

While the true perpetrators of the fire remain the subject of controversy, many Iranians at the time believed that SAVAK, the Shah's secret police, had deliberately set the fire as part of a broader campaign to crack down on opposition. The perception that the Shah's regime was responsible for such a horrific act further radicalized public opinion against him and his government. The Cinema Rex fire became a symbol of the regime's brutality, and it intensified the revolutionary fervor sweeping through the country.

For Khomeini and other revolutionary leaders, the incident was further proof of the regime's moral corruption and its willingness to use violence to maintain power. The event was widely covered in opposition media, and Khomeini used it in his sermons and writings to call for the Shah's overthrow, framing the tragedy as a manifestation of the regime's disregard for the lives of ordinary Iranians.

Media Portrayal and the Role of Intellectuals in Shaping Public Opinion

While incidents like the 1963 demonstrations and the Cinema Rex fire inflamed public sentiment, the media—both inside and outside of Iran—played a crucial role in shaping how these events were perceived. Iranian intellectuals, students, and leftist thinkers used every available platform to critique the Shah's regime, often portraying it as a puppet of Western imperialism. These intellectuals helped create a narrative that framed the Shah's authoritarianism as not merely a domestic issue, but as part of a larger Western project to dominate Iran and the broader Middle East.

One of the key vehicles for disseminating anti-Western and anti-Shah rhetoric was Iran's burgeoning underground press. Opposition groups published clandestine newspapers, pamphlets, and manifestos that criticized the Shah's close relationship with the United States, his lavish lifestyle, and his repressive policies. These publications often highlighted the growing inequality in Iranian society and the role that Western powers played in propping up the regime, making the argument that the West—particularly the U.S.—was complicit in the Shah's oppression of the Iranian people.

Intellectuals such as **Ali Shariati**, a prominent sociologist and revolutionary thinker, played a central role in articulating the ideological framework for the revolution. Shariati blended Islamic thought with Marxist theory, calling for a return to Islamic values while also critiquing the economic exploitation of Iran by Western imperial powers. His works, which were widely read by students and intellectuals, positioned Islam as a revolutionary force capable of challenging both the Shah's regime and the broader Western capitalist system.

The role of students in shaping public perception cannot be overlooked. Iran's university campuses became hotbeds of revolutionary activity, with students organizing protests, sit-ins, and strikes to demonstrate their opposition to the Shah and his Western backers. Many of these students had studied abroad in the West, particularly in the United States, where they had been exposed to anti-imperialist and leftist ideologies. Upon their return to Iran, they brought with them a heightened awareness of global political movements and framed their own struggle against the Shah as part of a broader fight against Western imperialism.

International media also played a role in shaping public perception, particularly as the revolution gained momentum. Western news outlets, while initially supportive of the Shah due to his alignment with U.S. interests, began to cover the growing unrest in Iran. Footage of protests, government crackdowns, and statements from opposition leaders were broadcast globally, further intensifying the anti-Western rhetoric of the revolution. Khomeini, who was in exile in France by the late 1970s, used international media to disseminate his messages, giving interviews to Western journalists and ensuring that his calls for revolution reached a global audience.

As the revolutionary movement grew, the lines between domestic discontent and anti-Western sentiment became increasingly blurred. For many Iranians, the Shah's repression was inextricably linked to the influence of the U.S. and other foreign powers, who were seen as enabling his regime. This perception, reinforced by the media and intellectual discourse, laid the groundwork for the overthrow of the Shah in 1979 and the establishment of a government defined by its opposition to Western imperialism.

The Iranian Revolution of 1979

a. Catalysts and Key Events

The Iranian Revolution of 1979 was the culmination of decades of political repression, social unrest, and widespread dissatisfaction with the Shah's regime. A complex tapestry of forces came together to bring about the fall of the monarchy and the rise of the Islamic Republic. The revolution was not the product of a single movement but rather the convergence of various social groups—including religious leaders, students, bazaar merchants (bazaaris), and the working class—each with their own grievances and aspirations. What united them was a shared desire to overthrow the Shah's authoritarian rule and end Iran's subservience to foreign powers, particularly the United States.

Timeline of Key Events

- **January 7, 1978: The Ettela'at Article Against Khomeini** The Iranian newspaper *Ettela'at* published an article that attacked Ayatollah Khomeini, referring to him as a "British agent" and accusing him of plotting against the state. The article sparked outrage among religious leaders and students, leading to widespread protests in the holy city of Qom. These protests were violently suppressed by the Shah's security forces, resulting in numerous deaths. This incident marked the beginning of a series of protests that would escalate over the following year.

- **February to August 1978: Waves of Protests** In the months following the protests in Qom, demonstrations spread to other cities, including Tabriz, Mashhad, and Isfahan. Each time the government cracked down on the protesters, new protests emerged in response. The cycle of protest and repression fueled the revolutionary fervor, with each martyr killed by the regime further galvanizing the opposition. During this period, the protests began to include not only religious students and clerics but also secular leftists, intellectuals, and workers, creating a broad-based movement against the Shah.

- **August 19, 1978: The Cinema Rex Fire** The Cinema Rex fire in Abadan, which killed over 400 people, became a major turning point in the revolution. Many Iranians blamed the Shah's regime for the fire, viewing it as an example of the government's willingness to use violence to suppress dissent. The tragedy sparked further protests, and the regime's failure to convincingly address the incident only deepened public anger.

- **September 8, 1978: Black Friday** As protests escalated, the Shah declared martial law and deployed the military to crush the demonstrations. On September 8, 1978, later known as *Black Friday*, the military opened fire on a large crowd of protesters in Tehran's Jaleh Square, killing hundreds of people. This massacre marked a turning point in the revolution. Any remaining hope of reconciliation with the Shah's regime evaporated, and even moderate groups began calling for the monarchy's overthrow. Black Friday also further radicalized the opposition, leading to mass strikes and demonstrations across the country.

- **October to December 1978: Nationwide Strikes** By the fall of 1978, strikes in key sectors of the economy —particularly the oil industry—brought the country to a standstill. Workers in oil refineries, factories, and public services joined the revolution, demanding the Shah's resignation and an end to foreign exploitation of Iran's resources. The bazaaris, Iran's traditional merchant class, also played a crucial role in financing the revolutionary movement. With their support, the revolutionary forces were able to maintain pressure on the regime while ensuring that essential goods continued to flow to the protesters.

- **January 16, 1979: The Shah Flees Iran** Facing widespread opposition and losing the support of the United States, the Shah fled Iran on January 16, 1979. His departure marked the collapse of the monarchy, although he insisted that he was leaving for a temporary "vacation." In reality, the Shah's reign was over. His departure was met with jubilation by millions of Iranians who had taken to the streets, seeing his exit as the definitive victory of the revolution.

- **February 1, 1979: Khomeini Returns** Two weeks after

the Shah's departure, Ayatollah Khomeini returned to Iran from his exile in France. He was greeted by millions of ecstatic Iranians who viewed him as the leader of the revolution. Khomeini immediately began to consolidate power, rejecting any attempts to form a coalition government that included moderates or supporters of the Shah's regime. His vision of an Islamic Republic became the dominant ideology of the revolution.

- **February 11, 1979: The Fall of the Pahlavi Regime** On February 11, 1979, the remnants of the Shah's regime collapsed. The military, which had been a key pillar of the Shah's power, declared its neutrality in the face of overwhelming opposition. Revolutionary forces took control of key government buildings, radio stations, and military bases, effectively ending the monarchy. The Islamic Revolution was now in full force, and Khomeini would soon begin the process of establishing a theocratic government based on Islamic principles.

Role of Social Groups in the Revolution

The Iranian Revolution succeeded in large part due to the involvement of diverse social groups, each contributing to the movement in different ways.

- **Students and Intellectuals**: University students were among the most vocal critics of the Shah's regime, organizing protests and sit-ins at campuses across the country. Many of these students had been influenced by leftist and anti-imperialist ideologies, which they had encountered while studying abroad or through underground movements. They saw the Shah not only as an autocratic ruler but also as a symbol of Western imperialism, particularly U.S. dominance in Iran. Intellectuals and academics helped shape the discourse of the revolution, providing ideological frameworks that linked the struggle against the Shah to global anti-colonial movements.

- **Bazaaris (Merchants):**
The traditional merchant class, or bazaaris, played a pivotal role in financing the revolution. The bazaaris had long been a powerful force in Iranian society, and many resented the Shah's economic policies, which favored large industrialists and foreign businesses at the expense of local merchants. Their financial support, combined with their ability to organize strikes and boycotts, made them a key pillar of the revolutionary movement. The alliance between the bazaaris and the religious clergy, particularly Khomeini, was crucial in mobilizing public support for the revolution.

- **The Working Class:**
Industrial workers, particularly those in the oil sector, were instrumental in bringing the Shah's regime to its knees. The nationwide strikes that paralyzed the country in the final months of 1978 demonstrated the power of the working class to disrupt the economy and challenge the state. Oil workers, in particular, were vital to the revolution's success. Their strike severely weakened the Shah's ability to maintain control, as Iran's oil exports were the primary source of revenue for the government. The participation of the working class signaled that the revolution was not just a political movement but also a social and economic one, with deep roots in the struggle for workers' rights and economic justice.

- **Clergy and Religious Leaders:**
The Shia clergy, led by Ayatollah Khomeini, were the ideological backbone of the revolution. While the clergy had initially been cautious about engaging in political opposition, the Shah's secularization policies and close ties to the West pushed them into active resistance. Khomeini's message of returning to Islamic values

and rejecting Western influence resonated deeply with the Iranian population, particularly in the rural areas where religious conservatism was strongest. The clergy's network of mosques and religious schools provided an effective means of organizing protests and spreading revolutionary ideas.

The convergence of these social groups, each with its own grievances and vision for the future, created a powerful and multifaceted revolutionary movement that ultimately succeeded in toppling the Shah's regime. While these groups had different motivations, they were united in their opposition to the Shah and their desire for a new political order —one that would be free from Western domination and rooted in Iranian values.

b. Khomeini's Leadership and Ideology

The return of Ayatollah Ruhollah Khomeini to Iran in February 1979 marked the beginning of a dramatic shift in the political and ideological landscape of the country. As the symbolic and spiritual leader of the Iranian Revolution, Khomeini's influence over the revolutionary movement was profound, and his vision for Iran would come to dominate the political framework of the post-revolutionary state. His return from exile signaled not only the fall of the Shah but also the transformation of Iran from a secular monarchy into an Islamic Republic.

Khomeini's leadership was defined by his ability to unite diverse factions under a single revolutionary cause, while his ideology centered on the establishment of an Islamic government based on the principles of Shia Islam. His rejection of both Western imperialism and secular nationalism paved the way for a new political order that would place Islamic jurisprudence, or *Velayat-e Faqih* (the guardianship of the Islamic jurist), at the center of governance.

Khomeini's Return from Exile

On **February 1, 1979**, after more than 14 years in exile, Khomeini returned to Iran from Paris, where he had been coordinating revolutionary activities and issuing directives to his followers. His return was met with jubilant celebrations, as millions of Iranians filled the streets of Tehran to welcome him home. For many, Khomeini represented a figure of moral authority, religious righteousness, and uncompromising opposition to the Shah's regime. He was seen not just as a political leader but as a symbol of spiritual renewal and a return to Islamic values.

Khomeini wasted no time in consolidating his power. Upon his arrival, he rejected the provisional government that had been established by the Shah's last prime minister, Shapour Bakhtiar, and declared it illegitimate. Khomeini quickly assumed control of the revolutionary forces, dismissing any possibility of a compromise with the remnants of the monarchy or with moderates who hoped to preserve a secular political system. For Khomeini, the revolution was not just about removing the Shah but about fundamentally transforming the political structure of Iran in accordance with Islamic principles.

Within weeks of his return, Khomeini and his supporters began the process of dismantling the institutions of the Pahlavi monarchy. Revolutionary committees and Islamic tribunals were established to purge the government, military, and security services of those loyal to the Shah. The old guard was systematically removed, and those deemed enemies of the revolution were arrested, tried, and, in many cases, executed. This period of consolidation was marked by a swift and often brutal effort to ensure that power remained firmly in the hands of Khomeini and his allies.

Establishment of the Islamic Republic

On **April 1, 1979**, following a national referendum in which an overwhelming majority of Iranians voted in favor of establishing an Islamic Republic, Khomeini declared the birth of a new political order in Iran. The Shah's monarchy was abolished, and the foundations were laid for a theocratic state in which religious leaders, rather than secular politicians, would hold the highest authority.

Khomeini's vision for the Islamic Republic was rooted in the concept of *Velayat-e Faqih*, or the guardianship of the Islamic jurist. According to this doctrine, a senior Islamic scholar, or *faqih*, would serve as the ultimate political and religious authority, guiding the state according to Islamic law (Sharia). Khomeini believed that only a religious leader with extensive knowledge of Islamic jurisprudence could ensure that the laws of the state were in accordance with the will of God. This represented a sharp departure from the secular nationalism that had characterized much of Iran's political history under the Pahlavi dynasty.

Under the new system, the *Supreme Leader*, as the *faqih* would be known, wielded unparalleled power. Khomeini himself assumed the role of Supreme Leader, giving him control over all branches of government, the military, and the judiciary. While Iran retained some elements of a republic, such as an elected president and parliament, these institutions were subordinate to the authority of the Supreme Leader and the religious establishment.

The creation of the Islamic Republic marked a profound ideological shift from the secular nationalism that had dominated Iranian politics during the Shah's reign. Secular nationalism, which had sought to modernize Iran by emulating Western political and economic models, was now replaced by a system that explicitly rejected Western influence and prioritized Islamic governance. Khomeini's Islamic

Republic was to be a state governed by divine law, where the teachings of Islam guided every aspect of life, from politics and economics to social and cultural norms.

From Secular Nationalism to Islamic Governance

The shift from secular nationalism to Islamic governance was not merely a change in political structure; it was a transformation of Iran's national identity. Under the Shah, Iran had been positioned as a modern, progressive state aligned with Western powers. The Shah had sought to create a society that mirrored Western secularism, where religion played a minimal role in public life and governance. This had been reflected in the Shah's efforts to curtail the power of the clergy, secularize the legal system, and promote Western cultural norms.

Khomeini's Islamic Republic represented a direct repudiation of this vision. In Khomeini's eyes, secular nationalism was not only incompatible with Islam but also a product of Western imperialism. He argued that the Shah's attempts to Westernize Iran had corrupted the nation, leading to moral decay, social injustice, and the loss of Iran's independence. For Khomeini, the solution was not to adopt Western models of governance but to return to Islamic principles that had been neglected under the Pahlavi dynasty.

In the new Islamic Republic, Shia Islam became the cornerstone of the state. The legal system was restructured to conform to Islamic law, and religious leaders played a central role in both the legislative and judicial processes. Religious observance was encouraged, if not enforced, in public life, and Islamic morality was promoted through laws that regulated behavior, dress, and cultural practices. For example, the consumption of alcohol was banned, women were required to wear the veil, and Islamic education was emphasized at all levels of schooling.

This ideological shift was not without its critics. Many secular intellectuals, leftists, and even some religious figures opposed the establishment of a theocratic state, arguing that it betrayed the democratic aspirations of the revolution. These groups had initially supported the overthrow of the Shah, believing that it would lead to greater political freedom and social justice. However, they quickly found themselves marginalized in the new political order, with many of their leaders imprisoned, exiled, or executed.

Despite this opposition, Khomeini's vision of an Islamic state took hold. His ability to unite religious fervor with a powerful critique of Western imperialism resonated with a broad cross-section of Iranian society, particularly the rural and working-class populations who had long felt alienated by the Shah's secular, Western-oriented policies. For these groups, Khomeini's promise of a government that would protect Islamic values and restore Iran's independence was a powerful antidote to the perceived corruption and tyranny of the Pahlavi regime.

Legacy of Khomeini's Ideology

Khomeini's leadership and ideology left a lasting impact on Iran and the broader Middle East. The establishment of the Islamic Republic not only transformed Iran's political landscape but also had significant implications for the region. Khomeini's anti-Western rhetoric and calls for Islamic governance inspired Islamist movements across the Muslim world, many of which sought to emulate the Iranian model of revolution.

In the years following the revolution, Iran became a major player in regional politics, using its newfound ideological legitimacy to support Shia movements and opposition groups in countries such as Lebanon, Iraq, and Bahrain. Khomeini's vision of exporting the revolution became a central tenet of Iranian foreign policy, as the Islamic Republic sought to challenge the influence of both the United States and Sunni-dominated Arab states in the region.

At home, Khomeini's legacy continued to shape Iranian politics long after his death in 1989. The system of *Velayat-e Faqih* remained intact, with subsequent Supreme Leaders wielding significant authority over the state. While some reformist movements emerged within the Islamic Republic, challenging the hardline interpretation of Islamic governance, the fundamental structure of the theocratic state remained in place.

Khomeini's vision of an Islamic state, free from Western influence and governed by religious principles, continues to define Iran's political identity and its place in the world. His leadership during the revolution not only brought about the downfall of the Pahlavi monarchy but also ushered in a new era of Islamic governance that would reshape the course of Iranian history.

c. Socio-Economic Reforms and Policies

With the establishment of the Islamic Republic, Ayatollah Khomeini and his government embarked on a series of socio-economic reforms that reflected both the revolutionary ideals of the movement and the practical needs of the newly formed state. These reforms aimed to address the economic inequalities that had plagued Iran under the Shah, while also consolidating Khomeini's vision of an Islamic society. Central to this effort were policies focused on redistributing wealth, nationalizing key industries, and reducing dependence on foreign powers. However, the implementation of these reforms was often complicated by the challenges of governing a country in the midst of political transformation and international isolation.

Redistribution Policies and Economic Reforms

One of the key promises of the Islamic Revolution was the

redistribution of wealth, particularly land and property, to the lower classes. Khomeini and the revolutionary leadership sought to address the socio-economic disparities that had worsened under the Shah's regime, where wealth had been concentrated in the hands of a small elite, while much of the population remained impoverished.

The first step in this process was the nationalization of large estates and the redistribution of land to the rural poor. This was part of a broader effort to break the power of the landed aristocracy and create a more equitable distribution of resources. However, these land reforms, much like those under the Shah's White Revolution, were only partially successful. While some land was redistributed, the reforms often fell short of their goals due to inefficiencies in implementation and the complex nature of Iranian property ownership. Many of the beneficiaries of the land redistribution were left with plots that were too small to be economically viable, and the agricultural sector remained underdeveloped.

Beyond land reform, the Islamic Republic also undertook efforts to nationalize key industries, particularly those related to oil, manufacturing, and banking. The nationalization of industries was seen as a way to wrest control of Iran's economy from foreign interests and corrupt domestic elites. This was especially significant in the oil sector, which had been central to the Iranian economy since the early 20th century. By taking control of the oil industry, the new government hoped to redirect the profits toward social welfare programs and infrastructure development, improving the lives of ordinary Iranians.

However, the nationalization efforts faced several challenges. While nationalizing the oil industry allowed the government to control one of its most valuable resources, it also led to inefficiencies and mismanagement. The loss of technical expertise and the exodus of many skilled workers, combined with the political instability of the post-revolutionary period, hampered the industry's productivity. Additionally, Iran's oil exports were severely affected by the international sanctions imposed after the U.S. embassy hostage crisis in 1979, which limited the country's ability to sell oil on the global market.

Despite these setbacks, Khomeini's government remained committed to the idea of economic justice and redistribution. The revolutionary leadership established **Bonyads**, or charitable foundations, to oversee the redistribution of wealth and resources. These semi-governmental organizations were tasked with managing nationalized assets and providing social services to the poor. While the Bonyads were intended to fulfill the revolution's promise of helping the underprivileged, they were often criticized for being inefficient and corrupt, with many of the funds being mismanaged or diverted to benefit political elites.

Impact on International Relations and Iran's Economic Position

The socio-economic reforms undertaken by the Islamic Republic had significant implications for Iran's international relations, particularly with the West. The nationalization of industries and the move away from reliance on foreign investment were key elements of Khomeini's broader rejection of Western influence. However, these policies also isolated Iran economically, as many Western companies, particularly in the oil and banking sectors, had previously played a significant role in Iran's economy.

In the immediate aftermath of the revolution, Iran's relationship with the United States, in particular, deteriorated rapidly. The **U.S. embassy hostage crisis**, which began in November 1979, marked a turning point in U.S.-Iranian relations. In response to the hostage-taking, the United States imposed economic sanctions on Iran, freezing Iranian assets and cutting off trade. These sanctions, combined with the nationalization of industries, made it difficult for Iran to access the global markets and foreign capital it needed to modernize its economy.

Iran's international isolation was further compounded by the outbreak of the **Iran-Iraq War** in 1980. The war, which lasted for eight years, devastated Iran's infrastructure and economy. The government was forced to divert much of its resources to the war effort, and the economic reforms that had been promised in the early days of the revolution were largely put on hold. The war also strained Iran's relations with other countries in the region, as many of its neighbors, including Saudi Arabia and Kuwait, supported Iraq in the conflict.

Despite these challenges, the Islamic Republic sought to reorient its economy away from dependence on the West and toward greater self-sufficiency. This policy, known as **"Resistance Economy"**, emphasized domestic production and the development of local industries. While this approach helped Iran weather the impact of international sanctions, it also led to economic stagnation, as the country struggled to maintain access to advanced technologies and foreign investment.

On the international stage, Iran's economic policies contributed to its strained relations with both the West and its regional neighbors. The nationalization of the oil industry and the regime's anti-Western rhetoric alienated Western countries, while Iran's support for revolutionary movements and Shia militias across the Middle East further isolated it diplomatically. By the mid-1980s, Iran was largely cut off from the global economy, relying on its oil revenues and domestic production to sustain itself.

Long-Term Impact of Iran's Economic Reforms

The economic strategies pursued by the Islamic Republic in the wake of the revolution had mixed results. While the redistribution of wealth and nationalization of industries were intended to promote social justice, they often fell short of their goals due to inefficiencies, corruption, and the strain of international isolation. The Bonyads, which were meant to oversee the redistribution of wealth, became sources of power for political elites, and many of the economic reforms failed to benefit the population as a whole.

Moreover, Iran's international isolation, exacerbated by the hostage crisis and the Iran-Iraq War, left the country economically vulnerable. While the policy of self-sufficiency allowed Iran to survive in the face of sanctions, it also limited its ability to grow and modernize its economy. The Islamic Republic's focus on ideological purity and anti-Western rhetoric often came at the expense of pragmatic economic policies, and this tension between ideology and economics has continued to shape Iran's economic trajectory in the decades since the revolution.

Despite these challenges, Khomeini's government was able to maintain a degree of economic stability, thanks in large part to its control of the oil industry. However, the promise of widespread economic reform and prosperity that had been central to the revolution was never fully realized, leaving many Iranians disillusioned with the new regime's ability to deliver on its socio-economic promises.

Long-Term Implications and Current Perspectives

a. U.S.-Iran Relations

The Iranian Revolution of 1979 fundamentally reshaped the relationship between the United States and Iran, transforming the two nations from close allies under the Shah to bitter adversaries in the decades that followed. The overthrow of the Pahlavi monarchy, the rise of Ayatollah Khomeini, and the establishment of the Islamic Republic created a new political order in Iran, one that rejected Western influence and placed anti-imperialism and Islamic governance at its core. This ideological shift set the stage for decades of tension, conflict, and sporadic attempts at rapprochement between the U.S. and Iran.

Ongoing Tensions: From the Hostage Crisis to Present Day

The roots of modern U.S.-Iranian tensions can be traced back to the **U.S. embassy hostage crisis** of 1979, in which 52 American diplomats and citizens were held hostage for 444 days by Iranian students loyal to Khomeini. This event, which followed the Islamic Revolution, deeply damaged relations between the two countries and created a lasting animosity that has continued to shape U.S. foreign policy toward Iran. For the Iranian regime, the hostage crisis was a symbol of resistance to American imperialism, while for the U.S., it marked Iran as a rogue state willing to defy international norms.

In the years following the revolution, the United States imposed a series of sanctions on Iran, aimed at weakening the regime and curtailing its influence. These sanctions, which were initially a response to the hostage crisis, expanded over time to include measures targeting Iran's nuclear program, its support for terrorist organizations, and its involvement in regional conflicts. U.S. sanctions have had a significant impact on the Iranian economy, limiting its access to global markets, restricting its ability to export oil, and isolating it from the international financial system.

Despite the deeply rooted tensions, there have been several attempts to engage in diplomatic negotiations between the two countries, particularly around the issue of Iran's nuclear program. Beginning in the early 2000s, the U.S. and its European allies became increasingly concerned about Iran's development of nuclear technology, fearing that Tehran was pursuing a nuclear weapon under the guise of a civilian energy program. The **Joint Comprehensive Plan of Action (JCPOA)**, also known as the **Iran nuclear deal**, was negotiated in 2015 under the Obama administration and represented a significant breakthrough in U.S.-Iranian relations.

The JCPOA was designed to limit Iran's nuclear activities in exchange for the lifting of economic sanctions. For a brief period, the deal appeared to create an opening for improved relations between the U.S. and Iran. However, the agreement was fraught with controversy from the outset, particularly in the United States, where critics argued that it did not go far enough in curbing Iran's nuclear ambitions or addressing its involvement in regional conflicts. In 2018, the Trump administration withdrew the U.S. from the nuclear deal, reimposing harsh sanctions on Iran and reigniting tensions.

The collapse of the JCPOA and the subsequent escalation of hostilities between the two countries brought U.S.-Iran relations back to a state of confrontation. Iran responded to the reimposition of sanctions by resuming its uranium enrichment activities, raising fears of a renewed nuclear crisis. The assassination of **Qassem Soleimani**, a top Iranian military commander, by a U.S. drone strike in 2020 further inflamed tensions, leading to retaliatory attacks by Iran on U.S. military bases in Iraq.

As of the early 2020s, relations between the U.S. and Iran remain strained, with both countries engaging in a cycle of sanctions, threats, and occasional diplomatic overtures. While the Biden administration has expressed interest in reviving the JCPOA, negotiations have been slow, hindered by mutual distrust and competing interests within each government. The nuclear issue continues to be a major point of contention, with Iran insisting on its right to develop nuclear energy while the U.S. and its allies demand guarantees that Tehran will not develop a nuclear weapon.

Sanctions and Their Impact on Iranian Economy

The U.S. strategy of using economic sanctions to pressure Iran has had a profound impact on the country's economy and its ability to engage in international trade. Over the past four decades, sanctions have targeted a wide range of sectors, including banking, oil exports, and military industries. While sanctions have succeeded in limiting Iran's access to global markets and isolating it from the international financial system, they have also contributed to significant economic hardship for ordinary Iranians.

The sanctions regime has led to inflation, unemployment, and shortages of essential goods, including medicine and food. Iran's oil exports, the lifeblood of its economy, have been severely restricted, reducing government revenues and limiting the country's ability to invest in infrastructure and social services. Despite these challenges, Iran has adapted to some extent, developing a parallel economy that relies on smuggling, barter trade, and partnerships with countries like China, Russia, and Venezuela to bypass sanctions.

Iran's leaders have long framed the sanctions as part of a broader Western conspiracy to weaken the Islamic Republic, and they have used this narrative to rally domestic support for the regime. However, the economic pain caused by the sanctions has also fueled discontent within Iran, particularly among the middle class and younger generations who have seen their prospects diminished by the country's isolation.

Iran's Role in Regional Conflicts and Relations with Other Middle Eastern Countries

In addition to its contentious relationship with the U.S., Iran has become a central player in many of the Middle East's most significant conflicts. The Islamic Republic's foreign policy, shaped by its revolutionary ideals and geopolitical ambitions, has been defined by its support for Shia movements and its opposition to the influence of the U.S., Israel, and Sunni Arab states, particularly Saudi Arabia.

One of the cornerstones of Iran's regional strategy has been its support for **proxy forces** in conflicts across the Middle East. The most prominent example of this is **Hezbollah**, the Lebanese Shia militant group and political party that receives substantial financial, military, and logistical support from Iran. Since its formation in the 1980s, Hezbollah has served as both a proxy for Iranian influence in Lebanon and a key actor in the broader Arab-Israeli conflict, frequently clashing with Israel and playing a major role in Lebanese politics.

Iran's involvement in Syria's civil war has also been a critical element of its regional strategy. Since the outbreak of the war in 2011, Iran has provided crucial support to the government of **Bashar al-Assad**, including deploying Iranian military forces and backing militias to fight against Syrian rebel groups. Iran's intervention in Syria, which is closely aligned with Russia's support for Assad, has helped to keep the Syrian regime in power, but it has also placed Iran at odds with much of the international community, particularly the U.S. and its allies.

Iran's role in **Iraq** is another major facet of its regional influence. Since the U.S. invasion of Iraq in 2003, Iran has worked to expand its influence in the country by supporting Shia militias and political groups. While Iran and the U.S. briefly cooperated to combat **ISIS** in Iraq, their rivalry over influence in the country has persisted, with Iran seeking to shape Iraq's political future in line with its own interests. The presence of Iranian-backed militias in Iraq has become a flashpoint in U.S.-Iran relations, particularly after the assassination of Soleimani, who was a key architect of Iran's Iraq strategy.

Iran's relationship with **Saudi Arabia**, the other dominant regional power in the Middle East, is characterized by deep rivalry and sectarian tension. The two countries, representing Shia and Sunni Islam respectively, have been engaged in a

proxy conflict for regional dominance, often referred to as the **Cold War of the Middle East**. This rivalry has played out in conflicts across the region, from **Yemen**, where Iran supports the Houthi rebels against a Saudi-led coalition, to **Bahrain**, where Iran has supported Shia opposition groups.

Iran's foreign policy has also involved closer ties with **Russia** and **China**, as both countries have sought to challenge U.S. dominance in the region. Iran's partnership with Russia has been particularly important in the context of the Syrian civil war, where the two countries have worked closely to prop up Assad's regime. Meanwhile, China has emerged as a critical economic partner for Iran, particularly as U.S. sanctions have limited Iran's ability to engage with Western markets.

A Long Road Ahead

The long-term implications of the 1979 revolution continue to shape U.S.-Iran relations and Iran's role in the Middle East. Despite decades of hostility, economic sanctions, and diplomatic isolation, the Islamic Republic has survived and, in many ways, thrived as a regional power. However, the country remains deeply isolated on the international stage, and its economy continues to suffer under the weight of sanctions. Meanwhile, the nuclear issue remains unresolved, with both sides reluctant to fully commit to a diplomatic solution.

As Iran continues to navigate its complex relationships with regional and global powers, the legacy of the revolution remains a defining force in its foreign policy and domestic governance. The tensions between Iran and the U.S., as well as between Iran and its regional rivals, are unlikely to dissipate in the near future, ensuring that the Islamic Republic will remain at the center of Middle Eastern geopolitics for years to come.

b. Lessons for U.S. Foreign Policy

The history of U.S. intervention in Iran and the broader Middle

East offers crucial lessons for understanding the long-term consequences of foreign interventions. The U.S. has repeatedly attempted to shape political outcomes in the region, often prioritizing short-term strategic gains over long-term stability and disregarding the complexities of local dynamics. The consequences of these interventions have frequently been unintended and counterproductive, fueling anti-Western sentiment, destabilizing governments, and empowering adversaries. Reflecting on the U.S. role in Iran, from the 1953 coup to the present-day sanctions regime, provides important insights into how American foreign policy might evolve in the future.

Reflections on the Long-Term Impacts of Foreign Interventions

The 1953 CIA-orchestrated coup against Prime Minister Mohammad Mosaddeq set the tone for U.S. involvement in Iran, laying the groundwork for decades of distrust and resentment. While the coup was seen as a Cold War victory at the time, ensuring Western control over Iran's oil resources and securing an ally in the Shah, it also had far-reaching consequences. The overthrow of Mosaddeq, a democratically elected leader, undermined Iranian democracy and created a perception that the U.S. valued its economic and geopolitical interests over the sovereignty of other nations. This perception would later be a critical factor in the rise of Ayatollah Khomeini and the Islamic Revolution of 1979.

In the years that followed, U.S. foreign policy in the Middle East frequently relied on similar strategies—supporting autocratic leaders, arming proxy forces, and intervening in local conflicts to protect American interests. However, as the Iranian case demonstrates, these tactics often produced unintended and damaging outcomes. The U.S. support for the Shah not only contributed to the rise of Khomeini but also to the formation of a regime that would challenge American influence in the region for decades. Similarly, U.S. interventions in Iraq,

Afghanistan, and Libya created power vacuums that were later filled by extremist groups, leading to prolonged instability and conflict.

One of the key lessons from the U.S. experience in Iran and elsewhere in the Middle East is that foreign interventions, particularly those that prioritize regime change or military solutions, tend to have unpredictable consequences. While they may achieve immediate tactical objectives, such as removing an unfriendly regime or securing access to resources, they often fail to account for the broader socio-political dynamics that shape long-term outcomes. In many cases, these interventions have fueled resentment, empowered adversaries, and destabilized entire regions, creating more problems than they solve.

The U.S. reliance on sanctions as a tool of foreign policy has also had mixed results. In the case of Iran, sanctions have undoubtedly weakened the country's economy, but they have also reinforced the regime's anti-Western rhetoric and created a rally-around-the-flag effect, in which ordinary Iranians blame external forces for their hardships rather than their own government. Sanctions have isolated Iran, but they have not succeeded in curbing its influence in the region or compelling it to abandon its nuclear ambitions. In fact, sanctions have often strengthened the resolve of the Iranian leadership to resist Western pressure and pursue policies that challenge U.S. interests in the Middle East.

Recommendations for Current and Future U.S. Policies in the Middle East

Given the long history of U.S. involvement in the Middle East, it is clear that future American foreign policy must be informed by the lessons of the past. While the U.S. cannot undo the consequences of previous interventions, it can adopt a more nuanced and pragmatic approach to the region—one that prioritizes diplomacy, local engagement, and long-term stability over short-term strategic gains.

1. **Emphasize Diplomacy and Multilateral Engagement** One of the key lessons from the Iran nuclear deal (JCPOA) is that diplomacy, while difficult, can be effective in addressing complex security issues. The JCPOA demonstrated that even in the face of deep mutual distrust, it is possible to reach agreements that serve the interests of both sides. Future U.S. policy in the Middle East should place greater emphasis on diplomatic engagement, working not only with regional actors but also with international partners to find solutions to conflicts and disputes.

   Multilateralism can help reduce the perception that the U.S. is acting unilaterally or in its own self-interest. By engaging with international organizations like the United Nations, the European Union, and regional bodies, the U.S. can build broader coalitions that share the burden of addressing regional challenges. This approach can help mitigate some of the negative consequences of past interventions and reduce the sense of American imperialism that has fueled anti-U.S. sentiment in the region.

2. **Avoid Regime Change as a Policy Objective** One of the most significant takeaways from U.S. involvement in Iran, Iraq, and Libya is that regime change often creates more problems than it solves. While removing hostile or authoritarian leaders may seem like a straightforward solution, the aftermath of such interventions is often chaotic, leading to power vacuums, civil wars, and the rise of extremist groups. In Iran, the 1953 coup set the stage for the Islamic Revolution and the establishment of a regime even more hostile to U.S. interests.

   Rather than pursuing regime change, U.S. policy should focus on fostering gradual reforms and supporting civil society in ways that empower local actors to drive political change from within. By promoting good governance, human rights, and economic development, the U.S. can contribute to more sustainable and stable outcomes without resorting to direct intervention or destabilizing military actions.

3. **Reassess the Use of Sanctions** While sanctions can be a powerful tool of economic coercion, they are not a panacea. The long-term effects of sanctions on Iran demonstrate that while they can weaken a regime's economy, they often fail to achieve broader political objectives. In many cases, sanctions have entrenched hardline positions, deepened the suffering of ordinary citizens, and limited the prospects for diplomatic engagement.

   Future U.S. policy should consider the selective use of sanctions, targeting specific individuals or entities involved in illicit activities, rather than imposing blanket sanctions that hurt entire populations. Sanctions should also be accompanied by clear diplomatic goals and exit strategies—an understanding of what specific behavior the U.S. wants to change and how sanctions relief can be used as leverage in negotiations.

4. **Support Regional Stability through Local Partnerships** U.S. policy in the Middle East has often been defined by its alliances with authoritarian regimes that promise stability in exchange for military or economic support. However, this approach has frequently backfired, as seen in Iran, Egypt, and Saudi Arabia, where popular discontent with autocratic leaders has led to revolutions, uprisings, or internal instability.

   Instead of relying on authoritarian regimes, the U.S. should invest in building partnerships with local actors who represent a broader cross-section of society. This could involve supporting grassroots organizations, democratic institutions, and moderate political movements that seek to address the needs of their populations. By aligning itself with actors who have legitimate popular support, the U.S. can foster more sustainable and inclusive governance structures.

5. **Recognize the Limits of Military Power** The U.S. has often turned to military force to achieve its objectives in the Middle East, whether through direct intervention or by arming proxy forces. However, the long-term consequences of these actions have demonstrated that military solutions rarely lead to lasting peace or stability. The wars in Iraq and Afghanistan, as well as the U.S. support for rebel groups in Syria and Libya, have shown that military interventions can create power vacuums, fuel extremism, and prolong conflicts.

Moving forward, U.S. policy should prioritize non-military approaches to conflict resolution, such as diplomacy, economic assistance, and peacebuilding efforts. While the U.S. must retain the ability to defend itself and its allies, military force should be seen as a last resort, used only when all other avenues have been exhausted.

A New Vision for U.S. Engagement

The lessons of U.S. involvement in Iran and the broader Middle East are clear: foreign interventions, particularly those aimed at regime change or imposing external solutions, often lead to unintended and damaging consequences. By adopting a more nuanced, pragmatic, and patient approach, the U.S. can begin to repair the damage caused by decades of failed policies and contribute to a more stable and peaceful Middle East.

Rather than seeking to impose its will through military power or economic coercion, the U.S. should focus on building long-term partnerships, promoting regional stability, and supporting local actors in their efforts to create inclusive and responsive governance. In doing so, the U.S. can avoid repeating the mistakes of the past and chart a new course for its role in the Middle East.

PART II: THE COLD WAR BATTLEGROUNDS

CHAPTER 4 - OPERATION CYCLONE: ARMING THE MUJAHIDEEN IN AFGHANISTAN

U.S. Motivations in Arming Afghan Forces Against the Soviet Union

The Soviet invasion of Afghanistan in 1979 marked a turning point in the Cold War, shifting the geopolitical dynamics in South Asia and prompting a significant response from the United States. In what would become one of the largest and most covert operations in CIA history, the U.S. launched **Operation Cyclone**, aimed at providing military and financial support to the Afghan **Mujahideen**, a coalition of insurgent groups fighting against the Soviet-backed Democratic Republic of Afghanistan. The U.S. motivations for arming the Mujahideen were deeply rooted in Cold War calculations, as well as regional and ideological interests that shaped American foreign policy at the time.

Containing Soviet Expansion

At the heart of U.S. motivations for intervening in Afghanistan was the Cold War rivalry between the United States and the Soviet Union. Since the end of World War II, both superpowers had been locked in a global struggle for influence, with the U.S. seeking to contain the spread of communism and the Soviet Union aiming to expand its ideological and geopolitical footprint. The Soviet invasion of Afghanistan in December 1979 was seen by the U.S. as an aggressive move that threatened to shift the balance of power in the region.

For the U.S., Afghanistan represented more than just a remote country in Central Asia. It bordered key U.S. allies, including Pakistan and Iran, and its proximity to the Persian Gulf made it strategically important in terms of controlling access to vital energy resources. The Soviet occupation of Afghanistan, therefore, raised the specter of Soviet dominance over the region and the potential for communist influence to spread further south into the oil-rich Gulf states, which were essential to global energy markets and to Western economies.

The U.S. was also concerned that the Soviet invasion could signal a broader Soviet strategy to expand its influence in the Third World. Throughout the 1970s, the Soviet Union had supported leftist movements and governments in various parts of the globe, including Africa, Latin America, and Southeast Asia. In places like Angola, Mozambique, and Nicaragua, Soviet-backed regimes had come to power, challenging U.S. influence and pushing the Cold War into the global South. Afghanistan, in the eyes of U.S. policymakers, was the latest example of Soviet expansionism and had to be confronted to prevent the further spread of communism.

For U.S. President Jimmy Carter, the Soviet invasion of Afghanistan was a turning point in his administration's foreign policy. Initially committed to pursuing détente with the Soviet Union—an effort to reduce tensions and promote cooperation between the two superpowers—Carter shifted to a more confrontational stance in the wake of the invasion. In his

State of the Union Address in January 1980, Carter outlined what became known as the **Carter Doctrine**, declaring that the U.S. would use military force if necessary to protect its interests in the Persian Gulf. This doctrine underscored the strategic importance of the region and signaled a new phase of U.S. engagement in the Cold War.

Zbigniew Brzezinski's Geopolitical Strategy

One of the chief architects of U.S. policy in Afghanistan was **Zbigniew Brzezinski**, Carter's National Security Advisor. Brzezinski was a staunch anti-communist who viewed the Soviet invasion of Afghanistan as an opportunity to weaken the Soviet Union by drawing it into a protracted and costly conflict. His geopolitical strategy was influenced by the idea of "bleeding" the Soviets through proxy warfare, forcing them to expend resources and military personnel in a country far from their own borders, much like the U.S. had been drained by the Vietnam War.

Brzezinski and other U.S. officials believed that supporting the Afghan resistance could turn Afghanistan into the Soviet Union's own Vietnam—a quagmire that would sap Soviet strength and morale. The idea was to provide enough support to the Mujahideen to keep the Soviet military bogged down in Afghanistan, thereby diverting Soviet attention and resources from other global theaters. By turning Afghanistan into a costly conflict for the Soviets, the U.S. hoped to weaken Soviet resolve, strain its economy, and expose the limits of its military power.

Brzezinski's view of the Soviet invasion as a major strategic blunder was encapsulated in his famous trip to Pakistan in 1980, where he stood on the Afghan border and addressed a group of Mujahideen fighters, declaring, "Your cause is right, and God is on your side." This symbolic gesture reflected the U.S. commitment to supporting the Afghan resistance, not only as a matter of geopolitical strategy but also as a moral imperative in the context of the Cold War.

Islam as a Tool in the Cold War

Another important motivation for the U.S. in arming the Mujahideen was the opportunity to use Islam as a counterbalance to Soviet communism. The Soviet Union was officially atheistic, and its communist ideology was seen as fundamentally incompatible with Islamic values. For the U.S., which had long viewed the Middle East and Central Asia through the lens of Cold War competition, the rise of Islamic fundamentalism was initially seen as a potential asset in the fight against communism.

In the context of the Afghan conflict, the U.S. framed its support for the Mujahideen as part of a broader struggle to defend Islamic civilization from Soviet oppression. The narrative of a jihad (holy war) against the atheistic Soviets resonated with many in the Muslim world, and the U.S. worked closely with Pakistan and Saudi Arabia to funnel financial and military support to the Afghan resistance. Islamic organizations, including the **Maktab al-Khidamat** (MAK), co-founded by **Osama bin Laden** and **Abdullah Azzam**, played a key role in recruiting fighters from across the Muslim world to join the Mujahideen in their fight against the Soviets.

For the U.S., the alignment with Islamic movements in Afghanistan was seen as a pragmatic strategy to counter Soviet influence, but it also reflected a broader willingness to engage with religious groups as part of the Cold War struggle. Throughout the 1980s, the U.S. and its allies, particularly Saudi Arabia, promoted the idea of jihad as a rallying cry for Muslims to resist Soviet occupation, helping to create a network of Islamic fighters that would later have profound consequences for global security.

Role of Pakistan and Saudi Arabia

Pakistan and Saudi Arabia played crucial roles in the

execution of Operation Cyclone, serving as intermediaries for U.S. assistance to the Mujahideen and providing additional financial and logistical support. Pakistan, under the leadership of **General Zia-ul-Haq**, was particularly important, as it shared a long border with Afghanistan and had a vested interest in preventing Soviet expansion into South Asia. For Zia, the Soviet invasion of Afghanistan represented a direct threat to Pakistan's security, and he was eager to support the Afghan resistance.

The **Inter-Services Intelligence** (ISI), Pakistan's powerful intelligence agency, became the primary conduit for U.S. aid to the Mujahideen. The ISI, with U.S. funding and technical assistance from the CIA, trained and equipped Afghan fighters, while also facilitating the flow of foreign volunteers into Afghanistan. Pakistan's role in the conflict allowed it to assert its influence over the Mujahideen and shape the direction of the insurgency, but it also had long-term consequences for Pakistan's own internal security, as the rise of Islamist militancy would later destabilize the country.

Saudi Arabia, as a major financial backer of the Mujahideen, played a key role in funding the jihad against the Soviets. The Saudis saw the conflict in Afghanistan as an opportunity to promote their own brand of Sunni Islam, **Wahhabism**, and to combat the spread of communism, which they viewed as a threat to the Islamic world. Saudi Arabia matched U.S. funding for the Mujahideen dollar for dollar, and wealthy Saudi individuals, including Osama bin Laden, provided additional support through private donations and fundraising efforts.

Covert Nature of Operation Cyclone

Operation Cyclone was one of the most covert and secretive operations in CIA history. The U.S. government, wary of escalating tensions with the Soviet Union and avoiding direct involvement in the conflict, kept its role in arming the Mujahideen largely hidden from the American public. The

CIA's involvement in Afghanistan began on a small scale in 1979, with only modest support for the resistance, but as the conflict escalated, the U.S. commitment grew significantly. By the mid-1980s, under the Reagan administration, U.S. funding for the Mujahideen had expanded to billions of dollars.

The CIA provided the Mujahideen with a wide range of military aid, including rifles, mortars, explosives, and **Stinger missiles**, which were particularly effective in countering Soviet helicopters. The introduction of Stinger missiles in 1986 was a game-changer, allowing the Mujahideen to shoot down Soviet aircraft and significantly reducing the Soviet military's air superiority. This, in turn, contributed to the increasing costs and casualties for the Soviet forces, making it more difficult for them to maintain control over Afghanistan.

Despite the covert nature of the operation, U.S. officials remained committed to avoiding direct military involvement in the conflict. The goal was to bleed the Soviet Union through a proxy war, using Afghan fighters and foreign volunteers to wage a guerrilla campaign that would tie down Soviet forces and prevent them from expanding their influence further. This strategy succeeded in many respects, as the Soviet Union was eventually forced to withdraw from Afghanistan in 1989, but the long-term consequences of Operation Cyclone were far more complex and troubling.

Long-Term Impact on U.S. Foreign Policy and Global Security

While Operation Cyclone achieved its immediate goal of weakening Soviet influence in Afghanistan, it also had unintended consequences that would come to haunt U.S. policymakers in the years that followed. The U.S. support for the Mujahideen, particularly the arming and training of Islamic militants, contributed to the rise of radical Islamist groups that would later turn their attention to the West. Many of the fighters who had been trained and funded by the U.S. during the Afghan conflict went on to form the core of **al-Qaeda** and other extremist organizations, including the **Taliban**, which would later take control of Afghanistan and provide a safe haven for terrorists.

The experience of fighting a superpower in Afghanistan gave these groups both the skills and the confidence to pursue their own ideological agendas, which often included opposition to the U.S. and its allies. The unintended consequence of Operation Cyclone was the creation of a global network of jihadists, who would use their experience in Afghanistan as a launching pad for future conflicts, including the **September 11, 2001** attacks on the U.S.

The U.S. intervention in Afghanistan also set a precedent for the use of proxy forces in conflicts, a strategy that would be employed in various other parts of the world. However, the Afghan case illustrated the dangers of relying on such forces without fully understanding their long-term goals or the broader implications of arming non-state actors. While Operation Cyclone succeeded in bleeding the Soviet Union, it also contributed to the rise of extremist ideologies that would challenge U.S. interests in the decades to come.

Historical Background on Al-Qaeda

Emergence of Al-Qaeda: The Role of Maktab al-Khidamat (MAK)

The roots of al-Qaeda can be traced back to the Soviet-Afghan War of the 1980s, a conflict that would not only transform the geopolitical landscape of Central Asia but also lay the foundation for the rise of modern jihadist networks. At the heart of this development was the **Maktab al-Khidamat (MAK)**, an organization co-founded by **Osama bin Laden** and **Abdullah Azzam**, which played a pivotal role in organizing foreign fighters, or "Afghan Arabs," to join the jihad against the Soviet Union.

The MAK was established in **1984** in **Peshawar, Pakistan**, as a logistical hub for funneling financial support and recruiting Muslim volunteers for the Afghan jihad. Its primary mission was to raise funds from across the Muslim world and channel those resources toward the anti-Soviet resistance in Afghanistan. While the Afghan mujahideen bore the brunt of the fighting, the MAK served as a critical infrastructure for recruiting foreign fighters and providing them with the necessary training and support.

Funded by the **Saudi government** as well as wealthy private donors, many of whom were Saudi businessmen, the MAK became the key organization that linked the broader Islamic world to the Afghan jihad. **Osama bin Laden**, hailing from a wealthy and influential Saudi family, played a central role in financing the organization and using his connections to sway public opinion in favor of the cause. Bin Laden and Azzam envisioned the MAK as a gateway for global jihad, where foreign Muslim volunteers could be trained, radicalized, and mobilized for future conflicts beyond Afghanistan.

By the mid-1980s, MAK had expanded its influence, establishing **guest houses** in **Peshawar**, near the Afghan border, to facilitate the flow of volunteers and resources. These guest houses served as transit points for recruits from across the Muslim world, and MAK's leadership oversaw the construction of **paramilitary training camps** in Afghanistan. These camps would prepare foreign fighters for guerrilla warfare on the Afghan front, although the foreign fighters never played a major role in the conflict. While it is estimated that over 250,000 Afghan mujahideen fought the Soviets and the Afghan communist government, there were never more than a few thousand foreign fighters active on the battlefield at any given time.

However, the foreign volunteers—known as **"Afghan Arabs"**— would prove significant in the long-term, as they became the core of a global jihadist movement that would eventually manifest as **al-Qaeda**. Between 1982 and 1992, an estimated 35,000 foreign fighters from 43 countries traveled to Afghanistan to participate in the jihad, creating a transnational network of militants. Although their numbers were relatively small compared to the Afghan mujahideen, their ideological fervor and dedication to the concept of global jihad would have lasting repercussions.

Emergence of Osama bin Laden and the Role of Ali Mohamed

Osama bin Laden's rise to prominence during the Afghan jihad was not merely a product of his financial contributions. He also cultivated relationships with key figures in the jihadist world, including individuals like **Ali Abdul Saoud Mohamed**, a complex figure who played a dual role as both a U.S. intelligence operative and a jihadist trainer. Mohamed, a former Egyptian army officer, became an important asset for both the **CIA** and **Egyptian Islamic Jihad**.

Ali Mohamed, born on **June 3, 1952**, operated as a double agent, using his access to both U.S. and jihadist networks to his advantage. After moving to the United States, Mohamed joined the U.S. Army as a sergeant, where he provided training to U.S. Special Forces. Simultaneously, he was an active member of jihadist circles, including those associated with **Egyptian Islamic Jihad**, an organization that would later merge with al-Qaeda. In the **1980s**, Mohamed trained anti-Soviet fighters who were en route to Afghanistan, becoming known for his role in teaching guerrilla warfare and insurgency tactics. **FBI Special Agent Jack Cloonan** would later describe Mohamed as "bin Laden's first trainer."

Mohamed's relationship with bin Laden was particularly significant. His ability to move between the worlds of U.S. intelligence and jihadist militancy gave him access to sensitive information and operational knowledge that he passed on to bin Laden's network. He played a key role in establishing training protocols for the fighters and helped to build a formidable infrastructure for future terrorist operations. His connection to bin Laden further cemented the foundation for what would later become al-Qaeda's global jihadist network.

Bin Laden's association with the **Muslim Brotherhood** also played a role in his early rise. He was sent to Pakistan as a **Muslim Brotherhood representative** to the **Jamaat-e-Islami**, an Islamist organization that was heavily involved in the Afghan jihad. It was during his time in Peshawar that bin Laden met **Abdullah Azzam**, a Palestinian Islamic scholar and a key figure in the global jihadist movement. Together, bin Laden and Azzam laid the groundwork for MAK, which would later serve as the precursor to al-Qaeda.

As MAK grew in influence, it began to attract more radical elements from across the Islamic world. One such figure was **Abu Musab al-Suri**, a Syrian jihadist who joined the MAK networks following the failed **Islamic uprising in Syria** in 1982. Al-Suri and others like him saw the Afghan jihad as a means of continuing their struggle against secular Arab regimes and Western imperialism. The radicalization of these foreign fighters in Afghanistan, combined with the organizational infrastructure provided by MAK, set the stage for the creation of a more permanent and global jihadist organization.

Role of Omar Abdel-Rahman and the Expansion of MAK into the West

By the mid-1980s, MAK's influence extended far beyond the Afghan-Pakistan border. The organization began setting up a network of **recruiting offices** across the globe, including in the United States. The most notable of these was the **Al Kifah Refugee Center**, located at the **Farouq Mosque** on Brooklyn's Atlantic Avenue. This center became a key hub for recruiting

Muslim volunteers for the Afghan jihad, as well as a nexus for fundraising and propaganda efforts in the West.

Among the figures associated with the Al Kifah center was the infamous **"Blind Sheikh" Omar Abdel-Rahman**, an Egyptian cleric who became a prominent recruiter of mujahideen for the Afghan conflict. Abdel-Rahman's radical sermons and calls for jihad attracted a following among young Muslims in the U.S., many of whom were inspired to join the fight in Afghanistan. He would later become infamous for his role in the **1993 World Trade Center bombing**, highlighting the long-term consequences of the jihadist networks built during the Afghan war.

The **Al Kifah center** also became a recruiting ground for individuals who would later be involved in al-Qaeda's global operations. Among them was **Ali Mohamed**, whose connections to both U.S. intelligence and jihadist networks made him a critical figure in bridging the gap between the Afghan jihad and future terrorist activities. The training and operational knowledge that Mohamed imparted to bin Laden and other fighters during this period would prove essential in the development of al-Qaeda's capabilities.

The Transition from MAK to Al-Qaeda

As the Soviet-Afghan war wound down in the late 1980s, the foreign fighters who had come to Afghanistan to participate in the jihad began to turn their attention to other conflicts. While the Afghan mujahideen had succeeded in driving out the Soviets, the infrastructure built by MAK—its guest houses, training camps, and networks of fighters—did not disappear. Instead, these assets were repurposed for a new, broader mission: the establishment of a global jihadist network aimed at confronting Western powers and secular regimes in the Islamic world.

In **1987**, bin Laden and Azzam began establishing more

permanent training camps in Afghanistan, formalizing the structures that would later become al-Qaeda. While MAK had originally been focused on supporting the Afghan jihad, bin Laden's vision expanded to include a broader fight against what he saw as Western imperialism and the corrupt regimes in the Muslim world. Al-Qaeda, meaning "the base" in Arabic, was born out of this shift in focus, becoming not just a network for foreign fighters but a global movement dedicated to jihad on a broader scale.

The assassination of Abdullah Azzam in **1989** marked a turning point in the evolution of the jihadist movement. Azzam had been a more traditional Islamist, focused primarily on fighting foreign occupiers like the Soviets, but bin Laden harbored more radical ambitions. With Azzam out of the picture, bin Laden took full control of the network and transformed it into **al-Qaeda**, a more aggressive and ideologically expansive organization that would soon launch attacks against Western targets, including the United States.

Legacy of MAK and the Rise of Global Jihad

The infrastructure built by Osama bin Laden and Abdullah Azzam during the Afghan jihad laid the foundation for al-Qaeda, which would emerge as the preeminent jihadist organization of the late 20th and early 21st centuries. What began as an effort to recruit and support foreign fighters in Afghanistan ultimately evolved into a global network of militants dedicated to confronting the West and overthrowing secular regimes in the Muslim world. Figures like Ali Mohamed, Omar Abdel-Rahman, and Osama bin Laden played crucial roles in this transition, leveraging their experiences and connections from the Afghan war to build a formidable terrorist organization.

The lessons from the emergence of al-Qaeda underscore the dangers of supporting non-state actors in foreign conflicts without fully understanding their long-term goals. The U.S. support for the Afghan jihad, while successful in driving out the Soviets, inadvertently contributed to the rise of a global jihadist movement that would later turn its sights on the West.

CHAPTER 5 - THE SOVIET WITHDRAWAL AND THE POWER VACUUM IN AFGHANISTAN

U.S. Disengagement and the Power Vacuum in Post-Soviet Afghanistan

When the Soviet Union finally withdrew its forces from Afghanistan in **1989**, after a decade of brutal conflict, it marked the end of one of the Cold War's most significant proxy wars. For the United States, the departure of Soviet troops was seen as a victory in its broader Cold War strategy of containing communism. Operation Cyclone, which funneled billions of dollars to Afghan mujahideen fighters through Pakistan's ISI, had succeeded in forcing a superpower into retreat. However, the U.S. quickly lost interest in the country once its Cold War objectives were fulfilled, leaving Afghanistan to face a turbulent future without the necessary political and economic support to rebuild.

The **U.S. disengagement from Afghanistan** in the early 1990s left a political and military vacuum in a war-ravaged country, where different factions of Afghan mujahideen began to compete for power. With the Soviet-backed Afghan government collapsing and no strong central authority to replace it, the country descended into civil war. Various warlords carved out their own territories, leading to widespread instability, violence, and lawlessness. The U.S., having achieved its Cold War goals, largely ignored the ensuing chaos, focusing instead on new global priorities after the fall of the Soviet Union.

This lack of post-war planning and investment in Afghanistan created fertile ground for the rise of militant groups, including **al-Qaeda**, which had begun to form from the networks established during the jihad against the Soviets. The U.S. had made little effort to secure a stable government or provide long-term assistance to the Afghan people, leaving them to cope with the aftermath of the war alone. In the absence of strong governance, radical Islamist factions, which had been emboldened and militarized during the fight against the Soviets, began to consolidate power.

It was in this context that **the Taliban** emerged, a movement that took advantage of the vacuum to establish itself as the dominant force in Afghanistan by the mid-1990s. While the Taliban initially gained support for restoring order to the war-torn country, it also harbored radical jihadist groups, including **Osama bin Laden's al-Qaeda**, which had relocated to Afghanistan after being expelled from Sudan in **1996**. The Taliban's willingness to offer sanctuary to bin Laden allowed al-Qaeda to grow its operational capabilities, plan future attacks, and cultivate its global network.

By withdrawing from Afghanistan without a coherent long-term strategy, the U.S. inadvertently contributed to the conditions that enabled radical groups to thrive. The power vacuum created in the wake of the Soviet withdrawal, compounded by years of civil war, laid the groundwork for Afghanistan to become a haven for global jihadist movements, with al-Qaeda emerging as the most prominent and dangerous among them.

Rise of the Taliban

As the Afghan civil war continued in the early 1990s following the Soviet withdrawal, Afghanistan descended into further chaos, with various mujahideen factions vying for control. The U.S., having accomplished its Cold War objective of defeating the Soviet Union in Afghanistan, largely disengaged from the country, leaving it without the resources or diplomatic attention necessary for stabilization. This power vacuum allowed the rise of new factions and the re-emergence of radical Islamist groups that would soon have profound consequences not just for Afghanistan, but for global security.

One of the most significant developments during this period was the rise of the **Taliban**, a militant Islamist group that would go on to dominate Afghan politics and provide a crucial sanctuary for Osama bin Laden and his growing al-Qaeda network. The Taliban emerged from the **madrassas** (Islamic religious schools) in Pakistan, where Afghan refugees and young men—many of them orphaned or displaced by war— were radicalized under the teachings of hardline, conservative clerics who adhered to a strict interpretation of **Deobandi Islam**. These madrassas were heavily funded by Saudi Arabia, which sought to spread its brand of **Wahhabi Islam** as a counterbalance to Shia Iran's influence in the region.

The **Taliban**, which means "students" in Pashto, began as a relatively small movement in southern Afghanistan, primarily composed of ethnic **Pashtuns**. They initially gained support by promising to restore order and security to a country ravaged by years of civil war and lawlessness. Disillusioned by the warlord-driven violence and corruption that had characterized much of post-Soviet Afghanistan, many Afghans—especially in rural areas—welcomed the Taliban's harsh but stable rule. By 1996, with the backing of Pakistan's **Inter-Services Intelligence (ISI)** and financial support from Saudi Arabia, the Taliban had seized control of **Kabul**, establishing the **Islamic Emirate of Afghanistan**.

While the Taliban claimed to offer stability, their rule was characterized by a brutal enforcement of **Sharia law**, particularly against women and ethnic minorities. The regime imposed draconian punishments for offenses such as adultery, theft, and blasphemy, while severely restricting women's rights, banning them from work and education. Despite these harsh measures, the Taliban's ability to restore relative peace in some parts of the country gave them a degree of legitimacy, at least in the eyes of their rural Pashtun base.

The rise of the Taliban also had international consequences, as the group provided sanctuary to a range of Islamist militants, including **Osama bin Laden** and his al-Qaeda network. After being expelled from Sudan in 1996, bin Laden returned to Afghanistan, where he had first fought during the Soviet-Afghan war. The Taliban, under the leadership of **Mullah Mohammed Omar**, welcomed bin Laden, offering him protection and allowing him to use Afghanistan as a base of operations for al-Qaeda's growing ambitions. Bin Laden's relationship with the Taliban would soon make Afghanistan the epicenter of global jihadist activities and set the stage for future conflicts with the West.

While the Taliban's focus was primarily domestic—aimed at consolidating power within Afghanistan and enforcing their vision of Islamic rule—bin Laden's ambitions were global. His growing network of militants and the infrastructure provided by the Taliban allowed al-Qaeda to pursue its broader agenda of targeting the United States and other Western powers. In offering refuge to al-Qaeda, the Taliban sowed the seeds of future conflict, as Afghanistan would become a haven for terrorist planning and training, ultimately culminating in the

9/11 attacks.

Bin Laden's Influence

Bin Laden's Vision and Anti-Western Sentiment

Osama bin Laden's experiences during the Afghan jihad against the Soviets had a profound impact on his worldview, shaping his belief in the power of armed jihad as a tool for confronting perceived enemies of Islam. Born into a wealthy and influential Saudi family, bin Laden had joined the Afghan jihad as a young man, initially motivated by a sense of religious duty to defend fellow Muslims against Soviet aggression. Over time, however, his experiences on the battlefield, coupled with his interactions with other radical Islamist thinkers like **Abdullah Azzam**, began to shape a more global and radical vision for jihad.

During the Afghan war, bin Laden witnessed firsthand how a relatively small group of mujahideen fighters, with support from external powers like the U.S., could successfully repel a superpower. This experience emboldened him and reinforced the idea that Muslim fighters, united by a common cause, could defeat much larger and better-equipped forces. The Soviet Union's eventual defeat validated bin Laden's belief in the effectiveness of guerrilla warfare and jihad as a means of achieving political and religious goals.

However, bin Laden's ideological evolution was not solely focused on local conflicts. Over time, he began to see the West, particularly the United States, as the primary enemy of Islam. This anti-Western sentiment was rooted in several key experiences and grievances that shaped his thinking during the 1990s and ultimately led to the formation of al-Qaeda as a global jihadist organization.

One of bin Laden's earliest sources of disillusionment with the U.S. came from its ongoing military presence in the Middle

East, particularly in **Saudi Arabia**. In the aftermath of the **1990 Iraqi invasion of Kuwait**, the U.S. deployed thousands of troops to Saudi Arabia as part of the **Gulf War coalition** to defend the kingdom and expel Iraqi forces from Kuwait. For bin Laden, the presence of U.S. troops on Saudi soil—the birthplace of Islam and home to its two holiest cities, Mecca and Medina—was an intolerable affront. He viewed the American presence as a form of occupation and a symbol of the broader Western influence that he believed was corrupting the Muslim world.

In a series of **fatwas** (religious decrees) issued during the mid-1990s, bin Laden articulated his growing opposition to the U.S. and its allies. He framed his jihad not just as a defense of Muslims in specific conflicts but as a global struggle against what he saw as a U.S.-led campaign to subjugate and humiliate the Islamic world. In a **1996 fatwa**, he declared that the presence of U.S. troops in Saudi Arabia violated the sanctity of Muslim lands and called for jihad against the "infidels" occupying the Arabian Peninsula. This fatwa marked a turning point in bin Laden's thinking, as he began to shift his focus from regional conflicts to a broader, global agenda.

Bin Laden's anti-Western sentiment was further fueled by U.S. support for **Israel** in the ongoing Israeli-Palestinian conflict. Like many in the Arab and Muslim world, bin Laden viewed the U.S. as complicit in the occupation of Palestinian territories, and he saw American support for Israel as a central grievance that justified violent resistance. He framed the U.S. not only as an enemy of Islam but as the chief backer of regimes and policies that oppressed Muslims worldwide.

By the mid-1990s, bin Laden had transformed his vision into a global jihadist ideology. In **1998**, he issued a joint fatwa with other Islamist leaders, declaring that it was the religious duty of all Muslims to kill Americans—both military and civilian—wherever they could be found. This fatwa, issued under the banner of the **World Islamic Front for Jihad Against Jews and Crusaders**, effectively formalized al-Qaeda's declaration of war against the United States and its allies.

Bin Laden's vision of global jihad took shape through a series of high-profile attacks that demonstrated al-Qaeda's capabilities and its willingness to strike at the heart of U.S. interests. In **1998**, al-Qaeda bombed the U.S. embassies in **Kenya** and **Tanzania**, killing more than 200 people. In **2000**, the group orchestrated a suicide attack on the **USS Cole** in Yemen, killing 17 U.S. sailors. These attacks were preludes to the most significant and devastating attack of all: the **September 11, 2001** attacks on the United States.

The **9/11 attacks**, in which al-Qaeda operatives hijacked commercial airliners and crashed them into the **World Trade Center** and **Pentagon**, killing nearly 3,000 people, marked the culmination of bin Laden's anti-Western vision. The attack was not only a symbolic blow against the U.S. but also a strategic move designed to provoke a military response. Bin Laden believed that by drawing the U.S. into prolonged conflicts in the Middle East, similar to the Soviet experience in Afghanistan, he could weaken American power and inspire a broader uprising across the Muslim world.

Al-Qaeda's Global Ambitions and the 9/11 Attacks

By the late 1990s, Osama bin Laden had transformed al-Qaeda from a loose network of jihadist fighters into a highly organized, ideologically driven terrorist group with a clear global mission: to wage jihad against the United States and its allies, whom he viewed as the primary oppressors of the Muslim world. Bin Laden's anti-Western sentiment had been crystallized by several key factors: the U.S. military presence in Saudi Arabia following the Gulf War, Washington's unwavering support for Israel, and the broader Western influence in the politics and economies of Muslim-majority countries. These grievances fueled his belief that violent jihad was the only way to combat the influence of the West and restore the Islamic caliphate.

In **1998**, bin Laden and several other jihadist leaders issued a **fatwa** under the banner of the **World Islamic Front for Jihad Against Jews and Crusaders**, which formally declared war on the United States. The fatwa stated that it was the religious duty of all Muslims to kill Americans—both military and civilian—wherever they could be found, framing the struggle as a defense of Islam against Western aggression. This declaration marked a significant escalation in al-Qaeda's global ambitions and signaled that the group would no longer limit its activities to regional conflicts but would directly target the U.S. on the global stage.

Al-Qaeda's operational reach expanded during this period, as bin Laden and his associates began planning attacks on U.S. interests abroad. In **1998**, al-Qaeda carried out the simultaneous bombings of the U.S. embassies in **Kenya** and **Tanzania**, killing over 200 people and injuring thousands more. These attacks demonstrated al-Qaeda's ability to coordinate large-scale operations and strike U.S. targets far beyond the Middle East. The bombings also drew the attention of the U.S. government, which responded with cruise missile strikes on suspected al-Qaeda facilities in **Afghanistan** and **Sudan**, but these efforts did little to curtail the group's activities.

In **2000**, al-Qaeda orchestrated another high-profile attack, this time targeting the **USS Cole**, a U.S. Navy destroyer docked in the Yemeni port of Aden. A small boat laden with explosives rammed into the side of the ship, killing 17 U.S. sailors and injuring dozens more. The attack on the Cole was another sign that al-Qaeda was increasingly focusing its efforts on targeting U.S. military assets, further signaling the group's growing capacity to strike at high-value targets.

However, these earlier attacks were merely precursors to al-Qaeda's most ambitious operation: the **September 11, 2001 attacks**. The 9/11 attacks, meticulously planned over several years, represented the culmination of bin Laden's vision of striking directly at the heart of the United States. On that fateful morning, 19 al-Qaeda operatives hijacked four commercial airliners. Two planes were flown into the **World Trade Center towers** in **New York City**, one crashed into the **Pentagon** in **Washington, D.C.**, and the fourth, **United Airlines Flight 93**, crashed into a field in Pennsylvania after passengers attempted to retake control of the aircraft.

The 9/11 attacks were the deadliest terrorist act in history, killing nearly 3,000 people and causing unprecedented devastation. For bin Laden and al-Qaeda, the attacks were not only a symbolic blow against the U.S. but also a strategic move designed to provoke a military response. Bin Laden believed that by drawing the U.S. into prolonged wars in the Muslim world, he could weaken American power, galvanize Muslims to join the jihad, and create the conditions for the eventual overthrow of Western-backed regimes in the Middle East.

The U.S. response to 9/11 was swift and decisive. In **October 2001**, the United States, with the support of NATO allies, launched **Operation Enduring Freedom**, a military campaign aimed at dismantling al-Qaeda and removing the Taliban from power in Afghanistan. The invasion quickly toppled the Taliban regime, but bin Laden and other al-Qaeda leaders managed to evade capture, retreating into the rugged mountains along the **Afghan-Pakistani border**. The war in Afghanistan would continue for two decades, with the U.S. and its allies facing a resilient Taliban insurgency and struggling to stabilize the country.

The 9/11 attacks fundamentally reshaped U.S. foreign policy and global security, leading to the **Global War on Terror** and a series of military interventions in the Middle East and beyond.

For al-Qaeda, the attacks marked both a major success in striking a blow against its primary enemy and the beginning of a protracted conflict with the U.S. and its allies. The group's global ambitions, combined with the sanctuary it had found in Afghanistan under the Taliban, set the stage for decades of violence, insurgency, and counterterrorism efforts that continue to this day.

The Seeds of Global Conflict

The rise of the Taliban and their alliance with al-Qaeda in post-Soviet Afghanistan laid the foundation for the global jihadist movement that would define the early 21st century. By providing sanctuary and operational freedom to bin Laden and his network, the Taliban unwittingly set Afghanistan on a collision course with the West, culminating in the catastrophic 9/11 attacks. Bin Laden's vision of a global jihad against the U.S. and its allies, shaped by his experiences in the Afghan jihad and his grievances against Western policies in the Muslim world, would leave a lasting legacy of conflict, instability, and terrorism that reverberates across the globe to this day.

Legacy of Bin Laden's Vision

Osama bin Laden's experiences during the Afghan jihad against the Soviets, coupled with his growing anti-Western sentiment, shaped the ideological foundation of al-Qaeda. His belief in the power of armed jihad, combined with his vision of a global struggle against the U.S. and its allies, set the stage for al-Qaeda's emergence as the world's most dangerous jihadist organization. The **post-Soviet power vacuum** in Afghanistan, left largely unaddressed by the U.S., provided bin Laden with the opportunity to grow and expand his network, ultimately leading to the tragic events of **9/11** and a new era of global terrorism.

The lessons from the rise of al-Qaeda underscore the

unintended consequences of U.S. foreign interventions and the need for a more comprehensive approach to post-conflict rebuilding and engagement. The failure to address the aftermath of the Afghan jihad allowed groups like al-Qaeda to thrive, and the consequences of that failure continue to reverberate across the world today.

CHAPTER 6 - PROXY WARS IN AFRICA: ANGOLA, MOZAMBIQUE, AND THE LEGACY OF U.S. SUPPORT FOR INSURGENTS

U.S. Involvement in Cold War-Era Conflicts in Africa

The African continent, rich in natural resources and strategically significant, became an important battleground during the Cold War as the United States and the Soviet Union sought to expand their influence through a series of **proxy wars**. From the **1960s** through the **1980s**, Angola and Mozambique, two former Portuguese colonies in southern Africa, became key flashpoints in this ideological struggle, with both the U.S. and the Soviet Union backing insurgent movements and governments aligned with their respective geopolitical interests.

For the U.S., the conflicts in Angola and Mozambique

represented an opportunity to counter Soviet expansion and protect American economic interests, particularly access to Africa's vast mineral wealth. However, the U.S. involvement in these conflicts—often through indirect means, such as funding, training, and arming insurgent groups—would leave a lasting legacy of instability, contributing to protracted civil wars and humanitarian crises. The U.S. support for insurgent movements in Africa during the Cold War mirrored its broader global strategy of using local forces to fight the spread of communism, as seen in other parts of the world like Latin America, Southeast Asia, and Afghanistan.

Decolonization and the Cold War in Africa

The period of **decolonization** that swept across Africa in the mid-20th century was deeply intertwined with the Cold War, as newly independent nations found themselves drawn into the geopolitical rivalry between the U.S. and the Soviet Union. African liberation movements, seeking to overthrow European colonial powers, often aligned themselves with one of the two superpowers based on ideology, strategic interests, and the availability of support.

Both the U.S. and the Soviet Union viewed Africa as an arena where they could extend their influence and prevent the other from gaining strategic footholds. For the Soviet Union, supporting revolutionary movements in Africa was part of a broader strategy to promote Marxist-Leninist ideologies and gain influence in the developing world. For the U.S., the rise of pro-Soviet or communist regimes in Africa was seen as a threat to Western interests, particularly access to key resources like oil, diamonds, and minerals.

In this context, the U.S. adopted a policy of **supporting insurgencies** and counter-revolutionary movements in Africa to weaken or overthrow governments aligned with the Soviet Union. This approach, part of the broader U.S. strategy of **containment**, often involved covert operations, financial assistance, and military support for anti-communist forces, much like in Afghanistan or Latin America.

Angola: The U.S. and the Angolan Civil War

Angola's struggle for independence from **Portugal** in the 1960s quickly escalated into a brutal and protracted civil war, which would last for decades and become one of the bloodiest conflicts in Africa. The **Angolan Civil War** (1975–2002) was marked by the involvement of multiple foreign powers, including the U.S., the Soviet Union, and Cuba, each backing different factions in the fight for control of the country.

After Angola gained independence from Portugal in **1975**, the country was divided between three main nationalist groups:

1. **MPLA (Popular Movement for the Liberation of Angola)** – A Marxist-Leninist group supported by the Soviet Union and Cuba.
2. **UNITA (National Union for the Total Independence of Angola)** – A pro-Western insurgent group led by **Jonas Savimbi**, which received support from the U.S., South Africa, and other Western allies.
3. **FNLA (National Front for the Liberation of Angola)** – Another nationalist group backed by the U.S. and Zaire (now the Democratic Republic of the Congo).

As the country slid into civil war, the U.S. saw Angola as a key battleground in the fight against the spread of communism in Africa. The **MPLA**, which had declared itself the ruling party in the capital, **Luanda**, was immediately recognized by the Soviet Union and Cuba, which sent thousands of Cuban troops to support the MPLA and help solidify its control over the country. The U.S., fearing the establishment of a Soviet-aligned government in such a resource-rich nation, began funneling covert military aid to **UNITA**, led by **Jonas Savimbi**.

The U.S. role in Angola was part of a broader Cold War strategy to counter Soviet influence in southern Africa, which was also aligned with South Africa's apartheid regime. For the U.S., supporting UNITA allowed it to challenge the Soviet-Cuban alliance in the region without committing American troops directly to the conflict. Instead, the U.S. provided arms, training, and financial support to UNITA, enabling Savimbi's forces to wage a guerrilla war against the MPLA government.

However, the U.S. support for Savimbi and UNITA had significant long-term consequences for Angola. While the aid prolonged the civil war and helped UNITA maintain its insurgency, it also contributed to massive civilian casualties, widespread destruction, and the displacement of millions of Angolans. The war became one of the most devastating conflicts in post-colonial Africa, fueled by the Cold War rivalry between the superpowers.

The U.S. backing of Savimbi, despite his brutal tactics and authoritarian leadership style, also tarnished America's image in the region. Savimbi, who was initially portrayed as a pro-democracy leader, increasingly used coercion, forced recruitment, and violence to maintain control over his forces. His pursuit of power at all costs contributed to the continuation of the conflict long after the Cold War ended, with Angola remaining embroiled in civil war until **2002**, well after the fall of the Soviet Union.

Mozambique: Cold War Proxies and the Fight for Independence

Like Angola, **Mozambique** experienced a bloody and prolonged civil war following its independence from **Portugal** in **1975**. The conflict was primarily between the **FRELIMO (Mozambique Liberation Front)** government, which was aligned with the Soviet Union, and the **RENAMO (Mozambique National Resistance)** insurgency, which received support from both the U.S. and apartheid-era South Africa.

FRELIMO, which had led the struggle for independence, took

power in Mozambique and aligned itself with the Soviet bloc, adopting Marxist-Leninist policies and receiving military and economic aid from the Soviet Union, Cuba, and East Germany. The U.S., concerned about the growing Soviet influence in southern Africa, indirectly supported RENAMO through its alliance with South Africa, which sought to destabilize Mozambique as part of its broader strategy to weaken neighboring governments sympathetic to anti-apartheid movements.

RENAMO, which was originally created by the **Rhodesian Intelligence Service** to fight against Zimbabwean guerrillas, became a major insurgent force in Mozambique, waging a brutal campaign against the FRELIMO government. The U.S., while not directly involved in arming RENAMO, provided support through its regional allies, viewing the group as a bulwark against the spread of communism in southern Africa. RENAMO used terror tactics, including the destruction of infrastructure, mass killings, and forced labor, to destabilize the FRELIMO government and gain control of rural areas.

The U.S. support for insurgencies like RENAMO and UNITA in southern Africa was part of a broader Cold War policy that prioritized defeating Soviet influence, even at the cost of supporting groups that engaged in human rights abuses and war crimes. Like the conflict in Angola, the war in Mozambique left a devastating legacy of destruction, with millions displaced and tens of thousands killed. The war also significantly hindered Mozambique's development, as RENAMO's attacks targeted key infrastructure, including roads, schools, and hospitals.

The **Mozambican Civil War** continued until **1992**, when a peace agreement was finally brokered, leading to multiparty elections and the formal end of the conflict. However, the war's legacy persisted, with many parts of the country left impoverished and underdeveloped due to years of fighting. The U.S. role in supporting RENAMO, much like its involvement in Angola, underscored the broader strategy of using proxy forces to fight ideological battles, regardless of the long-term humanitarian consequences.

Legacy of U.S. Support for Insurgents

The U.S. involvement in the proxy wars in Angola and Mozambique during the Cold War left a lasting impact on the region. By supporting insurgent movements like UNITA and RENAMO, the U.S. aimed to contain Soviet influence and protect Western economic interests, particularly access to Africa's natural resources. However, these interventions often prolonged conflicts, contributed to widespread destruction, and left deep scars on the societies involved.

The conflicts in Angola and Mozambique were part of a broader pattern of U.S. Cold War-era interventions in the Global South, where support for anti-communist insurgencies often came at the cost of long-term stability and development. The U.S. focus on defeating Soviet-aligned regimes sometimes meant backing authoritarian leaders and insurgent groups that engaged in human rights abuses, undermining America's stated commitment to democracy and freedom.

In both Angola and Mozambique, the Cold War proxy wars contributed to decades of instability, leaving these nations grappling with the legacies of civil war, poverty, and underdevelopment. The U.S. support for insurgents like Jonas Savimbi and RENAMO, while successful in achieving short-term geopolitical objectives, ultimately led to protracted conflicts that devastated local populations and delayed efforts at nation-building and reconciliation.

As the Cold War came to an end, the U.S. disengaged from many of its African proxy conflicts, leaving the countries involved to rebuild on their own. The long-term consequences of these wars—civilian casualties, displacement, destroyed infrastructure, and deeply divided societies—continue to affect Angola, Mozambique, and other parts of southern Africa today. The lessons from U.S. involvement in these conflicts underscore the dangers of using proxy forces to achieve geopolitical goals, particularly when those forces engage in tactics that undermine the broader principles of human rights and democracy.

How U.S. Support for Insurgent Groups Destabilized Entire Regions

During the Cold War, the United States frequently supported insurgent groups around the world as part of its broader strategy to contain communism and undermine Soviet influence. While these efforts sometimes yielded short-term strategic gains, they often had far-reaching and destructive consequences that destabilized entire regions, setting the stage for protracted conflicts, humanitarian crises, and the rise of radical movements. This chapter explores how U.S. support for insurgencies in various parts of the world—particularly in Africa, Latin America, and the Middle East—led to widespread instability, the collapse of local governance structures, and long-term challenges for regional and global security.

Containment Through Proxy Warfare

In the aftermath of World War II, the U.S. and the Soviet Union emerged as global superpowers, locked in an ideological struggle for dominance that would come to define the latter half of the 20th century. This global contest between capitalism and communism, commonly referred to as the **Cold War**, was characterized by an ongoing rivalry that played out not only through direct competition in Europe and Asia but also through **proxy wars** in the developing world. The U.S., determined to prevent the spread of communism, sought to counter Soviet-backed regimes and revolutionary movements by supporting anti-communist insurgents, often providing them with financial aid, military training, and weapons.

This policy of supporting insurgencies was part of a broader strategy of **containment**, articulated by U.S. policymakers such as **George Kennan**, who argued that the U.S. should prevent the spread of communism by any means necessary, including covert operations and indirect military support. As a result, the U.S. became deeply involved in a number of conflicts around the world, ranging from **Latin America** to **Africa** and **Southeast Asia**, in an effort to weaken Soviet influence and protect American economic and geopolitical interests. However, in many cases, this support for insurgent groups destabilized entire regions, with consequences that would resonate for decades.

Destabilization in Africa: Angola and Mozambique

The U.S. role in supporting insurgent movements in Africa during the Cold War exemplifies how such interventions could destabilize entire regions and prolong conflicts. In **Angola** and **Mozambique**, U.S. support for insurgencies not only fueled civil wars but also contributed to the spread of violence and instability across southern Africa.

In Angola, the U.S. provided significant support to **UNITA (National Union for the Total Independence of Angola)**, an insurgent group led by **Jonas Savimbi** that was fighting against the Soviet-aligned **MPLA (Popular Movement for the Liberation of Angola)**. The Angolan Civil War, which lasted from **1975** to **2002**, was one of the longest and deadliest conflicts in Africa, and the U.S. involvement helped to prolong the war by enabling UNITA to continue its insurgency. The war not only devastated Angola, causing the deaths of hundreds of thousands of people, but also had a destabilizing effect on neighboring countries.

The conflict in Angola spilled over into **Namibia**, which was then controlled by **South Africa** under apartheid rule, as well as into **Zaire** (now the Democratic Republic of the Congo), which supported UNITA in its fight against the MPLA. South Africa, which viewed the MPLA as a threat to its regional interests, provided military assistance to UNITA, while the Soviet Union and Cuba backed the MPLA with troops, weapons, and financial aid. This proxy war between East and West not only devastated Angola's economy and infrastructure but also fueled regional instability, as countries like Namibia, Zambia, and Zaire became drawn into the conflict.

Similarly, in **Mozambique**, the U.S. indirectly supported the **RENAMO (Mozambique National Resistance)** insurgency, which fought against the Soviet-backed **FRELIMO (Mozambique Liberation Front)** government. RENAMO, which was initially supported by **Rhodesia (modern-day Zimbabwe)** and later by apartheid South Africa, engaged in a brutal campaign of violence that targeted civilians, infrastructure, and government forces. The Mozambican Civil War, which lasted from **1977** to **1992**, resulted in the deaths of over a million people and displaced millions more.

The U.S. support for RENAMO, much like its support for UNITA in Angola, was part of a broader effort to counter Soviet influence in southern Africa. However, this support contributed to the continuation of a conflict that caused immense suffering and destruction. RENAMO's tactics, which included the use of child soldiers, mass killings, and the destruction of agricultural infrastructure, left Mozambique's economy in ruins and set back its development by decades.

The destabilizing effects of the Angolan and Mozambican civil wars were not limited to those countries alone. The conflicts spread violence and instability across southern Africa, weakening regional institutions, fueling cross-border insurgencies, and creating conditions for the emergence of new militant groups. The U.S. support for insurgents in these conflicts, while intended to counter Soviet influence, ultimately contributed to the destabilization of an entire region, with consequences that continue to affect southern Africa today.

Latin America: The Legacy of U.S. Support for Contras and Insurgents

In **Latin America**, U.S. support for insurgent groups and right-wing paramilitaries as part of its broader anti-communist strategy also had a destabilizing effect on the region. Nowhere was this more apparent than in **Nicaragua**, where the U.S. backed the **Contras**, an insurgent group that sought to overthrow the **Sandinista** government, which had come to power in **1979** after leading a successful revolution against the U.S.-backed dictatorship of **Anastasio Somoza**.

The **Sandinistas**, who had socialist leanings and were aligned with Cuba and the Soviet Union, quickly became a target of U.S. efforts to prevent the spread of communism in Central America. In response, the **Reagan administration** provided covert support to the **Contras**, a collection of anti-Sandinista forces that included former members of Somoza's National Guard, as well as other paramilitary groups.

The U.S. support for the Contras—most of which was provided covertly through the **CIA** and funded through illicit means, including the infamous **Iran-Contra scandal**—prolonged the conflict in Nicaragua and contributed to widespread violence. The Contras engaged in a campaign of sabotage, attacking civilian targets, destroying infrastructure, and using terror tactics to undermine the Sandinista government. This resulted in significant human rights abuses, including massacres of civilians, forced displacements, and the destruction of schools and healthcare facilities.

The **Nicaraguan Civil War** had a destabilizing effect not only within Nicaragua but also throughout Central

America, as the U.S. support for insurgencies in Nicaragua intersected with other conflicts in **El Salvador, Guatemala, and Honduras**. In **El Salvador**, the U.S. backed the **right-wing military government** in its fight against the **FMLN (Farabundo Martí National Liberation Front)**, a Marxist guerrilla group that sought to overthrow the government. The Salvadoran Civil War, which lasted from **1979** to **1992**, was marked by widespread atrocities committed by both the government and the insurgents, including the use of death squads and the massacre of civilians. The U.S. support for the Salvadoran military, including training provided by the **School of the Americas**, helped sustain the government's brutal counterinsurgency campaign, further destabilizing the region.

The destabilizing impact of U.S. involvement in Central America was not limited to the civil wars themselves. The violence and instability caused by these conflicts led to mass migrations, with hundreds of thousands of refugees fleeing to neighboring countries and to the U.S. These waves of migration, along with the destruction of infrastructure and social services, created long-term challenges for the region, including poverty, gang violence, and political corruption, which continue to affect Central America today.

The Middle East: Afghanistan and the Rise of Radical Movements

The U.S. support for insurgent groups in the **Middle East**, particularly in **Afghanistan**, also had a profound destabilizing effect that continues to reverberate across the region. During the **Soviet-Afghan War** (1979–1989), the U.S. provided significant support to the **Mujahideen**, a coalition of Afghan resistance fighters who sought to expel Soviet forces from Afghanistan. The U.S. viewed the Soviet invasion of Afghanistan as part of a broader Cold War struggle, and its goal was to "bleed" the Soviet Union by providing covert military aid to the Mujahideen through **Operation Cyclone**.

While the U.S. support for the Mujahideen contributed to the eventual withdrawal of Soviet forces from Afghanistan, it also had unintended consequences that destabilized the region for decades to come. After the Soviets withdrew in 1989, Afghanistan was left with a power vacuum, as various Mujahideen factions began fighting for control of the country. The U.S., having achieved its Cold War objectives, largely disengaged from Afghanistan, leaving it without the necessary support to rebuild and stabilize.

The result was a devastating civil war that led to the rise of the **Taliban**, a radical Islamist group that would go on to provide sanctuary to **al-Qaeda** and other jihadist movements. The U.S. support for insurgents in Afghanistan, while successful in defeating the Soviets, ultimately helped create the conditions for the rise of radical Islamist movements that would target the U.S. and its allies in the years that followed. The most notable consequence of this destabilization was the **9/11 attacks**, carried out by al-Qaeda operatives who had been trained and radicalized during the Afghan jihad.

The legacy of U.S. support for insurgent groups in Afghanistan is emblematic of the broader pattern of destabilization caused by Cold War-era interventions. By arming and empowering local forces to fight Soviet-backed regimes, the U.S. inadvertently contributed to the rise of non-state actors and radical movements that would go on to challenge U.S. interests and destabilize the region for decades.

The U.S. support for insurgent groups during the Cold War, while driven by the desire to contain Soviet influence and protect American interests, often had the unintended consequence of destabilizing entire regions. In Africa, Latin America, and the Middle East, the U.S. involvement in proxy wars fueled civil conflicts, prolonged violence, and contributed to the collapse of local governance structures.

These interventions often prioritized short-term strategic goals over long-term stability, leaving behind a legacy of broken states, impoverished populations, and radicalized movements. The consequences of U.S. support for insurgencies continue to affect the world today, as many of the regions destabilized during the Cold War remain mired in conflict, poverty, and underdevelopment.

Long-Term Effects on Governance and Regional Security

The long-term effects of U.S. support for insurgent groups during the Cold War reverberate through the political and security dynamics of the regions in which these proxy wars took place. By empowering insurgencies, often with little regard for the consequences beyond the immediate strategic objective of countering Soviet influence, the U.S. contributed to the erosion of state institutions, the proliferation of non-state actors, and the rise of radical movements. The destabilization of governance structures and the collapse of regional security frameworks have had enduring consequences, creating power vacuums, fostering corruption, and enabling the rise of warlordism and terrorism. This chapter delves into the enduring effects of these policies on governance and regional security in Africa, Latin America, and the Middle East.

Erosion of Governance Structures in Post-Conflict States

One of the most significant long-term effects of U.S. support for insurgent groups was the **erosion of governance structures** in the countries where these proxy wars took place. In many cases, insurgent groups, though nominally anti-communist or aligned with U.S. interests, were not equipped to govern effectively once they gained power, or their actions undermined existing institutions to such a degree that state collapse followed.

In **Angola**, U.S. support for **UNITA** in its fight against the **MPLA** helped fuel a civil war that devastated the country's infrastructure and institutions. The war not only destroyed physical assets such as roads, schools, and hospitals but also eroded the legitimacy of Angola's central government. The MPLA, though supported by the Soviet Union, had initially sought to establish a functioning state apparatus. However, continuous U.S. backing of UNITA, combined with the South African apartheid regime's support for anti-MPLA forces, ensured that Angola's governance structures were repeatedly undermined by insurgent attacks and internal divisions. When the war finally ended in **2002**, after the death of Jonas Savimbi, Angola was left with weak governance, a decimated economy, and a deeply divided society. Although the MPLA retained power, it presided over a state rife with corruption, where a small elite controlled the vast wealth generated by Angola's oil reserves, while the majority of the population remained impoverished.

Similarly, in **Mozambique**, U.S. indirect support for **RENAMO** insurgents during the civil war contributed to the destruction of Mozambique's state institutions. RENAMO's tactics, which included targeting infrastructure and terrorizing civilian populations, severely weakened the country's capacity to govern effectively. By the time a peace agreement was reached in **1992**, Mozambique's institutions were in shambles, and the government struggled to rebuild a nation that had been ravaged by 15 years of war. The central government's authority was limited in many parts of the country, where local warlords and insurgents retained significant influence. Even today, Mozambique remains one of the poorest countries in the world, and its fragile state institutions continue to struggle with corruption, poor governance, and insurgent violence, including the recent rise of Islamist extremism in the northern regions.

In **Latin America**, the U.S. support for insurgent groups and right-wing paramilitaries in countries like **Nicaragua** and **El Salvador** also had a corrosive effect on governance. In Nicaragua, the U.S.-backed **Contras** used guerrilla tactics to destabilize the **Sandinista** government, targeting state infrastructure and terrorizing rural populations. Although the Sandinistas were eventually voted out of power in **1990**, the civil war left the country deeply divided and its institutions weakened. The political polarization and mistrust fostered by the conflict continue to shape Nicaraguan politics, with the country cycling between periods of authoritarianism, corruption, and political unrest. Meanwhile, in **El Salvador**, the U.S. support for the right-wing military government during its civil war not only prolonged the conflict but also entrenched a culture of impunity and corruption within the country's military and political elite. Post-conflict El Salvador has struggled to build effective governance, with gang violence, corruption, and political instability continuing to plague the nation.

In the **Middle East**, the U.S. support for insurgent groups, particularly during the **Soviet-Afghan War**, played a key role in the **collapse of Afghan governance** following the Soviet withdrawal. While U.S.-backed mujahideen factions succeeded in expelling Soviet forces from Afghanistan, they subsequently turned on each other in a bloody civil war, contributing to the collapse of Afghanistan's state institutions. The war destroyed much of the country's infrastructure, weakened the central government, and left Afghanistan in a state of near-anarchy, ripe for the rise of the **Taliban**. U.S. disengagement from Afghanistan after the Soviet withdrawal left a power vacuum that insurgent groups, warlords, and extremist factions were quick to fill. The Taliban, which emerged from the madrassas in Pakistan, capitalized on this power vacuum, establishing its own form of governance based on a harsh interpretation of **Sharia law** and providing sanctuary to radical Islamist groups like **al-Qaeda**.

Another long-term consequence of U.S. support for insurgent groups during the Cold War was the **rise of warlordism** and the proliferation of **non-state actors**, many of whom retained significant influence long after the conflicts in which they fought had ended. In regions where insurgents gained power or continued to exert control after wars ended, governance was often fragmented, with warlords, militias, and local strongmen wielding de facto power over territories.

In **Afghanistan**, the U.S. support for a decentralized network of mujahideen fighters during the Soviet occupation contributed to the fragmentation of the country after the war. As various mujahideen commanders seized control of different regions, Afghanistan became a patchwork of fiefdoms, each controlled by local warlords. These warlords, many of whom had been armed and funded by the U.S. during the Soviet-Afghan War, resisted efforts to build a centralized government, leading to years of civil war. The rise of the **Taliban** was in part a reaction to the warlordism that had taken root in the country, as the Taliban sought to impose order through its strict interpretation of Islamic law. However, even after the Taliban was toppled by the U.S. in **2001**, warlordism persisted in parts of Afghanistan, undermining efforts to build a stable, democratic state.

In **Africa**, the U.S. support for insurgent groups also contributed to the rise of warlordism, particularly in **Angola** and **Mozambique**. In Angola, Jonas Savimbi, the leader of **UNITA**, ruled over vast swaths of the country as a warlord, using the resources provided by the U.S. and South Africa to maintain his control. Even after the end of the Cold War, Savimbi continued his insurgency, fighting against the MPLA government and prolonging the conflict. The persistence of warlordism in Angola hampered efforts to rebuild the country after the civil war, as rival factions competed for control of resources, particularly diamonds, which had been a major source of funding for UNITA.

In **Somalia**, U.S. involvement in the 1980s and early 1990s —primarily in the form of supporting various warlord factions to counter Soviet-backed groups—contributed to the fragmentation of the country. After the fall of Somali dictator **Siad Barre** in **1991**, Somalia descended into chaos, with competing warlords carving out territories and engaging in brutal battles for control. U.S. military intervention in Somalia, which culminated in the **Battle of Mogadishu** in 1993 (popularly known as "Black Hawk Down"), failed to stabilize the country, and warlordism persisted for years. Somalia became a failed state, with no effective central government, creating a power vacuum that allowed radical Islamist groups like **al-Shabaab** to emerge and grow.

One of the most far-reaching consequences of U.S. support for insurgent groups during the Cold War has been the **rise of terrorism** and **radical Islamist movements**, particularly in the Middle East and Central Asia. In its efforts to counter Soviet influence in places like Afghanistan, the U.S. provided arms, training, and financial support to groups that would later evolve into some of the most dangerous terrorist organizations in the world.

The **Soviet-Afghan War** was a turning point in the radicalization of Islamist movements. The U.S. support for the mujahideen fighters—many of whom were drawn from across the Muslim world and radicalized during their time fighting in Afghanistan—helped create a global jihadist network that would later become **al-Qaeda**. Figures like **Osama bin Laden**, who played a central role in organizing foreign fighters during the Afghan jihad, used the infrastructure built during the war to establish al-Qaeda as a global terrorist organization. The U.S.

support for the mujahideen, while successful in driving the Soviets out of Afghanistan, had the unintended consequence of fostering the growth of a radical Islamist movement that would go on to target the U.S. and its allies in the years that followed.

In the aftermath of the Soviet withdrawal from Afghanistan, many of the foreign fighters who had participated in the jihad returned to their home countries, where they began to spread the ideology of **global jihad**. The **Afghan Arabs**, as they were called, became the nucleus of al-Qaeda and other Islamist groups, which used the experience and networks developed during the war to launch terrorist attacks against Western targets. The most significant of these attacks, the **September 11, 2001** attacks on the U.S., demonstrated the long-term dangers of supporting insurgent groups without fully understanding the consequences of their ideologies or long-term goals.

The long-term effects of U.S. support for insurgent groups also extended to **regional security**, as the destabilization of individual states often had a **ripple effect** on neighboring countries. In many cases, insurgent movements spilled over borders, contributing to cross-border conflicts, refugee crises, and the proliferation of arms and militias.

In **Central America**, the U.S. support for the **Contras** in Nicaragua had a destabilizing effect on the entire region. The violence and instability in Nicaragua spilled over into neighboring countries like **El Salvador**, **Honduras**, and **Guatemala**, which were already grappling with their own civil wars and insurgencies. The U.S. support for right-wing paramilitaries and military governments in these countries, as part of its broader Cold War strategy, contributed to regional instability and created an environment in which violence, corruption, and impunity flourished. Even after the wars ended, the legacy of U.S. involvement in Central America persisted in the form of weak governance, rampant gang violence, and mass migration, as people fled the poverty and insecurity that these conflicts had engendered.

In **southern Africa**, the U.S. involvement in Angola and Mozambique contributed to **regional destabilization**, particularly through the cross-border involvement of apartheid South Africa. The wars in Angola and Mozambique, which were fueled in part by U.S. support for insurgents, created instability in neighboring countries like **Namibia** and **Zambia**, which became drawn into the conflict. The flow of arms and fighters across borders further weakened regional security, making it difficult for post-conflict governments to establish control and rebuild.

The U.S. support for insurgent groups during the Cold War, while motivated by the strategic goal of containing communism, had far-reaching and often unintended consequences for governance and regional security. The collapse of state institutions, the rise of warlordism, and the proliferation of terrorism are all part of the legacy of these proxy wars, which destabilized entire regions and created long-term challenges for global security.

The overarching conclusion that can be drawn from all these historical instances is that the destabilization caused by U.S. support for insurgents continually leaves behind a legacy of violence, poverty, and weak governance that continues to affect the world today. All these historical examples are a cautionary tale about the dangers of short-term thinking in foreign policy. While these interventions may have achieved immediate geopolitical goals, they leave behind a legacy of broken states, impoverished populations, and radicalized movements.

PART III: POST-9/11 ERA: THE WAR ON TERROR

CHAPTER 7 - REVISITING AFGHANISTAN: OPERATION ENDURING FREEDOM AND THE FALL OF THE TALIBAN

U.S. Motivations for Re-engaging in Afghanistan After 9/11

The **September 11, 2001 attacks** fundamentally reshaped U.S. foreign policy and set the stage for a renewed military intervention in **Afghanistan**, a country that had largely faded from America's strategic focus after the Cold War. For nearly a decade following the withdrawal of Soviet forces in 1989, Afghanistan had been mired in civil war and had eventually fallen under the control of the **Taliban**, an Islamist militant group that enforced a strict version of Sharia law and provided sanctuary to **al-Qaeda**. The rise of the Taliban and the subsequent use of Afghanistan as a safe haven for Osama bin Laden and his jihadist network were largely ignored by the U.S.

government until the devastating attacks on U.S. soil in 2001.

The **9/11 attacks**, in which al-Qaeda operatives hijacked commercial airliners and crashed them into the **World Trade Center** and the **Pentagon**, killing nearly 3,000 people, represented a direct challenge to U.S. national security. In the immediate aftermath of the attacks, the U.S. public and policymakers demanded swift action to bring those responsible to justice and to prevent further attacks. President **George W. Bush**, in a now-famous address to Congress on September 20, 2001, declared a global "war on terror," vowing to hunt down the terrorists and their supporters. Afghanistan, as the base of operations for **Osama bin Laden** and **al-Qaeda**, was the first target in this new conflict.

The **U.S. invasion of Afghanistan**, launched on **October 7, 2001**, under the banner of **Operation Enduring Freedom**, had two primary objectives: to dismantle the **Taliban regime** that had provided sanctuary to al-Qaeda, and to capture or kill Osama bin Laden and other senior al-Qaeda leaders. The decision to invade Afghanistan was driven by a combination of immediate security concerns and broader geopolitical considerations. First and foremost, the U.S. needed to respond decisively to the attacks, and striking at the heart of al-Qaeda's operations in Afghanistan was seen as the most direct way to eliminate the threat. Secondly, the U.S. sought to demonstrate its resolve in the face of international terrorism, sending a clear message to both state and non-state actors that harboring terrorists would not be tolerated.

In addition to these security objectives, the U.S. invasion was also framed within the broader context of **nation-building**. American policymakers believed that toppling the Taliban would create an opportunity to establish a stable, democratic government in Afghanistan, which would, in turn, serve as a model for political reform in the wider Middle East and Central Asia. This idea was rooted in the **neoconservative** belief that the promotion of democracy and free markets would help counter the appeal of radical Islamist ideologies. However, the immediate focus of the invasion was on military objectives, particularly the elimination of al-Qaeda's leadership and the overthrow of the Taliban regime.

Early Successes of Operation Enduring Freedom

The initial phase of **Operation Enduring Freedom** was marked by rapid military success. The U.S. military, in partnership with the **Northern Alliance**, a coalition of Afghan rebel groups that had been fighting the Taliban for years, quickly gained the upper hand. The Northern Alliance, which had been significantly weakened after years of fighting against the better-armed Taliban forces, welcomed U.S. air strikes and special forces assistance. By coordinating air strikes with ground assaults, U.S. forces helped the Northern Alliance capture key Taliban strongholds across northern Afghanistan.

On **November 13, 2001**, just a month after the start of the invasion, the Northern Alliance entered the capital city of **Kabul**, and the Taliban regime collapsed. By December, the Taliban had been driven from power, its fighters scattered, and much of Afghanistan was under the control of Northern Alliance forces, supported by U.S. special operations and air power.

The collapse of the Taliban regime was a significant achievement for the U.S. and its allies. The Taliban had controlled much of Afghanistan since **1996**, enforcing a brutal and repressive regime that had isolated the country from the international community. Their swift defeat by a combination of U.S. forces and Afghan rebels was seen as a vindication of the Bush administration's strategy of using limited ground forces in conjunction with overwhelming air power and local proxies. However, while the Taliban had been toppled from power, the ultimate goal of the war—the capture of **Osama bin**

Laden and the dismantling of al-Qaeda—remained elusive.

The Battle of Tora Bora: A Missed Opportunity

In the weeks following the fall of Kabul, U.S. intelligence agencies began to focus on the whereabouts of **Osama bin Laden** and other senior al-Qaeda leaders. By mid-November 2001, reports indicated that bin Laden and his followers had retreated to the **Tora Bora** region, a mountainous area in eastern Afghanistan near the **Pakistan border**. Tora Bora had long been a favored hiding place for Afghan mujahideen fighters, including bin Laden, who had used the caves in the region during the **Soviet-Afghan War**. The rugged terrain and network of caves provided natural defenses against aerial bombardment and ground assaults, making it an ideal location for a final stand by al-Qaeda.

The **Battle of Tora Bora**, which took place in December 2001, was a critical moment in the early stages of the war in Afghanistan. U.S. and coalition forces, along with Afghan tribal militias, launched an assault on the Tora Bora cave complex in an effort to capture bin Laden and other top al-Qaeda leaders. **CIA intelligence** had indicated that bin Laden was in the area, and **Gary Berntsen**, the CIA officer in charge of the mission, requested that **U.S. Army Rangers** be deployed to seal off the mountainous border region and prevent bin Laden's escape into Pakistan. Berntsen believed that a swift deployment of American forces could have successfully eliminated bin Laden, potentially bringing a quick end to the conflict.

However, the Bush administration decided against sending U.S. ground forces in significant numbers, relying instead on Afghan militias to conduct the ground assault, supported by U.S. air strikes. The administration argued that **Pakistani forces** would intercept bin Laden if he attempted to flee across the border, and there was a reluctance to commit large numbers of U.S. troops to what was seen as a high-risk operation in difficult terrain. In hindsight, this decision proved to be a crucial mistake.

While U.S. air strikes inflicted heavy casualties on al-Qaeda fighters, bin Laden and many of his senior lieutenants managed to escape, likely crossing into Pakistan's **tribal areas**, where they would remain hidden for years. Former CIA officer **Gary Schroen** later echoed Berntsen's assessment, arguing that the deployment of U.S. Rangers could have sealed off the mountains and captured bin Laden. Schroen believed that this missed opportunity allowed al-Qaeda's leadership to regroup and continue its global operations, ultimately prolonging the **War on Terror**.

Other analysts, such as **Carter Malkasian**, a historian and former adviser to U.S. military commanders in Afghanistan, have suggested that bin Laden's escape was almost inevitable, given the complex terrain and the vast network of caves in the Tora Bora region. Malkasian argued that even if U.S. forces had been deployed in larger numbers, sealing off the mountainous region completely would have been a nearly impossible task, and bin Laden would likely have found a way to escape into Pakistan. Nevertheless, the failure to capture or kill bin Laden at Tora Bora would have profound consequences for the U.S. mission in Afghanistan.

Could the Decade-Long Afghan Occupation Have Been Avoided?

The failure to capture **Osama bin Laden** at Tora Bora set the stage for a protracted U.S. military presence in Afghanistan, one that would last nearly two decades. Many have argued that had bin Laden been eliminated in the early months of the war, the U.S. might have avoided the long and costly occupation of Afghanistan that followed. Without the need to continue the hunt for al-Qaeda's leadership, the U.S. could have focused its efforts on stabilizing Afghanistan and withdrawing its forces relatively quickly, leaving behind a less militarized, but still supportive, diplomatic and development footprint.

The prolonged U.S. military presence in Afghanistan, however, became increasingly entangled in efforts to rebuild the country's political and economic systems, while also combating a **Taliban insurgency** that re-emerged in the mid-2000s. The Bush administration, followed by the Obama administration, became committed to the broader goals of counterinsurgency and nation-building, believing that a stable, democratic Afghanistan would prevent the country from becoming a haven for terrorists in the future.

As the U.S. military became more deeply involved in Afghanistan, the conflict evolved from a limited counterterrorism mission focused on eliminating al-Qaeda to a comprehensive effort to defeat the Taliban and rebuild Afghanistan's institutions. The insurgency, fueled by the Taliban's resilience and their ability to find sanctuary in **Pakistan**, prolonged the war and made a swift U.S. exit impossible. While bin Laden remained at large until he was finally killed by U.S. Navy SEALs in **Pakistan** in 2011, his escape at Tora Bora ensured that al-Qaeda would continue to pose a global threat, and the War on Terror would drag on for years to come.

The **Battle of Tora Bora** and the failure to capture Osama bin Laden in the early months of the war stand as pivotal moments in the U.S. invasion of Afghanistan. Had the U.S. succeeded in eliminating bin Laden and the senior al-Qaeda leadership at Tora Bora, the War on Terror might have taken a very different trajectory. The decision not to deploy U.S. ground forces in sufficient numbers, based on the belief that local militias and Pakistani forces would be able to seal off the area, allowed bin Laden to escape and prolong the conflict.

The U.S. invasion of Afghanistan, which initially appeared to be a swift and successful campaign to topple the Taliban, ultimately evolved into a long and costly occupation that lasted nearly two decades. The missed opportunity at Tora Bora set the stage for this prolonged conflict, as U.S. forces became bogged down in a counterinsurgency campaign and the effort to build a stable Afghan state. The consequences of that early decision continue to shape U.S. foreign policy and military strategy today.

Challenges of Nation-Building After Ousting of the Taliban

Collapse of the Taliban Regime

The swift collapse of the **Taliban regime** in the fall of 2001 initially seemed like a decisive victory for the United States and its coalition partners. In the weeks following the launch of **Operation Enduring Freedom** on **October 7, 2001**, U.S. airstrikes, special operations, and Northern Alliance ground forces rapidly pushed Taliban fighters out of key cities, culminating in the capture of **Kabul** on **November 13, 2001**. By December, the Taliban leadership had fled into the mountains or across the border into **Pakistan**, and the formal government of the Islamic Emirate of Afghanistan had effectively ceased to exist.

However, while the removal of the Taliban from power was accomplished with relative ease, the long-term task of rebuilding Afghanistan as a stable, democratic state would prove to be far more difficult. The fall of the Taliban did not mark the end of conflict in Afghanistan. Instead, it marked the beginning of a new phase of **nation-building**, which would be plagued by significant challenges, from the re-emergence of the Taliban as an insurgent force to the deep-rooted issues of corruption, ethnic tensions, and weak governance.

The Bonn Agreement and the Formation of the Interim Government

In the immediate aftermath of the Taliban's collapse, the United States and its allies turned their attention to the task of forming a new government for Afghanistan. This effort began with the **Bonn Agreement**, a U.N.-sponsored conference held in **December 2001** in **Bonn, Germany**. The agreement brought together representatives from the various Afghan factions that had opposed the Taliban, including the **Northern Alliance**, as well as exiled political figures and members of Afghanistan's ethnic groups.

The Bonn Agreement established the framework for an **interim government** to lead Afghanistan during the transition period until national elections could be held. The Northern Alliance, which had played a key role in toppling the Taliban, secured significant positions in the interim government, with **Hamid Karzai**—a prominent Pashtun leader who had worked with the CIA and U.S. Special Forces—appointed as **interim president**. Karzai, a politically moderate figure, was seen as a unifying choice who could help bridge the country's deep ethnic and political divides.

The Bonn Agreement also outlined a timeline for the establishment of a **Constitutional Loya Jirga** (a grand assembly) to draft a new constitution for Afghanistan, which would lay the foundation for democratic governance. Additionally, the agreement called for the creation of an **International Security Assistance Force (ISAF)** to provide stability and security in the capital, Kabul, and surrounding areas. The ISAF, initially led by NATO, would later expand its mandate to cover the entire country.

While the Bonn Agreement was seen as a significant diplomatic achievement, it also highlighted some of the inherent challenges of nation-building in Afghanistan. The agreement's reliance on warlords and ethnic factions that had fought against the Taliban, many of whom had their own local power bases and militias, meant that the new government was often beholden to regional strongmen rather than being a truly unified national authority. This reliance on factional leaders would undermine efforts to establish a strong central government, setting the stage for future instability.

Challenges of Nation-Building

The U.S. and its allies faced several significant challenges as they embarked on the process of rebuilding Afghanistan. The scope of these challenges quickly became apparent, as the initial optimism surrounding the defeat of the Taliban gave way to the harsh realities of governing a deeply divided and war-torn country. Several key issues emerged as obstacles to the success of nation-building efforts.

1. Weak Central Governance and the Role of Warlords

One of the most persistent challenges in post-Taliban Afghanistan was the weakness of the central government, which struggled to assert control over the country's vast and often inaccessible rural areas. Although the Bonn Agreement established an interim government under **Hamid Karzai**, the new administration lacked the resources and authority to govern effectively outside of Kabul. Much of Afghanistan remained under the control of local warlords and tribal leaders, many of whom had been empowered by U.S. support during the campaign against the Taliban.

These warlords, who commanded their own militias and controlled significant portions of the country's economy—particularly through the **opium trade**—often resisted efforts to build a strong central government. While they had been valuable allies in the fight to oust the Taliban, their continued influence posed a significant challenge to the stability and unity of Afghanistan. The warlords maintained de facto control over many provinces, collecting taxes, dispensing justice, and exerting authority independently of the central government.

Efforts to rein in these warlords and disarm their militias, such as the **Disarmament, Demobilization, and Reintegration (DDR)** program launched in 2003, met with limited success. Many warlords were reluctant to give up their military power, and in some cases, they were simply incorporated into the government as regional governors or military commanders, perpetuating a system of patronage and corruption. This fragmentation of authority made it difficult to establish the rule of law or create a functioning national government capable of providing services to the Afghan population.

2. Ethnic and Sectarian Divisions

Afghanistan's deeply entrenched **ethnic and sectarian divisions** also complicated efforts to create a cohesive and inclusive government. The country is home to a diverse population that includes **Pashtuns, Tajiks, Hazaras, Uzbeks**, and other ethnic groups, each with its own political and cultural traditions. Historically, Afghanistan's rulers, including the Taliban, had been dominated by the Pashtun ethnic group, which constitutes the largest portion of the population, particularly in the southern and eastern provinces.

The Northern Alliance, which played a central role in the U.S.-led effort to overthrow the Taliban, was primarily composed of **Tajiks, Uzbeks**, and **Hazaras** from northern Afghanistan, many of whom had long-standing grievances against Pashtun-dominated governments. Although the Bonn Agreement sought to create a government that included representatives from all of Afghanistan's major ethnic groups, tensions between these factions persisted.

The rivalry between Pashtuns and non-Pashtuns was a

particular source of tension. The appointment of Hamid Karzai, a Pashtun, as interim president was intended to placate the Pashtun population and prevent ethnic fragmentation, but it also alienated some of the non-Pashtun factions that had been instrumental in toppling the Taliban. The **Hazaras**, who had faced brutal persecution under the Taliban, were especially wary of Pashtun dominance in the new government.

These ethnic tensions hindered efforts to build a unified national identity and contributed to the fragmentation of Afghan politics. As different ethnic groups vied for power and influence within the government, the risk of factionalism and civil conflict remained high, making it difficult to establish a stable political system.

3. Insurgency and Taliban Resurgence

Perhaps the most significant challenge to nation-building in Afghanistan was the resurgence of the **Taliban insurgency**, which began to gain momentum in the mid-2000s. While the Taliban had been ousted from power, many of its leaders and fighters had found refuge in **Pakistan's tribal areas**, where they regrouped and began organizing a guerrilla campaign against the U.S.-backed Afghan government and international forces.

The Taliban insurgency was fueled by several factors. First, the continued presence of U.S. and NATO forces in Afghanistan was used as a rallying cry by Taliban leaders, who framed the conflict as a struggle against foreign occupation. The Taliban exploited nationalist sentiments and resentment toward Western military operations, particularly in rural areas where civilians were often caught in the crossfire.

Second, the Afghan government's failure to provide basic services and security in many parts of the country created a vacuum that the Taliban was able to fill. The weakness of the central government, combined with widespread corruption and the inability to deliver on promises of development, eroded public confidence in the Karzai administration. The Taliban took advantage of these grievances, offering an alternative form of governance based on Sharia law and providing services in areas where the government was absent.

The re-emergence of the Taliban as a potent insurgent force posed a direct challenge to U.S. and NATO efforts to stabilize the country. As the insurgency intensified, the U.S. and its allies were forced to shift their focus from nation-building to counterinsurgency, launching large-scale military operations to combat Taliban fighters in the southern and eastern provinces. The escalation of the conflict made it increasingly difficult to implement the political and economic reforms necessary to rebuild Afghanistan, as resources were diverted to the military campaign.

4. Corruption and the Opium Economy

Corruption became a pervasive problem in post-Taliban Afghanistan, undermining efforts to build effective governance and contributing to public disillusionment with the new government. Many Afghan officials, including those in key positions of power, were involved in corrupt practices such as embezzlement, bribery, and nepotism. The distribution of international aid and reconstruction contracts often benefited well-connected elites, while ordinary Afghans saw little improvement in their living conditions.

The persistence of corruption was closely tied to the **opium trade**, which became a major driver of the Afghan economy after the fall of the Taliban. Afghanistan quickly regained its position as the world's largest producer of **opium** poppies, and the profits from the drug trade flowed into the hands of warlords, insurgents, and corrupt government officials. The **Taliban**, which had previously curtailed opium production as part of its efforts to impose strict Islamic rule, began to profit from the trade by taxing opium farmers and providing protection to traffickers.

The nexus between the opium trade, corruption, and insurgency made it difficult for the Afghan government to establish the rule of law or assert its authority in rural areas. The international community's efforts to combat the opium trade through eradication campaigns and alternative development programs met with limited success, as many rural farmers depended on opium cultivation for their livelihoods.

5. Role of International Forces

While the presence of **international forces** under NATO's **ISAF** provided a measure of stability in Kabul and other key areas, their presence also became a source of tension. The ongoing military operations, particularly U.S. airstrikes that sometimes resulted in civilian casualties, contributed to anti-Western sentiment and fueled the insurgency. At the same time, the reliance on foreign troops to maintain security underscored the weakness of Afghanistan's own security forces, which were slow to develop and struggled with issues of training, equipment, and loyalty.

The international community's focus on building a viable **Afghan National Army (ANA)** and **Afghan National Police (ANP)** was essential to the long-term goal of transferring security responsibilities to Afghan forces. However, these efforts were hindered by the lack of experienced officers, poor morale, and widespread corruption within the security forces. As a result, the ANA and ANP remained heavily dependent on U.S. and NATO support for many years, delaying the transition to Afghan-led security.

The ousting of the Taliban in 2001 was only the beginning of a long and difficult process of nation-building in Afghanistan. While the initial military campaign succeeded in toppling the regime, the subsequent efforts to establish a stable, democratic state were fraught with challenges. The weakness of the central government, the persistence of ethnic divisions, the resurgence of the Taliban insurgency, and the pervasive influence of corruption all contributed to the difficulties of rebuilding Afghanistan.

As the conflict dragged on and international forces became more deeply entrenched in counterinsurgency operations, the broader goals of political reform and economic development were often overshadowed. The challenges of nation-building in Afghanistan would remain a central issue for U.S. and international policymakers for nearly two decades, with no easy solutions in sight.

Resurgence of the Taliban After Two Decades of Conflict

The return of the **Taliban** to power in **August 2021**, following the collapse of the U.S.-backed Afghan government, marked a dramatic reversal of fortunes for a group that had operated as an insurgent force for nearly two decades. After being ousted from power by the U.S. invasion in **2001**, the Taliban waged a relentless guerrilla war against U.S. and NATO forces, Afghan security personnel, and the Western-backed government in Kabul. Despite overwhelming firepower and financial support provided to the Afghan National Army (ANA), the Taliban persisted in their fight, ultimately seizing control of the country in a lightning-fast campaign that culminated in the chaotic withdrawal of U.S. forces.

The **fall of Kabul** on August 15, 2021, signaled not just the collapse of the Afghan government but also the beginning of a new chapter for the Taliban, one in which they transformed from an insurgent group to the de facto rulers of Afghanistan once again. The group's rapid consolidation of power has been bolstered by their acquisition of a massive stockpile of **U.S.-made weapons and equipment** left behind by the retreating Afghan army, which has enabled them to make the transition from a guerrilla force to a standing army. This transformation was vividly displayed in November 2021, when the Taliban held a **military parade** in **Kabul**, showcasing American-made armored vehicles and Russian helicopters, signaling their return to power and their ability to field a conventional military force.

Taliban's Transformation From Insurgency to Standing Army

For nearly two decades, the Taliban operated as an **insurgent group**, relying on guerrilla tactics such as ambushes, roadside bombings, and hit-and-run attacks against both Afghan government forces and NATO troops. Their fighters were often clad in traditional Afghan clothing, blending into rural communities to evade detection. However, since their return to power, the Taliban have worked to professionalize their military, integrating captured equipment and skilled personnel from the disbanded Afghan National Army into their ranks.

The **Kabul military parade** on November 2021 marked a significant shift in the Taliban's military posture. Taliban forces, now equipped with **U.S.-made M117 armored security vehicles** and other advanced military hardware, paraded through the streets of Kabul as helicopters—also of U.S. and Russian origin—patrolled overhead. The event celebrated the graduation of 250 newly trained soldiers, who marched in **American-made M4 assault rifles**. This show of strength underscored the Taliban's ongoing efforts to transition from a loosely organized insurgency to a conventional military force capable of enforcing their control over Afghanistan.

The Taliban's ability to seize this equipment stems from the rapid disintegration of the Afghan National Army in the face of their final offensive in the summer of 2021. The **Afghan government**, led by President **Ashraf Ghani**, collapsed under the weight of the Taliban's advance, with Ghani fleeing the country as the Taliban closed in on Kabul. In the ensuing chaos, Afghan military forces abandoned vast quantities of military equipment supplied by the **U.S.** over the course of two decades.

According to a report from the **Special Inspector General for Afghanistan Reconstruction (SIGAR)**, between **2002** and **2017**, the U.S. provided more than **$28 billion** in defense articles and services to the Afghan government, including **weapons, vehicles, night-vision devices, aircraft**, and **surveillance systems**. This equipment, which had been intended to build an Afghan military force capable of defending the country against the Taliban, fell into the hands of the very group it was meant to defeat. The Taliban quickly seized control of these military assets, incorporating them into their own forces and displaying them during military parades to project their newfound strength.

Given U.S. failure to destroy or retrieve these equipments as they withdrew, including more than **70 aircraft** and dozens of armored vehicles, a significant amount remained intact and fell under Taliban control. The **Bagram military parade**, held at the site of the former **Bagram Air Base**, was the Taliban's most grandiose display of military power since taking over the country. Soldiers clad in newly acquired **military uniforms** marched in formation, while **motorcycle brigades** carried the Taliban flag through the streets. Pickup trucks, crammed with men brandishing rifles, drove in celebration of the Taliban's victory.

This public display of force was not only a celebration of the Taliban's military victory but also a symbolic rejection of the two-decade-long U.S. occupation. By using American-made equipment, the Taliban showcased how they had repurposed the material remnants of the U.S. military presence to their own advantage. The parade also served as a warning to both internal and external actors that the Taliban were no longer merely a guerrilla movement—they were now the rulers of Afghanistan, with a standing army capable of defending their rule.

Legacy of U.S. Military Interventions in Afghanistan

The Taliban's current military capabilities are in large part a direct consequence of the **decades-long U.S. investment** in the Afghan military. Between 2001 and 2021, the U.S. and its NATO allies poured billions of dollars into building up Afghan security forces in the hopes of creating a force capable of defending the country against the Taliban. The idea was that a well-equipped and well-trained Afghan National Army would allow the U.S. to withdraw its forces while leaving behind a stable, secure Afghanistan.

However, the **collapse of the Afghan government** in 2021 revealed the fragility of this effort. Despite the vast sums spent on training and equipping Afghan forces, the ANA disintegrated in the face of the Taliban's final offensive. Morale among Afghan soldiers plummeted as it became clear that their government was losing the war. When President Ghani fled the country, many Afghan units simply laid down their arms and surrendered, allowing the Taliban to seize key military installations, including **Bagram Air Base**, which had been the largest U.S. military installation in Afghanistan.

The vast stockpiles of U.S.-supplied weapons and equipment left behind in the wake of the ANA's collapse have been a boon for the Taliban. By incorporating these assets into their own forces, the Taliban have been able to dramatically enhance their military capabilities. The U.S.-supplied **M117 armored vehicles**, **Humvees**, **night-vision equipment**, and

helicopters have transformed the Taliban from an insurgent group into a conventional military force. They have also integrated experienced pilots, mechanics, and other personnel from the former Afghan National Army into their ranks, further strengthening their capacity to operate and maintain the equipment left behind by U.S. forces.

The transformation of the Taliban's military capabilities raises significant concerns for **regional security**. With access to advanced weaponry and a newfound sense of legitimacy as the rulers of Afghanistan, the Taliban are better equipped than ever before to project power within the country and potentially beyond its borders. While it remains unclear how many of the aircraft and other high-tech systems left behind by the U.S. are operational, the Taliban's ability to use these assets in military parades and training exercises demonstrates their intent to develop a professional military force capable of maintaining internal control and defending Afghanistan's borders.

Broader Implications for Afghanistan and Regional Stability

The Taliban's resurgence and their transformation into a conventional military force have profound implications for Afghanistan's future and the broader region. As the Taliban consolidate their control over the country, they face the challenge of governing a deeply divided society and maintaining order in the face of potential internal dissent. The Taliban's reliance on military parades and public displays of force, such as the one at **Bagram Air Base**, reflects their awareness that they must project strength and legitimacy to maintain their grip on power.

However, the militarization of the Taliban also poses risks for **regional security**. Afghanistan shares borders with several countries, including **Pakistan**, **Iran**, **China**, and the **Central Asian republics**, all of which have a vested interest in preventing Afghanistan from becoming a source of instability. The Taliban's acquisition of advanced weaponry, combined with their history of providing sanctuary to extremist groups like **al-Qaeda**, raises concerns that Afghanistan could once again become a haven for jihadist movements that threaten regional and global security.

Furthermore, the **economic collapse** and **humanitarian crisis** that have followed the Taliban's return to power could exacerbate instability both within Afghanistan and across the region. The country's economy, already heavily dependent on international aid, has been severely impacted by the withdrawal of Western support and the freezing of Afghan assets abroad. As poverty and hunger worsen, the Taliban may struggle to maintain order, and the potential for internal uprisings or insurgencies against their rule could grow.

The Taliban's parade in Kabul, featuring **U.S.-made military equipment**, was not only a show of strength but also a reminder of the unintended consequences of two decades of U.S. intervention in Afghanistan. The vast stockpile of weapons left behind by the U.S. has now become a critical asset for the Taliban as they transition from insurgents to rulers, highlighting the complex legacy of America's longest war.

As the Taliban consolidate their control over Afghanistan and continue to transform into a conventional military force, they face significant challenges in maintaining stability and addressing the country's economic and social crises. The legacy of U.S. military assistance, in the form of the weapons and equipment left behind, has allowed the Taliban to project power and authority in the short term. However, the question remains whether they can translate their military dominance into effective governance and long-term stability.

The Taliban's reliance on displays of military strength, such as the Bagram parade, underscores the fragility of their rule. While they may have won the war, the challenge of governing

Afghanistan—one of the most complex and divided nations in the world—will require more than just weapons and soldiers. Whether the Taliban can overcome these challenges remains to be seen, but their return to power and their transformation into a standing army mark a significant turning point in the history of Afghanistan and the broader region.

Lessons for U.S. Foreign Policy

The return of the Taliban to power in Afghanistan after two decades of U.S. involvement offers significant lessons for American foreign policy, particularly regarding the challenges of long-term military engagements, nation-building, and the unintended consequences of intervention. The events leading up to the Taliban's resurgence, including the collapse of the Afghan government and the rapid disintegration of Afghan security forces, underscore the limitations of foreign-led efforts to impose stability and democracy in complex, deeply divided societies. These lessons are critical not only for future engagements in Afghanistan but for U.S. involvement in other regions where it seeks to combat insurgencies or support fragile states.

One of the most glaring lessons from Afghanistan is the inherent difficulty in building and sustaining a foreign-backed military force in the absence of strong, legitimate political institutions. Over two decades, the U.S. invested heavily in training, equipping, and funding the Afghan National Army (ANA) with the expectation that it would be able to defend the country against insurgents like the Taliban. Despite the billions of dollars spent, the Afghan military crumbled in the face of the Taliban's final offensive. The collapse was swift and decisive, illustrating that no amount of material support could compensate for the lack of political cohesion, motivation, and effective leadership within the Afghan government and its security forces.

This failure points to a deeper issue in U.S. foreign policy: the tendency to prioritize military solutions over political ones. While the U.S. military succeeded in toppling the Taliban regime and significantly weakening al-Qaeda in the early years of the war, it struggled to create a stable political environment capable of sustaining these gains. The Afghan government, plagued by corruption and deeply divided along ethnic and tribal lines, failed to gain the trust of its people. The lack of legitimacy and widespread corruption within the Afghan government meant that, for many Afghans, the Taliban—despite its harsh ideology—was viewed as a more authentic representation of Afghan society than the government in Kabul, which was seen as a puppet of foreign powers.

The lesson here is clear: sustainable peace and security cannot be achieved through military means alone. The U.S. effort in Afghanistan reveals the limitations of relying on military power to achieve political objectives in complex environments. Building durable political institutions, fostering local governance, and addressing underlying social and economic grievances are essential components of any long-term strategy. Without these foundations, military victories will be short-lived, as evidenced by the rapid resurgence of the Taliban after the U.S. withdrawal.

The chaotic U.S. exit from Afghanistan also raises important questions about the efficacy of nation-building as a component of foreign intervention. The U.S. attempted to create a Western-style democratic state in Afghanistan, complete with elections, a constitution, and a centralized government. However, Afghanistan's political culture, deeply rooted in local tribal structures and decentralized governance, was ill-suited to this model. The disconnect between the political system that the U.S. sought to build and the realities on the ground meant that many Afghans did not see the government in Kabul as a legitimate authority. Instead, power often remained in the hands of local warlords and tribal leaders, many of whom operated independently of the central government and maintained their own militias.

This experience should serve as a cautionary tale for future U.S. efforts at nation-building. Imposing a foreign political model without taking into account local traditions, power structures, and social dynamics is unlikely to succeed. The U.S. must recognize that each country has its own unique political and cultural context, and efforts to build state institutions must be rooted in an understanding of those contexts. In Afghanistan, the attempt to graft a centralized, democratic state onto a deeply fragmented and tribal society proved to be a fundamental miscalculation.

One of the most ironic and troubling aspects of the U.S. intervention in Afghanistan is the extent to which **American-made weapons** and military equipment ended up in the hands of the Taliban following the collapse of the Afghan government. The U.S. spent more than **$28 billion** supplying the Afghan National Army with advanced weaponry, vehicles, and aircraft, much of which was either abandoned or captured by the Taliban as Afghan forces melted away in the face of their final offensive.

The Taliban's ability to field **American-made armored vehicles**, helicopters, and small arms in military parades in **Kabul** and **Bagram** is a stark reminder of the unintended consequences of providing massive amounts of military aid to fragile governments. Just as the U.S. support for the **mujahideen** during the **Soviet-Afghan War** in the 1980s inadvertently contributed to the rise of the Taliban and al-Qaeda, the billions of dollars in military aid provided to the Afghan government have now been repurposed by the Taliban for their own use.

For U.S. foreign policy, this raises important questions about the long-term implications of arming proxy forces and building foreign militaries. The risks of these weapons falling into the wrong hands, particularly in unstable regions, should be carefully considered when providing military aid. Future policies should include safeguards to ensure that weapons and equipment are not easily captured or repurposed by hostile actors in the event of a government collapse.

The U.S. war in Afghanistan, which spanned nearly 20 years, became the longest military engagement in American history. The conflict, which began as a targeted counterterrorism mission, evolved into a protracted counterinsurgency and nation-building effort that consumed vast amounts of resources and political capital. The war cost the U.S. trillions of dollars and the lives of thousands of American and allied soldiers, while also causing immense suffering among the Afghan population.

The long-term costs of the war far outweighed the initial objectives of eliminating al-Qaeda and removing the Taliban from power. By the time the U.S. withdrew in 2021, many policymakers and military leaders questioned whether the mission had ever been achievable in the first place. The **Afghan government's collapse** and the Taliban's return to power raised the question of whether the U.S. could have avoided a two-decade-long occupation if its goals had remained more narrowly focused on counterterrorism.

For U.S. foreign policy, the lesson is clear: military engagements must be clearly defined, limited in scope, and tied to achievable political objectives. The risk of mission creep —where the goals of an intervention expand beyond their original intent—can lead to long-term entanglements that are difficult to exit. Policymakers should be wary of committing U.S. forces to open-ended conflict.

Another critical lesson from Afghanistan is the long-term impact of insurgent groups evolving into powerful political and military entities. The Taliban's ability to return to power after two decades of conflict demonstrates the resilience of ideologically driven insurgencies that have deep ties to local communities and a clear vision of governance. For years, the U.S. focused on military strategies aimed at defeating the Taliban on the battlefield, but it underestimated the group's capacity to regenerate and adapt. The Taliban's survival was not only due to its ability to carry out guerrilla warfare but also because it provided services, security, and a sense of order in areas where the Afghan government was absent.

The U.S. experience in Afghanistan highlights the importance of understanding the local context in which insurgent movements operate. Insurgencies thrive in environments where the central government is weak or illegitimate, and where local grievances—whether political, economic, or social—are not addressed. Counterinsurgency strategies must therefore go beyond military operations and focus on addressing the root causes of instability. In Afghanistan, the failure to create a functioning government that could meet the basic needs of its people allowed the Taliban to maintain its foothold in rural areas, even as U.S. forces targeted its leadership and fighters.

Moreover, the events in Afghanistan raise important considerations about the long-term consequences of military withdrawals. The rapid collapse of the Afghan government following the U.S. withdrawal illustrates the fragility of many U.S.-backed governments and security forces. Once U.S. forces left, the Afghan government was unable to stand on its own, and the Taliban swiftly moved to fill the power vacuum. This pattern has been seen in other parts of the world, where U.S. military disengagement has led to a resurgence of insurgent or terrorist groups.

This brings into focus the difficult question of how and when the U.S. should disengage from military interventions. While there is broad recognition that indefinite military occupations are unsustainable, the U.S. must carefully plan and execute its exits to avoid creating power vacuums that can be exploited by adversaries. In Afghanistan, the lack of a clear strategy for transitioning security responsibilities to Afghan forces, coupled with the rapid pace of the withdrawal, left the government ill-prepared to defend itself, leading to the Taliban's return to power. Future U.S. interventions must ensure that local security forces are fully capable of maintaining stability before U.S. forces depart, and that political solutions are in place to manage the transition.

One of the notable aspects of the U.S. intervention in Afghanistan was the broad coalition of international partners that supported the mission. **NATO**, through its **International Security Assistance Force (ISAF)**, played a crucial role in maintaining security in Afghanistan, and many U.S. allies contributed troops, resources, and expertise to the effort. However, as the war dragged on, international support began to wane, and the burden of the conflict increasingly fell on the U.S.

The lesson for U.S. foreign policy is the importance of **multilateralism** and global partnerships in addressing complex security challenges. The success of any long-term military engagement or nation-building effort depends on the sustained commitment of international partners and the ability to share the burdens of security, governance, and development. While the U.S. led the intervention in Afghanistan, it could not have maintained its presence there for as long as it did without the support of NATO allies and other international actors.

Going forward, the U.S. should prioritize working within international frameworks and alliances to address global security challenges. Multilateralism not only helps distribute the costs of intervention but also lends legitimacy to military operations and enhances the prospects for long-term success.

Lastly, Afghanistan underscores the limits of U.S. influence when it comes to shaping the internal politics of other countries. For years, the U.S. attempted to engineer a political system in Afghanistan that would align with its own values and strategic interests. However, the failure to establish a stable government capable of commanding widespread loyalty among the Afghan population shows that external powers have limited ability to control the political trajectories of other nations. While the U.S. can provide support and guidance, ultimately, the success of political institutions depends on the will of the local population and the legitimacy of the government in the eyes of its people.

The lessons from Afghanistan should prompt a broader rethinking of U.S. foreign policy, particularly in relation to military interventions, counterinsurgency strategies, and nation-building efforts. The U.S. must recognize the limits of its power and focus on approaches that prioritize long-term political solutions, rather than short-term military gains. By learning from the mistakes of Afghanistan, the U.S. can develop more effective strategies for engaging with fragile states and preventing the kind of protracted conflicts that have defined its involvement in the region for the past two decades.

CHAPTER 8 - OPERATION IRAQI FREEDOM: THE FALL OF SADDAM HUSSEIN AND THE RISE OF ISIS

> *"And it's no secret to you that the thinkers and perceptive ones from among the Americans warned Bush before the war and told him: "All that you want for securing America and removing the weapons of mass destruction - assuming they exist - is available to you, and the nations of the world are with you in the inspections, and it is in the interest of America that it not be thrust into an unjustified war with an unknown outcome."*
>
> Osama bin Laden,
> Founder of Al-Qaeda

The 2003 Invasion of Iraq and the Removal of Saddam Hussein

The **2003 invasion of Iraq**, led by the United States and

its coalition partners, remains one of the most controversial military interventions in modern history. The U.S. decision to invade Iraq and remove its long-time dictator, **Saddam Hussein**, was driven by a combination of strategic, political, and ideological factors, many of which have been debated extensively since the operation. The invasion, launched under the banner of **Operation Iraqi Freedom**, resulted in the swift toppling of Hussein's regime. However, the aftermath of his removal—characterized by sectarian violence, the rise of insurgent groups, and the eventual emergence of **ISIS**—revealed the deep complexities and unintended consequences of the U.S. intervention.

The invasion marked the beginning of a prolonged and destabilizing conflict in Iraq that not only reshaped the country's political landscape but also had profound ramifications for the entire **Middle East**. Understanding the motivations behind the invasion and the steps leading to Saddam Hussein's removal is critical for comprehending the broader geopolitical consequences that followed.

U.S. Motivations for Invading Iraq

The U.S. invasion of Iraq in **March 2003** was primarily justified on the grounds that **Saddam Hussein's regime** posed an imminent threat to global security. The **Bush administration**, particularly in the aftermath of the **September 11, 2001** terrorist attacks, argued that Hussein possessed **weapons of mass destruction (WMDs)** and had links to terrorist organizations, including **al-Qaeda**. These claims, though later discredited, were central to the U.S. rationale for military intervention.

Several key motivations drove the U.S. decision to invade Iraq:

1. **Weapons of Mass Destruction (WMDs):** The Bush administration claimed that Saddam Hussein was actively developing chemical, biological, and possibly

nuclear weapons, which posed a direct threat to the U.S. and its allies. Despite the absence of conclusive evidence, intelligence reports suggested that Iraq had stockpiles of WMDs and had continued to pursue weapons programs in violation of **United Nations Security Council** resolutions. The U.S. argued that preemptive action was necessary to prevent Hussein from using these weapons or providing them to terrorist organizations.

2. **Iraq's Noncompliance with U.N. Resolutions**: Since the end of the **Gulf War** in 1991, Iraq had been subject to a series of **U.N. Security Council** resolutions that required it to dismantle its WMD programs and submit to international weapons inspections. However, Hussein's regime had repeatedly obstructed U.N. inspectors and failed to fully account for its weapons stockpiles. The U.S. and its allies viewed Iraq's defiance of U.N. resolutions as evidence of its continued pursuit of WMDs and a justification for military action.

3. **Links to Terrorism**: In the wake of the 9/11 attacks, the Bush administration sought to connect Hussein's regime to global terrorism, particularly **al-Qaeda**. Although no direct operational links between Saddam Hussein and al-Qaeda were ever proven, the administration argued that Hussein's support for other terrorist groups, such as **Palestinian militants**, and his history of using violence against his own people made him a potential ally for terrorist organizations.

4. **Regime Change and Democratization**: Beyond the immediate security concerns, the U.S. invasion was also framed as part of a broader strategy to **reshape the Middle East** by promoting democracy and regime change. Neoconservative policymakers within the Bush administration believed that by removing Saddam Hussein and establishing a democratic government in

Iraq, the U.S. could set off a wave of democratization across the region. This vision of Iraq as a model for democratic reform was a key ideological underpinning of the invasion, though it underestimated the complexity of Iraq's social and political landscape.

5. **Control of Oil and Strategic Resources**: While not openly acknowledged as a primary motivation, control over Iraq's vast **oil reserves** was also seen as a factor in the decision to invade. Iraq, which holds some of the largest proven oil reserves in the world, was viewed as a critical player in the global energy market. Some analysts argued that the U.S. sought to secure access to Iraq's oil resources and reduce the influence of **OPEC** and other oil-producing states.

Operation Iraqi Freedom: The Fall of Saddam Hussein

The invasion of Iraq, launched on **March 20, 2003**, began with a massive **air and missile campaign** designed to target key military installations and decapitate the leadership of Saddam Hussein's regime. This initial phase of the war, often referred to as "**shock and awe**," was intended to overwhelm Iraqi forces and swiftly bring about the collapse of the government. The U.S. and coalition forces, numbering more than 300,000 troops, rapidly advanced into Iraq from bases in **Kuwait**.

Within weeks, coalition forces had taken control of key cities, including **Basra** and **Baghdad**. The **Iraqi military**, despite its size, proved no match for the technologically superior U.S. forces, which employed precision air strikes, armored assaults, and special operations to dismantle Iraq's defenses. By **April 9, 2003**, U.S. troops had entered Baghdad, and the iconic images of **Iraqis toppling statues** of Saddam Hussein in the capital's **Firdos Square** became symbolic of the regime's downfall.

Saddam Hussein himself went into hiding, and for several months his whereabouts remained unknown. In **December**

2003, after an extensive manhunt, U.S. forces captured Hussein in a small underground bunker near his hometown of **Tikrit**. His capture marked the formal end of his rule, and he was later tried by an **Iraqi tribunal** for crimes against humanity and executed in **December 2006**.

The swift removal of Saddam Hussein was initially hailed as a success by U.S. policymakers, who had achieved their objective of toppling the regime with minimal casualties among coalition forces. However, the real challenges of the Iraq invasion lay not in the removal of Hussein but in the occupation and rebuilding of a deeply divided country.

Aftermath of Iraqi Regime Change: Power Vacuum and Sectarian Violence

With the removal of Saddam Hussein, Iraq faced a **power vacuum** that quickly descended into chaos. The **Ba'ath Party**, which had ruled Iraq for decades under Hussein's leadership, was dismantled as part of the U.S.-led **de-Ba'athification** policy. This decision, which barred former Ba'athists from holding government or military positions, removed many of Iraq's most experienced bureaucrats and military officers from power, contributing to a breakdown in governance and security.

At the same time, the **disbanding of the Iraqi military** left hundreds of thousands of armed and trained soldiers unemployed and disenfranchised. Many of these former soldiers, particularly those from the **Sunni** Arab minority who had been favored under Hussein's regime, became disillusioned with the new U.S.-backed government, which was dominated by **Shia** political parties. The combination of de-Ba'athification and the dismantling of the Iraqi military sowed the seeds for the insurgency that would emerge in the years following the invasion.

The **U.S. occupation** also failed to address the deep-seated

sectarian divisions within Iraq. Saddam Hussein's regime, though brutal, had maintained a tenuous balance between Iraq's Sunni minority, Shia majority, and Kurdish population in the north. The removal of Hussein and the subsequent empowerment of Shia political factions—particularly the **Dawa Party** and the **Supreme Council for Islamic Revolution in Iraq (SCIRI)**—exacerbated tensions between Iraq's Sunni and Shia communities.

Sectarian violence escalated rapidly, as Shia militias, such as the **Mahdi Army**, clashed with Sunni insurgents and remnants of the Ba'athist regime. **Al-Qaeda in Iraq (AQI)**, a Sunni extremist group founded by **Abu Musab al-Zarqawi**, capitalized on the chaos to incite further sectarian violence and target U.S. forces. AQI's brutal tactics, including bombings, kidnappings, and assassinations, contributed to a cycle of violence that engulfed Iraq in the years following the invasion.

The Surge and Temporary Stability

In response to the growing insurgency and sectarian violence, the U.S. launched a major counterinsurgency campaign in **2007** known as the **Iraq Surge**. Under the leadership of **General David Petraeus**, U.S. forces adopted a new strategy that involved deploying an additional 30,000 troops to Iraq, improving security in Baghdad and other key cities, and working more closely with local tribal leaders and militias to combat AQI.

The **surge** initially succeeded in reducing violence and restoring a degree of stability to Iraq. Sunni tribal leaders in **Anbar Province**, who had grown disillusioned with AQI's extremism, joined forces with the U.S. in what became known as the **Anbar Awakening**, helping to drive AQI out of key areas. However, this period of relative calm proved to be short-lived, as underlying sectarian tensions remained unresolved, and the U.S. began to reduce its troop presence in Iraq following the election of **President Barack Obama in 2008**.

A Fragile Peace and the Seeds of Future Conflict

While the U.S. achieved its immediate objective of removing Saddam Hussein, the invasion of Iraq created a deeply unstable environment that allowed extremist groups like **al-Qaeda in Iraq** to thrive. The disbanding of Iraq's military and the marginalization of its Sunni population contributed to the rise of an insurgency that would eventually give birth to **ISIS**, the most dangerous and effective jihadist organization of the 21st century.

The challenges of rebuilding Iraq after the fall of Hussein exposed the difficulties of regime change as a strategy for promoting democracy and stability. The unintended consequences of the U.S. intervention in Iraq, including the rise of ISIS, serve as a cautionary tale for future foreign policy decisions, illustrating the risks of military intervention in complex and deeply divided societies.

Destabilization of Iraq and Creation of a Power Vacuum

The **2003 U.S.-led invasion of Iraq** not only resulted in the swift removal of **Saddam Hussein** from power, but it also set into motion a series of events that would profoundly destabilize the country and the broader **Middle East** for years to come. While the initial military operation, **Operation Iraqi Freedom**, successfully toppled the regime, the **aftermath of the invasion** proved far more chaotic and destructive. The **power vacuum** created by the removal of Saddam Hussein and the dismantling of Iraq's state institutions left the country vulnerable to **sectarian violence, insurgencies**, and **foreign intervention**. These dynamics, in turn, laid the groundwork for the eventual rise of **ISIS** and the further unraveling of regional stability.

This unit explores the key factors that contributed to the destabilization of Iraq following the invasion, focusing on the mismanagement of post-war governance, the alienation of the **Sunni population**, the rise of sectarian militias, and the broader consequences of U.S. policies that dismantled the Iraqi state.

De-Ba'athification and Disbanding of the Iraqi Military

One of the most significant and controversial decisions made by the U.S. **Coalition Provisional Authority (CPA)** in the early days of the occupation was the policy of **de-Ba'athification**. The **Ba'ath Party**, which had ruled Iraq for decades under Saddam Hussein, was a deeply entrenched political organization that had dominated nearly every aspect of Iraqi life. The CPA, led by **Paul Bremer**, sought to dismantle the Ba'athist infrastructure as part of a broader effort to rid Iraq of its authoritarian past and pave the way for democratic governance.

On **May 16, 2003**, Bremer issued **CPA Order No. 1**, which effectively barred members of the Ba'ath Party from holding government or military positions. While the policy was aimed at preventing former regime loyalists from regaining power, it had the unintended consequence of removing thousands of experienced bureaucrats, civil servants, and military officers from their posts. Many of these individuals, particularly those in the **Sunni Arab minority**, were not ideologically committed to the Ba'ath Party but had joined it as a requirement for employment under Hussein's regime. The sweeping nature of the de-Ba'athification policy, which reached down to the local government and administrative levels, left Iraq without the skilled professionals needed to manage the country's institutions during the critical post-invasion period.

The de-Ba'athification policy was compounded by **CPA Order**

No. 2, issued on **May 23, 2003**, which disbanded the **Iraqi military** and other security forces. This decision, which effectively dissolved the **Iraqi Army, Republican Guard**, and **Ministry of Defense**, left hundreds of thousands of armed and trained soldiers without employment. Many of these soldiers, particularly those from Sunni Arab backgrounds, had been the backbone of Iraq's security apparatus under Saddam Hussein. The sudden and complete disbanding of the military created a vast pool of disaffected former soldiers who felt betrayed and abandoned by the new U.S.-backed government.

The consequences of these decisions were immediate and far-reaching. The removal of Ba'ath Party members from government positions created a governance vacuum, particularly in Sunni-majority areas, where local leaders and administrators had been predominantly Ba'athist. The disbanding of the military, meanwhile, left Iraq without a functioning security force at a time when order and stability were desperately needed. As a result, large swathes of Iraq descended into lawlessness, with criminal gangs, militias, and insurgent groups quickly filling the void left by the absence of state authority.

Alienation of Iraq's Sunni Population

The **Sunni Arab minority**, which had dominated Iraq's political and military institutions under Saddam Hussein, was disproportionately affected by the policies of de-Ba'athification and the disbanding of the military. As Iraq's new U.S.-backed government, dominated by **Shia** political factions and **Kurdish** leaders, began to take shape, many Sunnis felt marginalized and excluded from the political process. This sense of alienation was exacerbated by the fact that the **Sunni heartland**, particularly in regions such as **Anbar Province**, had been strongholds of support for Saddam Hussein's regime.

The **Iraqi Governing Council**, established by the CPA in **July 2003** as a transitional governing body, was composed primarily of Shia and Kurdish leaders, with limited Sunni representation. The political disenfranchisement of the Sunni population contributed to a growing sense of resentment and opposition to the new government. Sunni leaders, many of whom had been removed from their positions of power, viewed the post-invasion order as illegitimate and saw the U.S.-led occupation as an affront to their community's historical dominance in Iraq.

This growing sense of disenfranchisement among Sunnis fueled the rise of an **insurgency** that would come to define the post-invasion period. Sunni insurgent groups, many of which were composed of former Ba'athists and disbanded military officers, began organizing attacks against U.S. forces and the newly established Iraqi government. These groups, which operated primarily in Sunni-majority regions such as **Fallujah**, **Ramadi**, and **Mosul**, framed their resistance as a struggle against foreign occupation and Shia dominance.

The insurgency quickly gained momentum, with Sunni fighters targeting U.S. convoys, Iraqi security forces, and government buildings in a series of escalating attacks. The violence reached a peak in **2004** with the **Battle of Fallujah**, in which U.S. Marines fought a brutal urban campaign against Sunni insurgents who had taken control of the city. The battle, which resulted in heavy casualties on both sides, underscored the deepening rift between Iraq's Sunni population and the U.S.-backed government.

Rise of Sectarian Militias and Civil War

As the insurgency spread, Iraq became increasingly engulfed in **sectarian violence**, with Shia and Sunni militias engaging in retaliatory attacks that further destabilized the country. The **Shia majority**, which had long been oppressed under

Saddam Hussein's Sunni-dominated regime, saw the post-invasion period as an opportunity to assert their political dominance. Shia political parties, such as the **Dawa Party** and the **Supreme Council for Islamic Revolution in Iraq (SCIRI)**, formed militias that sought to protect Shia communities and expand their influence.

One of the most prominent Shia militias was the **Mahdi Army**, led by **Moqtada al-Sadr**, a young and radical Shia cleric who emerged as a key figure in post-invasion Iraq. The Mahdi Army, which initially formed as a response to perceived threats against Shia civilians, quickly evolved into a powerful paramilitary force that operated outside the control of the Iraqi government. Sadr's militia clashed with U.S. forces on multiple occasions, most notably during the **Sadr City Uprising** in 2004, when Mahdi Army fighters took control of large parts of Baghdad's Shia neighborhoods.

The rise of Shia militias, many of which were aligned with Iran, further exacerbated sectarian tensions and contributed to the descent into **civil war**. Sunni insurgent groups, including **al-Qaeda in Iraq (AQI)**, capitalized on these tensions by launching attacks against Shia civilians and holy sites, including the **2006 bombing of the Al-Askari Mosque** in **Samarra**, one of the holiest sites in Shia Islam. The bombing triggered a wave of sectarian reprisals, with Shia militias carrying out retaliatory attacks against Sunni neighborhoods and mosques.

By **2006**, Iraq had descended into a full-scale civil war, with Sunni and Shia militias engaging in daily violence that claimed thousands of lives. The sectarian conflict, which pitted Sunni insurgents and al-Qaeda-linked fighters against Shia militias and government forces, tore apart the social fabric of Iraq and left entire cities in ruins. **Baghdad**, once a diverse and cosmopolitan city, became a battleground for sectarian violence, with neighborhoods becoming segregated along sectarian lines.

Foreign Influence and Regional Destabilization

The power vacuum created by the fall of Saddam Hussein also opened the door for foreign powers to exert influence in Iraq, further complicating the situation. **Iran**, which had long viewed Saddam Hussein's regime as a regional rival, saw the U.S. invasion as an opportunity to expand its influence in Iraq, particularly through its support for Shia militias and political factions. Iranian-backed militias, such as the **Badr Organization**, played a key role in the sectarian conflict, and Iranian operatives provided weapons, training, and financial support to Shia fighters.

At the same time, Iraq became a battleground for **Sunni jihadist groups**, including **al-Qaeda in Iraq** (AQI), which sought to establish a foothold in the country and drive out both U.S. forces and Shia "apostates." AQI, led by the notorious jihadist **Abu Musab al-Zarqawi**, waged a campaign of terror against both U.S. forces and Iraqi civilians, carrying out bombings, assassinations, and kidnappings. Zarqawi's brutal tactics, which targeted Shia civilians in particular, were designed to incite sectarian violence and destabilize the country further.

The presence of these foreign-backed militias and insurgent groups contributed to the destabilization of Iraq and made it increasingly difficult for the U.S.-backed government to assert control. The conflict in Iraq also had a destabilizing effect on the broader region, as neighboring countries, including **Syria**, **Jordan**, and **Saudi Arabia**, were drawn into the conflict, either through the flow of foreign fighters or through their support for various factions.

Creation of a Power Vacuum

The **destabilization of Iraq** following the 2003 invasion and the removal of Saddam Hussein can be traced to a series of critical missteps, including the de-Ba'athification policy, the disbanding of the military, and the failure to address sectarian tensions. The power vacuum left by the dismantling of Iraq's institutions created the conditions for widespread insurgency, sectarian violence, and the rise of militias that operated outside the control of the government. This vacuum not only plunged Iraq into years of civil war but also created the environment in which extremist groups like **al-Qaeda in Iraq** and later **ISIS** could flourish.

The lessons of Iraq's destabilization are a stark reminder of the unintended consequences of regime change and the challenges of post-war reconstruction in deeply divided societies. As Iraq descended into chaos, the broader **Middle East** felt the ripple effects, as regional powers and jihadist groups sought to exploit the vacuum left by Saddam Hussein's removal. The legacy of the U.S. invasion of Iraq continues to shape the region's politics and security dynamics to this day.

Rise of ISIS as a Terrorist Caliphate

The rise of the **Islamic State of Iraq and Syria (ISIS)**, also known as **Daesh**, stands as one of the most consequential developments in the modern Middle East. Emerging from the ashes of the **Iraq War** and the Syrian civil war, ISIS rapidly transformed from a local insurgent group into a global jihadist movement that captured territory, established a self-proclaimed **caliphate**, and carried out a campaign of terror that shook the region and reverberated across the world. At the height of its power in 2014, ISIS controlled large swaths of territory in Iraq and Syria, governing millions of people under its brutal interpretation of Islamic law and attracting tens of thousands of foreign fighters.

The rise of ISIS can be traced back to the conditions created by the **U.S. invasion of Iraq** in 2003 and the subsequent power vacuum left by the removal of **Saddam Hussein**. However, it was the collapse of state institutions in **Syria** following the outbreak of the Syrian civil war in 2011 that allowed ISIS to expand beyond Iraq's borders and become a transnational threat. This chapter will explore the origins of ISIS, its rise as a terrorist caliphate, and the profound impact it had on regional stability, as well as the broader geopolitical consequences of its emergence.

Origins of ISIS in Iraq

The origins of ISIS can be traced back to **al-Qaeda in Iraq (AQI)**, a Sunni extremist group founded by the Jordanian militant **Abu Musab al-Zarqawi** in the aftermath of the 2003 U.S. invasion of Iraq. Zarqawi, a veteran of the **Afghan jihad** against the Soviet Union, had aligned himself with **Osama bin Laden** and the broader al-Qaeda network but pursued his own brutal tactics that often went beyond al-Qaeda's traditional methods. Under Zarqawi's leadership, AQI carried out a campaign of bombings, kidnappings, and assassinations aimed at destabilizing the U.S.-backed Iraqi government and inciting sectarian conflict between Iraq's Sunni and Shia populations.

Zarqawi's strategy of targeting Shia civilians, as well as U.S. forces, was designed to provoke a cycle of sectarian violence that would weaken the Iraqi state and create fertile ground for AQI to expand its influence. His tactics, which included the 2006 bombing of the **Al-Askari Mosque** in **Samarra**, succeeded in plunging Iraq into a bloody civil war, with Sunni and Shia militias engaging in retaliatory attacks that left thousands dead. However, Zarqawi's extremism also alienated many Sunni Iraqis, including tribal leaders in **Anbar Province**, who eventually turned against AQI and aligned with U.S. forces during the **Anbar Awakening** in 2007.

Despite the death of Zarqawi in a U.S. airstrike in 2006 and the subsequent weakening of AQI, the group persisted under new leadership. In 2010, **Abu Bakr al-Baghdadi** assumed control of AQI, which had by then rebranded itself as the **Islamic State of Iraq (ISI)**. Baghdadi, a religious scholar and experienced militant, sought to rebuild the group by taking advantage of the instability in Iraq and neighboring Syria. The U.S. withdrawal from Iraq in 2011, coupled with the growing Sunni disenfranchisement under the Shia-dominated government of **Nouri al-Maliki**, provided an opening for ISI to reassert itself as a major player in Iraq's insurgency.

Syrian Civil War and the Expansion of ISIS

While ISI was rebuilding in Iraq, the outbreak of the **Syrian civil war** in 2011 provided the group with a new opportunity to expand its influence across borders. The collapse of central authority in Syria, coupled with the fragmentation of opposition forces fighting against the regime of **Bashar al-Assad**, created a chaotic environment in which jihadist groups could thrive. In 2013, ISI formally expanded into Syria, rebranding itself as the **Islamic State of Iraq and Syria (ISIS)** and absorbing smaller jihadist factions operating in the war-torn country.

The group's ability to operate freely in both Iraq and Syria, two countries now engulfed in civil conflict, allowed ISIS to establish a transnational insurgency that defied traditional state boundaries. Baghdadi's vision for ISIS went beyond the tactics of al-Qaeda; he sought to establish a full-fledged **caliphate**—a theocratic state governed by Sharia law, with himself as the **caliph** (leader of the Muslim world). In 2014, ISIS captured the Iraqi city of **Mosul**, the country's second-largest city, in a lightning offensive that saw Iraqi security forces melt away in the face of the group's advance. The fall of Mosul marked a turning point for ISIS, as the group declared the establishment of its caliphate, with **Raqqa** in Syria serving as its de facto capital.

Establishment of the ISIS Caliphate

In **June 2014**, ISIS declared the establishment of its **caliphate**, with **Abu Bakr al-Baghdadi** as the self-proclaimed **caliph** of all Muslims. The caliphate was more than just a symbolic gesture; it represented the group's territorial ambitions and its intention to govern according to its strict interpretation of Islamic law. At its height, the ISIS caliphate controlled a vast swath of territory stretching from western Iraq to eastern Syria, encompassing major cities such as Mosul, Raqqa, and **Fallujah**.

ISIS quickly imposed its brutal version of Sharia law in the territories it controlled. Public executions, amputations, and floggings became common, as the group sought to enforce its rigid moral code. Religious minorities, including **Yazidis** and **Christians**, were targeted for extermination or forced conversion, while women were subjected to draconian restrictions, including forced marriages and sexual slavery. The group's use of social media to broadcast its atrocities—such as the beheadings of Western hostages—helped spread fear and attract recruits from around the world.

ISIS's ability to govern the territories it controlled was partly due to its use of sophisticated bureaucratic structures. The group established a range of administrative departments to manage everything from education and healthcare to taxation and infrastructure. ISIS also exploited the resources of the territories it captured, particularly oil, to finance its operations. At its height, the group was earning millions of dollars per day from oil sales, extortion, and smuggling, making it one of the wealthiest terrorist organizations in history.

Foreign Fighters and Global Recruitment

One of the defining features of ISIS's rise was its ability to attract tens of thousands of foreign fighters from across the globe. The group's declaration of a caliphate resonated with jihadists worldwide, many of whom saw it as the fulfillment of long-standing ideological aspirations. The **caliphate's promise of an Islamic utopia** appealed to a broad range of individuals, from disillusioned youth in the Middle East and North Africa to radicalized individuals in Europe, Asia, and even the United States.

ISIS used **social media** and online propaganda to recruit foreign fighters, portraying life in the caliphate as a noble and adventurous endeavor. The group's slickly produced videos and publications, such as its **Dabiq** magazine, glorified martyrdom and jihad while demonizing Western nations and their regional allies. Many foreign fighters were lured by the promise of status, purpose, and belonging, while others were motivated by ideological fervor or personal grievances.

The influx of foreign fighters not only bolstered ISIS's ranks but also helped to globalize its operations. The group began launching attacks outside the Middle East, either through coordinated operations or by inspiring so-called "lone wolf" attacks. Notable examples include the **November 2015 Paris attacks**, the **2016 Brussels bombings**, and the **2016 Orlando nightclub shooting**. These attacks, carried out by ISIS operatives or individuals radicalized by the group's propaganda, underscored the global reach of the caliphate's ideology.

Regional Impact of ISIS

The rise of ISIS had a profound impact on the Middle East, exacerbating existing conflicts and creating new challenges for regional governments. In **Iraq**, the group's capture of Mosul and its expansion into Sunni-majority areas threatened to further destabilize the fragile post-Saddam Hussein political order. The Iraqi government, under **Prime Minister Nouri al-Maliki**, struggled to respond effectively to the ISIS threat, particularly given the deep sectarian divisions that plagued the country's politics. Many Sunni Iraqis, alienated by the Shia-dominated government in Baghdad, initially viewed ISIS as a preferable alternative to the corrupt and ineffective central government.

In **Syria**, ISIS's rise compounded the chaos of the ongoing civil war, drawing resources and attention away from the fight against the **Assad regime**. The group's brutal tactics and expansionist ambitions alienated other Syrian rebel factions, including those aligned with **al-Qaeda's Syrian affiliate, Jabhat al-Nusra**. This led to infighting between jihadist groups and further fragmentation of the Syrian opposition. At the same time, ISIS's control of territory in eastern Syria allowed it to exploit Syria's oil fields, providing the group with a valuable source of revenue.

ISIS's presence in Syria and Iraq also heightened tensions between regional powers. **Iran**, which viewed the rise of ISIS as a direct threat to its influence in both countries, deployed **Shiite militias** and the **Iranian Revolutionary Guard Corps (IRGC)** to combat the group, particularly in Iraq. **Turkey**, meanwhile, became increasingly concerned about the presence of Kurdish forces in northern Syria, some of whom were aligned with the U.S.-backed **Syrian Democratic Forces (SDF)** in the fight against ISIS. The resulting geopolitical dynamics complicated international efforts to defeat the group and contributed to the ongoing instability in the region.

Decline of ISIS and Its Legacy

Although the ISIS caliphate reached its peak in 2014 and 2015, its territorial expansion was unsustainable in the face of concerted military pressure from a coalition of international and regional forces. **U.S.-led airstrikes**, combined with ground offensives by Iraqi forces, Kurdish militias, and Syrian rebel groups, gradually chipped away at ISIS's territorial holdings. In **2017**, Iraqi forces recaptured Mosul, dealing a major blow to the caliphate, and by **2019**, ISIS had lost control of all its territory in Iraq and Syria.

However, the defeat of ISIS as a territorial entity did not mark the end of the group's influence. ISIS fighters dispersed into the desert or went underground, continuing to launch insurgent attacks and guerrilla operations in both countries. Moreover, the group's ideology continued to inspire lone-wolf attacks and the formation of ISIS-affiliated cells in regions as far afield as **Libya**, **Nigeria**, and the **Philippines**.

The legacy of ISIS is one of destruction, sectarianism, and radicalization. Its rise exposed the fragility of the post-invasion order in Iraq and Syria, as well as the limits of Western military intervention in the Middle East. The group's brutal reign of terror, its appeal to foreign fighters, and its ability to carve out a quasi-state in the heart of the region will continue to influence the security landscape of the Middle East for years to come.

Lessons for U.S. Foreign Policy

The emergence, rapid expansion, and eventual territorial defeat of the **Islamic State of Iraq and Syria (ISIS)** provide a wealth of lessons for **U.S. foreign policy**, particularly in terms of intervention, counterterrorism, nation-building, and the unintended consequences of regime change. The rise of ISIS highlighted the dangers of **power vacuums**, **sectarianism**, and the challenges of governing post-conflict societies. Additionally, the global impact of ISIS—from its recruitment of foreign fighters to its ability to inspire lone-wolf terrorist attacks across the world—underscored the limits of traditional military strategies in countering transnational jihadist movements. The following section explores key lessons for U.S. policymakers derived from the rise and fall of ISIS, as well as the broader implications for U.S. engagement in the Middle East and beyond.

1. Dangers of Power Vacuums After Regime Change

The rise of ISIS is inextricably linked to the **power vacuum** created by the **2003 U.S.-led invasion of Iraq** and the subsequent dismantling of Iraq's **Ba'athist government** under **Saddam Hussein**. While the U.S. successfully removed a brutal dictator, it also unintentionally dismantled the institutions necessary for governing a deeply divided and fragile society. The disbanding of the **Iraqi military** and the de-Ba'athification policy, which purged former Ba'athists from government positions, created a vacuum in which state authority collapsed. The result was the marginalization of Iraq's **Sunni population**, many of whom turned to insurgent groups, including **al-Qaeda in Iraq (AQI)**, as a means of resistance.

This vacuum, combined with the withdrawal of U.S. forces in **2011** and the failure of the Iraqi government under **Nouri al-Maliki** to reconcile with its Sunni population, created fertile ground for the rise of ISIS. The fall of key Iraqi cities like **Mosul** in 2014 was not only a military defeat but also a reflection of deep-rooted political dysfunction, exacerbated by the absence of effective governance and security structures in Sunni-majority regions.

For U.S. foreign policy, this highlights the dangers of **regime change** without a comprehensive plan for post-conflict reconstruction and governance. The removal of autocratic regimes, whether in Iraq, Libya, or Syria, often leads to a destabilizing power vacuum if institutions are not preserved or quickly rebuilt. Future interventions must consider the long-term consequences of regime change, with a focus on preventing the collapse of governance and ensuring that new political systems are inclusive and capable of providing security and basic services.

2. Limits of Military Solutions in Counterterrorism

The U.S. and its allies employed overwhelming military force to defeat ISIS territorially, including **airstrikes**, **special operations**, and support for local forces like the **Syrian Democratic Forces (SDF)** and the **Iraqi military**. These efforts ultimately succeeded in recapturing key cities like **Raqqa** and **Mosul**, dismantling ISIS's territorial caliphate by 2019. However, the military defeat of ISIS did not eliminate the group as a threat. ISIS fighters dispersed into the desert, reverted to guerrilla warfare, and continued to carry out bombings, assassinations, and insurgent operations in Iraq and Syria. Meanwhile, ISIS-inspired attacks persisted in Europe, Asia, and the United States, carried out by lone-wolf actors radicalized by the group's online propaganda.

The lesson here is that while military force can degrade terrorist groups, it cannot eliminate the **underlying conditions** that give rise to extremism. The U.S. has learned, both in Iraq and Afghanistan, that defeating an insurgency or terrorist group on the battlefield is only one part of the equation. **Counterterrorism** must be integrated with broader political, social, and economic strategies that address the root causes of radicalization, such as **poverty**, **political exclusion**, **sectarianism**, and **poor governance**.

In the case of ISIS, the group's ability to attract recruits from disenfranchised Sunni communities in Iraq and Syria—many of whom saw the Shia-dominated governments as corrupt and illegitimate—underscored the importance of political inclusion and reconciliation. Military victories against groups like ISIS are often fleeting if the underlying grievances that drive support for extremism are not addressed.

3. Perils of Sectarianism in Nation-Building

One of the most significant factors contributing to the rise of ISIS was the deep-seated **sectarian tensions** between Iraq's **Sunni** and **Shia** populations. Under Saddam Hussein, the Sunni minority held disproportionate power, while the Shia majority and the **Kurdish** minority were marginalized and repressed. The post-invasion government, dominated by Shia political factions, reversed this dynamic, leading to the marginalization of Sunnis. **Prime Minister Nouri al-Maliki's** government was seen by many Sunnis as authoritarian, corrupt, and beholden to Iran.

The U.S. failed to address these sectarian divisions effectively during its occupation, and the subsequent Iraqi governments, under Maliki and others, exacerbated them through **sectarian policies**, such as the targeting of Sunni leaders and the exclusion of Sunnis from political power. ISIS, with its virulent anti-Shia ideology, capitalized on Sunni grievances to gain support in Sunni-majority areas, portraying itself as the defender of Sunni interests against both the Shia-led government and foreign (U.S. and Iranian) forces.

For U.S. foreign policy, the lesson is clear: **sectarianism** can be a powerful driver of instability, and nation-building efforts must be inclusive to prevent one group from dominating another. In countries with deep ethnic or sectarian divides, post-conflict political systems should ensure power-sharing arrangements and representation for all major groups. The failure to do so in Iraq directly contributed to the rise of ISIS and prolonged instability.

4. Global Nature of Jihadist Ideologies

The rise of ISIS underscored the global nature of **jihadist movements** and the challenges of combating transnational terrorism. Unlike traditional insurgencies that are primarily localized, ISIS was able to project its influence far beyond the borders of Iraq and Syria. Through its **sophisticated use** of social media, ISIS recruited tens of thousands of foreign fighters from across the globe, including Europe, North Africa, Central Asia, and even the United States. At the height of its power, ISIS-controlled territories served as a magnet for jihadists seeking to fight for the caliphate.

Moreover, ISIS's ability to inspire **lone-wolf attacks** in countries far from the battlefield demonstrated the difficulty of containing the spread of extremist ideologies. The group's propaganda, disseminated through encrypted messaging apps, social media platforms, and online forums, radicalized individuals in their home countries, leading to attacks in places like **Paris, Brussels, Orlando**, and **London**.

This global reach highlighted the **limitations of traditional counterterrorism approaches**, which often focus on eliminating leaders and degrading terrorist networks through military means. The U.S. and its allies must also focus on **countering violent extremism** (CVE) by addressing the social and ideological factors that drive radicalization. This includes promoting **deradicalization programs**, enhancing **community engagement** to prevent radicalization, and working with tech companies to disrupt the online platforms used by jihadist groups to spread their message.

5. Role of Regional Powers in Proxy Conflicts

Another lesson from the rise of ISIS is the role that **regional powers** play in shaping conflicts and influencing the outcome of U.S. foreign policy interventions. In both Iraq and Syria, regional actors—including **Iran, Turkey, Saudi Arabia**, and **Qatar**—played significant roles in either supporting or opposing various factions, often complicating U.S. efforts to build a cohesive strategy for defeating ISIS.

Iran, in particular, emerged as a key player in Iraq's fight against ISIS, deploying **Shiite militias** and **Iranian Revolutionary Guard Corps (IRGC)** operatives to assist the Iraqi government. While Iranian-backed militias were instrumental in reclaiming territory from ISIS, their presence also deepened sectarian tensions and raised concerns about Iran's growing influence in Iraq. This complicated U.S. relations with both the Iraqi government and Sunni populations, as well as with regional allies like Saudi Arabia, which viewed Iran's involvement with suspicion.

In **Syria**, the conflict became even more complex as multiple regional powers supported different factions. **Turkey** focused on containing Kurdish forces, Saudi Arabia and Qatar backed various rebel groups, and Russia intervened on behalf of the **Assad regime**. These overlapping and often conflicting interests turned the fight against ISIS into a broader regional struggle for influence.

For U.S. foreign policy, the lesson is that military interventions in the Middle East often draw in **regional actors** who have their own agendas, which can complicate U.S. objectives. Future interventions must consider the role of neighboring countries and work to engage regional powers in diplomatic efforts to prevent proxy conflicts from exacerbating local tensions.

6. Need for a Comprehensive Post-Conflict Strategy

The territorial defeat of ISIS, while a significant military achievement, did not mark the end of instability in Iraq and Syria. In the aftermath of ISIS's collapse, both countries faced the enormous challenge of rebuilding their cities, economies, and political systems, which had been ravaged by years of conflict. **Mosul**, once Iraq's second-largest city, was left in ruins after the battle to liberate it from ISIS, and the reconstruction of Raqqa, the former ISIS capital in Syria, has been slow and underfunded.

The failure to plan for the **post-conflict phase** of military operations is a recurring theme in U.S. interventions, from Iraq in 2003 to Libya in 2011. In the case of ISIS, the absence of a coherent strategy for post-ISIS governance, reconstruction, and reconciliation left many areas vulnerable to renewed violence, lawlessness, and the resurgence of extremist groups. The power vacuum left by ISIS's defeat was quickly filled by competing factions, including Shia militias, Kurdish forces, and Sunni tribal groups, each with its own interests.

For U.S. foreign policy, the lesson is that **post-conflict planning** must be an integral part of any military intervention. Defeating an enemy on the battlefield is only the first step; ensuring long-term stability requires investment in **governance**, **reconstruction**, and **reconciliation**. The international community must be prepared to provide financial and technical assistance for rebuilding war-torn societies, while also working to address the root causes of conflict, such as political exclusion and economic inequality.

7. Importance of Multilateral Cooperation

The fight against ISIS demonstrated the value of **multilateral cooperation** in addressing complex global security challenges. The U.S.-led **Global Coalition to Defeat ISIS**, which included more than 80 countries, played a critical role in coordinating military, financial, and humanitarian efforts to degrade and ultimately defeat ISIS. This coalition, which brought together a diverse group of nations—including NATO allies, Gulf states, and regional actors—highlighted the importance of burden-sharing and international collaboration in counterterrorism efforts.

However, the complexities of the Syrian and Iraqi conflicts also underscored the limitations of unilateral U.S. action in the face of transnational threats. The rise of ISIS was not confined to one country, and its defeat required cooperation from a range of actors, including those with divergent interests. Future U.S. foreign policy must prioritize **multilateral engagement** and work within international frameworks to address security challenges that transcend borders.

Adapting U.S. Foreign Policy to a Changing Landscape

The rise and fall of ISIS offer a sobering reminder of the challenges the U.S. faces in an increasingly volatile and interconnected world. The group's ability to exploit power vacuums, sectarianism, and weak governance to establish a terrorist caliphate underscores the importance of comprehensive, long-term strategies that go beyond military intervention. As the U.S. continues to engage with the Middle East and other regions affected by jihadist movements, the lessons from the ISIS experience must guide future foreign policy decisions. These include the need for **post-conflict planning**, **political reconciliation**, and **multilateral cooperation**, as well as a recognition of the limits of military power in addressing complex ideological threats.

CHAPTER 9 -. SYRIA: CIVIL WAR AND PROXY CONFLICT

The Syrian civil war, which began in 2011, has become one of the most devastating and complex conflicts in modern history, transforming from an internal uprising into a protracted civil war and a theater for **proxy conflict** involving numerous regional and international actors. The war has resulted in hundreds of thousands of deaths, displaced millions of people, and left much of Syria in ruins. The conflict's roots are deeply embedded in Syria's authoritarian political system, social and economic discontent, and the wave of protests that swept across the **Middle East** during the **Arab Spring**. However, what began as a popular revolt against the regime of **Bashar al-Assad** quickly morphed into a multifaceted war, drawing in foreign powers and militant groups vying for control and influence.

Syria's civil war has provided a critical case study in how internal conflicts can become entangled in broader geopolitical struggles, turning local grievances into global confrontations. The war has highlighted the dangers of **sectarianism**, the challenges of **nation-building**, and the consequences of **foreign intervention**, both direct and indirect. This chapter examines the causes of the Syrian civil war, the role of foreign powers in shaping the conflict, and the broader lessons for U.S. foreign policy.

Origins of the Syrian Civil War

The roots of the Syrian civil war can be traced back to the **authoritarian rule** of the **Assad family**, which has governed Syria since 1970, when **Hafez al-Assad**, a military officer and member of the **Ba'ath Party**, seized power in a bloodless coup. Under Hafez, Syria became a **one-party state** dominated by the **Ba'athist ideology**, which combined **Arab nationalism** with **socialism** and promised economic development and social justice. In reality, however, the Assad regime became synonymous with **political repression, corruption**, and **sectarian favoritism**.

The Assad regime relied heavily on its **security apparatus**, including the **Mukhabarat** (intelligence services), to suppress dissent and maintain control. Power was concentrated in the hands of the Assad family and a small elite, many of whom hailed from the **Alawite** sect, a minority offshoot of **Shia Islam** to which the Assads belonged. The majority of Syrians, however, were **Sunni Muslims**, and while the regime portrayed itself as secular, it systematically favored the Alawites and other minorities, such as **Christians** and **Druze**, in government and the military. This sectarian imbalance contributed to simmering resentment among Syria's Sunni majority.

By the time **Bashar al-Assad** inherited power in **2000** following his father's death, Syria was already facing significant social and economic challenges. Bashar, who had been trained as an ophthalmologist in the **United Kingdom**, initially presented himself as a reformer and modernizer. However, hopes for meaningful political reform were quickly dashed, as the younger Assad maintained the authoritarian structures of his father's regime. Over the next decade, Syria's economy stagnated, unemployment soared, and corruption became endemic. These economic difficulties, combined with widespread political repression and a lack of basic freedoms, fueled discontent across the country.

The Arab Spring and the Outbreak of Protests

The spark for the Syrian civil war came in **2011**, when popular uprisings swept across the Middle East and North Africa in what became known as the **Arab Spring**. Inspired by the successful overthrow of autocratic regimes in **Tunisia** and **Egypt**, Syrians began to protest against their own government, demanding an end to corruption, political repression, and economic hardship. The initial protests, which began in the southern city of **Daraa** after the arrest and torture of several teenagers for anti-government graffiti, were peaceful and largely focused on calls for reform rather than regime change.

However, the Assad regime responded to the protests with **brutal force**, deploying security forces to crack down on demonstrators. Protesters were beaten, arrested, and, in many cases, killed. The regime's violent response only fueled the anger of the protesters, and demonstrations quickly spread to other cities, including **Homs**, **Aleppo**, and **Damascus**. What began as a popular movement for reform soon escalated into a broader revolt, with protesters calling for the downfall of Bashar al-Assad.

As the regime's crackdown intensified, opposition groups began to organize and arm themselves, setting the stage for a full-scale civil war. By the end of 2011, the conflict had transformed from a peaceful protest movement into an armed insurgency. Opposition groups, many of them composed of defectors from the **Syrian military**, formed the **Free Syrian Army (FSA)**, which sought to overthrow the Assad regime through armed resistance. At the same time, various Islamist groups, including **Jabhat al-Nusra**, an al-Qaeda affiliate, began to emerge as significant players in the conflict.

Sectarianism and the Fragmentation of the Opposition

One of the defining features of the Syrian civil war has been the role of **sectarianism** in fueling the conflict. While the initial protests were largely secular and focused on political and economic grievances, the Assad regime quickly portrayed the uprising as a **Sunni Islamist** insurgency aimed at toppling a secular government. This narrative resonated with many of Syria's minorities, particularly the Alawites, who feared that a Sunni-dominated government would lead to persecution and retribution for their historical dominance under the Assad regime.

The regime's sectarian rhetoric, combined with its brutal suppression of the largely Sunni protest movement, deepened the divisions within Syrian society. Sunni-majority towns and cities became the centers of resistance, while many Alawites, Christians, and Druze remained loyal to the regime, fearing that the fall of Assad would result in chaos and sectarian violence. The conflict thus became increasingly polarized along sectarian lines, with Sunni opposition groups pitted against a regime dominated by Alawites and supported by other minority communities.

The opposition itself became deeply fragmented as the war progressed. While the FSA initially sought to represent a broad-based, secular opposition to the Assad regime, it struggled to unite the various factions fighting against the government. Islamist groups, including **Jabhat al-Nusra** and later **ISIS**, gained prominence within the opposition, attracting foreign fighters and financial support from regional powers. These groups often pursued their own agendas, clashing with secular opposition forces and further complicating efforts to present a unified front against Assad.

The fragmentation of the opposition also reflected the broader regional dynamics of the conflict. As the war dragged on, Syria became a battleground for competing **proxy forces**, each backed by foreign powers with their own interests in the outcome of the conflict.

Role of Foreign Powers in Escalation of the Conflict

The Syrian civil war quickly became a proxy conflict involving a wide range of **regional** and **international actors**, each with its own strategic interests in the outcome. From the beginning of the conflict, foreign powers provided military, financial, and logistical support to both the Assad regime and various opposition groups, turning Syria into a theater for **geopolitical competition**.

Iran was one of the Assad regime's earliest and most steadfast supporters. Tehran viewed Syria as a crucial ally in its regional strategy, particularly in its efforts to counterbalance **Saudi Arabia** and **Israel**. The fall of Assad, Iran feared, would weaken its axis of influence stretching from **Lebanon** (through its proxy **Hezbollah**) to Iraq and Syria. In response, Iran provided substantial military and financial support to the regime, including deploying units from the **Islamic Revolutionary Guard Corps (IRGC)** and mobilizing **Shia militias** from **Iraq**, **Lebanon**, and **Afghanistan** to fight on Assad's behalf.

Russia, too, became a critical ally of the Assad regime. Moscow had long-standing ties to Syria, dating back to the **Cold War**, when the Soviet Union supported **Hafez al-Assad**. Russia's interests in Syria were both geopolitical and economic: the country provided Moscow with a foothold in the Middle East and access to its only naval base in the **Mediterranean**, located in the Syrian port city of **Tartus**. In **2015**, after the Assad regime appeared to be on the verge of collapse, Russia intervened directly in the conflict, launching an air campaign to support the Syrian military. Russian airpower, combined with Iranian ground forces, helped turn the tide in favor of Assad, allowing the regime to recapture key cities such as **Aleppo**.

On the other side of the conflict, **Turkey**, **Saudi Arabia**, **Qatar**, and other **Gulf States** provided support to various opposition groups, particularly Islamist factions. Turkey, which shares a long border with Syria, sought to oust Assad and supported both the FSA and Islamist groups such as **Ahrar al-Sham**. At the same time, Turkey sought to counter the influence of Kurdish militias in northern Syria, which it viewed as an extension of the **PKK**, a Kurdish separatist group that has waged a decades-long insurgency inside Turkey.

Saudi Arabia and **Qatar** viewed the conflict through the lens of their rivalry with Iran, seeing the fall of Assad as a way to weaken Tehran's influence in the region. Both countries provided financial and military support to Islamist groups fighting against the regime, although their efforts were often hampered by the fractured nature of the opposition.

The United States, for its part, initially took a more cautious approach to the conflict. While the Obama administration expressed support for the Syrian opposition and called for Assad to step down, it was reluctant to become deeply involved in another Middle Eastern war following the U.S. withdrawal from **Iraq**. However, as the conflict escalated and jihadist groups such as ISIS gained prominence, the U.S. became increasingly involved, particularly through its support for the **Syrian Democratic Forces (SDF)**, a coalition of Kurdish and Arab fighters that became the primary U.S. ally in the fight against ISIS.

Emergence of ISIS in Syria and the Transformation of the War

One of the most significant developments in the Syrian civil war was the rise of **ISIS** in Syria, which took advantage of the chaos in both Syria and Iraq to establish its self-proclaimed **caliphate**. ISIS's brutal tactics and rapid territorial expansion transformed the conflict from a civil war between the Assad regime and the opposition into a broader regional struggle against jihadist extremism. The group's capture of **Raqqa** in 2014, which it declared the capital of its caliphate, made it a major player in the Syrian war and drew international attention.

The U.S.-led **Global Coalition to Defeat ISIS** launched a sustained military campaign against the group, targeting its strongholds in both Syria and Iraq. The **SDF**, backed by U.S. airpower, played a key role in recapturing Raqqa in 2017, effectively ending ISIS's control of major urban centers. However, ISIS fighters continued to operate in both countries as an insurgent force, carrying out bombings, assassinations, and guerrilla attacks.

The rise of ISIS further complicated an already chaotic conflict, as various factions—including the Assad regime, the opposition, Kurdish militias, and foreign powers—shifted their focus to fighting the group. At the same time, the war against ISIS brought the U.S. and Russia into an uneasy and often conflicting relationship, as both powers pursued their own interests in the region.

Complexity of Proxy Conflict in Syria

The Syrian civil war, which began as a popular uprising against an authoritarian regime, quickly morphed into one of the most complex and destructive conflicts of the 21st century. The involvement of multiple foreign powers, each with its own strategic goals, turned Syria into a battleground for proxy warfare, with devastating consequences for the Syrian people. The conflict has also raised important questions about the limits of foreign intervention, the challenges of nation-building in fractured societies, and the long-term consequences of sectarianism.

As the war continues, Syria remains deeply divided, with large parts of the country still outside the control of the central government. The long-term impact of the conflict will likely shape the region for decades to come, and the lessons learned from the Syrian civil war are critical for understanding the broader dynamics of proxy conflict and foreign intervention in the Middle East.

U.S. Arming of Syrian Rebels and the Complexities of the Syrian Civil War

The decision by the **United States** to arm Syrian rebels in the country's protracted civil war represented a major development in American foreign policy, reflecting the complexities and risks of intervention in a highly fractured and volatile conflict. Initially hesitant to become directly involved in the Syrian conflict, the U.S. eventually embraced the strategy of arming and supporting opposition groups as a means of weakening the regime of **Bashar al-Assad**, countering the growing influence of **ISIS**, and fostering conditions for a political transition. However, the program faced significant challenges, including the difficulty of vetting and controlling rebel factions, the overlap between moderate rebels and extremist groups, and the geopolitical complications of a multi-sided proxy war.

The U.S. decision to arm Syrian rebels is emblematic of the broader dilemmas that have defined American involvement in civil wars and insurgencies across the Middle East and beyond. This chapter explores the U.S. rationale for arming the Syrian opposition, the operational and political challenges of the program, and the broader consequences for both the Syrian conflict and U.S. foreign policy.

The U.S. Hesitation and Initial Response

When the Syrian civil war broke out in 2011, the **Obama administration** faced a difficult decision: whether to intervene directly in the conflict or remain on the sidelines. The war was a part of the broader **Arab Spring** uprisings, which had already seen the fall of autocratic regimes in **Tunisia**, **Egypt**, and **Libya**. However, the situation in Syria was more complex, given the entrenchment of the Assad regime, the country's deep sectarian divisions, and its strategic importance to regional powers like **Iran** and **Russia**.

Early in the conflict, the U.S. expressed support for the Syrian opposition's calls for political reform but refrained from direct military involvement. The U.S. stance was primarily shaped by a desire to avoid another protracted and costly Middle Eastern conflict following the **Iraq War** and the ongoing war in **Afghanistan**. Instead, the Obama administration initially pursued a strategy of **diplomatic engagement** and **economic sanctions** against the Assad regime, hoping to isolate the government and encourage a negotiated solution.

However, as the conflict intensified and Assad's security forces escalated their use of violence against civilians, the U.S. faced increasing pressure to do more. The regime's use of chemical weapons in 2013, most notably in an attack on the Damascus suburb of **Ghouta**, where hundreds of civilians were killed, further heightened calls for intervention. The Obama administration had previously stated that the use of chemical weapons by Assad would constitute a "red line," but in the end, the U.S. chose not to respond with military force, instead opting for a diplomatic agreement with Russia to remove Assad's chemical weapons stockpiles.

Despite this, the tide of U.S. policy gradually began to shift. By mid-2012, the administration had begun providing limited non-lethal assistance to rebel groups, such as communications equipment, medical supplies, and food. This support was framed as part of an effort to strengthen moderate elements within the opposition and build a foundation for future governance once Assad was removed from power.

The Decision to Arm the Rebels

The turning point for U.S. policy came in **2013**, when the Obama administration approved a secret program, known as **Timber Sycamore**, to arm and train Syrian rebels. This program was run by the **Central Intelligence Agency (CIA)** and involved the provision of arms, ammunition, and training to carefully vetted groups within the **Free Syrian Army (FSA)** and other moderate factions fighting against Assad's forces. The decision to arm the rebels was motivated by several factors:

1. **Countering Assad's Military Superiority**: The Assad regime had a significant military advantage over the opposition, thanks in part to the support it received from **Iran** and **Hezbollah**, as well as **Russia**. The U.S. viewed arming the rebels as a way to level the playing field and increase pressure on Assad to negotiate a political settlement.

2. **Preventing the Expansion of Extremist Groups**: By 2013, jihadist groups like **Jabhat al-Nusra** (an al-Qaeda affiliate) and later **ISIS** were gaining influence within the Syrian opposition. The U.S. hoped that by supporting moderate factions, it could prevent extremist groups from dominating the opposition and from taking control of territory within Syria.

3. **Creating Leverage for Diplomatic Negotiations**: The U.S. believed that increasing support for the rebels could create leverage in future diplomatic negotiations, such as the **Geneva peace talks**, by demonstrating to Assad and his allies that they could not achieve a military victory.

4. **Humanitarian Concerns**: The mounting civilian death toll, widespread displacement, and reports of war crimes committed by Assad's forces contributed to growing pressure on the U.S. to act. Arming the rebels was seen as a way to support the Syrian people's fight for freedom while avoiding the direct costs of a U.S. military intervention.

Complexities of Arming the Opposition

While the decision to arm the Syrian rebels was motivated by a desire to strengthen moderate opposition forces and pressure Assad, the program was fraught with challenges from the outset. The Syrian conflict was highly fragmented, with hundreds of opposition groups operating independently and often pursuing divergent goals. This made it extremely difficult for the U.S. to identify reliable partners on the ground, let alone ensure that the weapons and resources it provided were used effectively.

One of the primary difficulties was the **vetting process** for rebel groups. The U.S. wanted to avoid arming groups that were linked to extremist organizations, such as al-Qaeda or ISIS. However, the reality on the ground was far more complicated. Many rebel factions, particularly those affiliated with the FSA, were loosely organized and often cooperated with Islamist groups for tactical reasons. In some cases, weapons provided by the U.S. ended up in the hands of extremist groups through battlefield alliances, defections, or outright theft.

The **fluidity of alliances** among rebel groups also posed a significant challenge. Rebel factions frequently shifted their loyalties, and some groups that were initially vetted as moderate later aligned with more radical elements. This undermined U.S. efforts to build a cohesive, moderate opposition capable of challenging both Assad and ISIS. Additionally, the fragmentation of the opposition meant that U.S. support was often spread too thin, with no single group able to achieve significant gains against the regime.

Geopolitical Complexities and Regional Rivalries

The U.S. decision to arm the Syrian rebels also intersected with the broader **geopolitical dynamics** of the Middle East, further complicating the conflict. **Regional powers** such as

Turkey, **Saudi Arabia**, **Qatar**, and **Jordan** were all involved in supporting various factions within the Syrian opposition, each pursuing its own strategic objectives. Turkey, for example, was focused on preventing the rise of Kurdish forces near its border, while Saudi Arabia and Qatar sought to counter Iran's influence in Syria by backing Islamist factions opposed to Assad.

This multiplicity of foreign sponsors created a situation in which opposition groups were often beholden to external actors, rather than united by a common Syrian national interest. The result was a patchwork of rebel factions, some of which were supported by multiple foreign powers with conflicting agendas. This fragmentation not only weakened the overall effectiveness of the opposition but also made it nearly impossible for the U.S. to control the flow of arms and resources.

The involvement of **Russia** and **Iran** on the side of the Assad regime further complicated the conflict. Russia's direct military intervention in **2015**, through an intensive bombing campaign in support of Assad's forces, tipped the balance in favor of the regime and significantly undermined the U.S.-backed rebels 'ability to hold territory. Iran, for its part, continued to provide critical support to the regime through **Hezbollah** fighters and Shia militias, ensuring that Assad remained in power despite international opposition.

As the conflict escalated into a full-blown proxy war, the U.S. found itself facing the dual challenge of supporting its rebel partners while avoiding a direct confrontation with Russia and Iran. This limited the scope and effectiveness of U.S. support, as Washington sought to balance its involvement in Syria with its broader strategic priorities in the Middle East.

Rise of ISIS and the Shift in U.S. Strategy

The emergence of **ISIS** as a dominant force in both Syria and

Iraq fundamentally altered the dynamics of the Syrian civil war and prompted a shift in U.S. strategy. By **2014**, ISIS had captured large swaths of territory, including the Iraqi city of **Mosul** and the Syrian city of **Raqqa**, which it declared the capital of its self-proclaimed caliphate. The group's rapid territorial gains, brutal tactics, and ability to inspire global terror attacks shifted U.S. priorities from supporting the Syrian opposition against Assad to defeating ISIS.

In response to ISIS's rise, the U.S. launched **Operation Inherent Resolve**, a multinational military campaign aimed at degrading and ultimately defeating the group. The U.S. began conducting airstrikes against ISIS targets in both Iraq and Syria, while simultaneously expanding its support for local ground forces, including the **Syrian Democratic Forces (SDF)**, a coalition of Kurdish and Arab fighters.

The focus on defeating ISIS meant that U.S. support for the Syrian opposition became increasingly limited to groups that were actively fighting ISIS, rather than those solely focused on opposing the Assad regime. This shift in strategy further complicated U.S. relations with rebel groups, many of which viewed the Assad regime as their primary enemy. The prioritization of the anti-ISIS campaign also led to tensions with regional allies like Turkey, which was more concerned about the rise of Kurdish forces near its border than the defeat of ISIS.

End of the Timber Sycamore Program and the Legacy of U.S. Support

By **2017**, the U.S. had largely abandoned its program to arm and train Syrian rebels, with the **Trump administration** officially ending the **Timber Sycamore** program. The decision to wind down the program reflected the shifting priorities of U.S. foreign policy, as the fight against ISIS took precedence over efforts to topple Assad. It also signaled a recognition that the U.S. had limited influence over the outcome of the Syrian civil war, particularly in light of Russia's military intervention and Assad's resurgence.

The legacy of U.S. support for Syrian rebels is one of mixed results. While the program provided some short-term gains for the opposition, it ultimately failed to achieve its broader goals of weakening Assad, fostering a unified moderate opposition, or creating leverage for a political settlement. Instead, the Syrian conflict continued to escalate, with Assad remaining in power and extremist groups like ISIS and al-Qaeda-linked factions gaining strength.

For U.S. foreign policy, the experience of arming Syrian rebels underscores the **complexities and risks** of intervening in civil wars where local dynamics are deeply intertwined with regional and global power struggles. The challenges of vetting and controlling rebel groups, the fluidity of alliances, and the involvement of foreign powers all made the U.S. strategy in Syria difficult to execute and ultimately unsustainable. As the Syrian civil war continues, the lessons of U.S. involvement will shape future discussions on the limits of arming opposition forces in volatile and fragmented conflicts.

Rise of Jihadist Factions and the Role of ISIS in Syria

The Syrian civil war, which began in 2011 as a popular uprising against the regime of **Bashar al-Assad**, quickly morphed into a complex, multifaceted conflict that attracted a wide array of local, regional, and international actors. Among the most significant developments in the war was the rise of **jihadist factions**, which sought to exploit the chaos of the conflict to further their own ideological and territorial ambitions. Of these factions, none had a more profound impact on the course of the war—and on global security—than the **Islamic State of Iraq and Syria (ISIS)**.

ISIS's meteoric rise in Syria, alongside other jihadist groups like **Jabhat al-Nusra** (an al-Qaeda affiliate), transformed the conflict from a civil war into a battleground for extremist groups seeking to establish a fundamentalist **caliphate**. The presence of these factions not only complicated the dynamics of the war but also drew in foreign powers, including the United States, Russia, and European nations, each seeking to neutralize the global threat posed by ISIS. This chapter examines the emergence of jihadist factions in Syria, the role of ISIS in the war, and the broader implications of their rise for the region and international security.

Emergence of Jihadist Factions in Syria

The initial protests that sparked the Syrian civil war in 2011 were largely secular in nature, driven by popular discontent with Assad's authoritarian rule, economic stagnation, and government corruption. However, as the regime responded with brutal force, the conflict escalated into an armed insurgency, with various factions taking up arms against the government. As the conflict deepened, jihadist groups—many of which had been previously active in Iraq and other parts of the Middle East—began to gain a foothold in Syria.

The vacuum created by the collapse of state authority in large parts of the country provided fertile ground for jihadist groups to operate. Many of these groups were well-funded, experienced in guerrilla warfare, and ideologically motivated to establish an Islamic state. Among the first jihadist groups to emerge in Syria was **Jabhat al-Nusra**, formed in **2012** as an affiliate of **al-Qaeda**. Led by **Abu Mohammad al-Julani**, Jabhat al-Nusra quickly became one of the most effective opposition forces, conducting high-profile suicide bombings and military operations against the Assad regime.

Jabhat al-Nusra's success on the battlefield, combined with its ability to provide basic services in areas it controlled, helped it gain significant support among local populations. However, its hardline Islamist ideology and its affiliation with al-Qaeda alienated other opposition groups, particularly those affiliated with the secular **Free Syrian Army (FSA)**. As a result, the opposition in Syria became increasingly fragmented, with jihadist groups like Jabhat al-Nusra and secular factions often fighting against both the regime and each other.

While Jabhat al-Nusra was the most prominent jihadist faction in the early years of the conflict, it would soon be overshadowed by the rise of **ISIS**, which brought a new level of brutality and ambition to the war.

Origins of ISIS in Syria

The origins of ISIS can be traced back to **al-Qaeda in Iraq (AQI)**, which was founded by **Abu Musab al-Zarqawi** during the U.S. occupation of Iraq in the early 2000s. Zarqawi's group, known for its extreme violence and sectarian attacks against Shia Muslims, played a major role in the insurgency against U.S. forces and the Iraqi government. After Zarqawi's death in 2006, AQI rebranded itself as the **Islamic State of Iraq (ISI)** and continued to wage a brutal insurgency.

By 2010, ISI had come under the leadership of **Abu Bakr al-Baghdadi**, who sought to expand the group's influence beyond Iraq's borders. The outbreak of the Syrian civil war in 2011 provided Baghdadi with the perfect opportunity to do so. In 2013, ISI expanded into Syria, rebranding itself as the **Islamic State of Iraq and Syria (ISIS)**. Baghdadi's vision for ISIS was not limited to fighting Assad; he aimed to establish a transnational **caliphate** that would span the Middle East and impose a strict interpretation of **Sharia law**.

One of the key factors behind ISIS's success in Syria was its ability to recruit foreign fighters from across the world. Unlike Jabhat al-Nusra, which remained focused on the Syrian conflict, ISIS presented itself as the vanguard of a global jihad, attracting recruits from as far afield as Europe, North Africa, and Central Asia. These foreign fighters, many of whom were radicalized online, provided ISIS with a steady stream of manpower as it sought to expand its control over territory in both Syria and Iraq.

The Capture of Raqqa and the Declaration of the Caliphate

ISIS's most significant territorial gains in Syria came in **2014**, when the group captured the city of **Raqqa**, which it declared the capital of its self-proclaimed caliphate. The capture of Raqqa marked a turning point in the Syrian civil war, as ISIS consolidated its control over large swaths of territory in eastern Syria and western Iraq, including key cities such as **Mosul** in Iraq.

In June 2014, Baghdadi declared the establishment of the **caliphate**, with himself as the **caliph** (leader of all Muslims). This declaration was more than just a symbolic gesture; it represented a significant shift in ISIS's goals and ambitions. Unlike other jihadist groups that focused on fighting local regimes, ISIS sought to create a state—complete with its own governance structures, taxation systems, and military forces. The group's propaganda, disseminated through slickly produced videos and online publications, portrayed life in the caliphate as a utopia for devout Muslims, attracting thousands of foreign fighters.

The caliphate's rapid territorial expansion, combined with its brutal tactics—including public executions, crucifixions, and the enslavement of religious minorities such as the **Yazidis**— made ISIS one of the most feared and reviled jihadist groups in the world. Its atrocities shocked the international community and prompted a coordinated military response led by the **United States** and its allies.

Role of ISIS in the Syrian Civil War

While ISIS's primary goal was the establishment of its caliphate, the group also played a significant role in shaping the dynamics of the Syrian civil war. From its stronghold in Raqqa, ISIS launched offensives against both the Assad regime and other opposition groups, seeking to expand its territory and consolidate its power. The group's ability to operate across the porous border between Syria and Iraq allowed it to move fighters and resources between the two countries, giving it a strategic advantage over other factions.

In Syria, ISIS clashed frequently with **Jabhat al-Nusra** and other Islamist groups, as well as with the secular FSA. These intra-opposition conflicts further fragmented the anti-Assad forces and weakened the overall opposition effort. While some rebel groups initially saw ISIS as a potential ally in the fight against Assad, they quickly became disillusioned by the group's brutal tactics and its refusal to cooperate with other factions.

ISIS's expansion into Syria also had significant implications for the broader regional and international response to the conflict. The group's rapid territorial gains, combined with its ability to inspire terrorist attacks across the world, prompted the United States and its allies to shift their focus from supporting the Syrian opposition to defeating ISIS. The **U.S.-led coalition** launched **Operation Inherent Resolve** in **2014**, targeting ISIS positions in both Syria and Iraq with airstrikes and providing support to local ground forces, such as the **Syrian Democratic Forces (SDF)**.

The rise of ISIS also provided a pretext for increased foreign intervention in Syria. **Russia**, which had long been a staunch supporter of the Assad regime, used the threat of ISIS to justify its direct military intervention in **2015**. While Russia claimed its airstrikes were targeting ISIS, much of its military effort was directed against other rebel groups, allowing the Assad regime to regain territory and strengthen its position.

By **2017**, the tide had turned against ISIS. The group faced mounting pressure from the U.S.-led coalition, which had successfully reclaimed large parts of Iraq and Syria from ISIS control. The recapture of **Mosul** in July 2017 and **Raqqa** in October 2017 marked the beginning of the end for the caliphate. As ISIS lost territory, its ability to govern and recruit diminished, and the group was forced to revert to its origins as a guerrilla insurgency.

However, while the territorial caliphate was defeated, ISIS continued to pose a threat, both in the region and globally. Many ISIS fighters went underground, carrying out insurgent attacks in Iraq and Syria. Others returned to their home countries, where they either carried out or inspired lone-wolf attacks. The group's ideology, disseminated through online propaganda, continued to attract followers long after its territorial defeat.

ISIS's Regional Impact

The rise of ISIS had a profound impact on the Middle East, exacerbating existing conflicts and reshaping the regional security landscape. In Syria, the group's territorial ambitions and extreme tactics further fragmented the opposition, making it more difficult for anti-Assad forces to present a unified front. ISIS's rise also intensified the sectarian dimensions of the Syrian civil war, as the group's virulent anti-Shia rhetoric and its targeting of religious minorities fueled wider sectarian violence.

In Iraq, the group's capture of Mosul and other cities deepened the country's sectarian divide and led to widespread displacement and destruction. The Iraqi government, backed by U.S. forces and Iranian militias, eventually reclaimed the territory lost to ISIS, but the damage done to Iraq's social fabric has been lasting.

Moreover, the rise of ISIS had global implications, as the

group's ability to inspire and direct terrorist attacks extended far beyond the Middle East. From the **2015 Paris attacks** to the **2016 Brussels bombings**, ISIS-linked or inspired attacks demonstrated the global reach of the group's ideology. This global threat prompted a coordinated international response, but it also raised difficult questions about how to combat a jihadist movement that could operate both as a territorial state and as a decentralized network of cells and lone-wolf actors.

ISIS's Enduring Legacy in Syria

While the territorial caliphate established by ISIS has been dismantled, the group's legacy in Syria and the broader Middle East endures. The rise of ISIS fundamentally altered the trajectory of the Syrian civil war, turning what was initially a conflict between the Assad regime and the opposition into a broader struggle against jihadist extremism. The group's brutal tactics, territorial ambitions, and ability to inspire global terrorism left a lasting impact on both the region and the world.

For U.S. foreign policy, the rise and fall of ISIS underscores the challenges of combating extremist movements that thrive in failed or failing states. The Syrian civil war, with its mix of sectarianism, foreign intervention, and jihadist extremism, highlights the difficulties of finding lasting solutions to conflicts where local grievances are intertwined with global ideological movements.

Iranian and Russian Involvement in Supporting Assad's Regime

The **Syrian civil war**, which erupted in 2011, quickly became a battleground for regional and international powers with vested interests in the outcome. Among the most significant players backing the regime of **Bashar al-Assad** were **Iran** and **Russia**. Their involvement fundamentally shaped the trajectory of the conflict, tipping the balance in Assad's favor and ensuring his survival against both domestic insurgents and international opposition. This chapter explores the motivations behind Iranian and Russian support for Assad, the nature of their involvement in the conflict, and the broader geopolitical implications of their actions for the **Middle East** and beyond.

Iranian Involvement in Syria

Iran's support for Assad predates the Syrian civil war and is rooted in a long-standing strategic alliance that dates back to the rule of **Hafez al-Assad**, Bashar's father. The relationship between Iran and Syria has been central to **Iran's regional strategy**, especially in its efforts to project power across the **Levant** and counterbalance regional rivals such as **Saudi Arabia** and **Israel**. For Tehran, Syria represents a key part of the **"Axis of Resistance"**, a network of Shia-aligned governments and militias that includes **Hezbollah** in Lebanon and **Shia militias** in Iraq. Maintaining Assad in power was thus seen as essential to preserving Iran's influence in the region and securing its strategic foothold in the Eastern Mediterranean.

1. Iran's Motivations for Supporting Assad

Iran's involvement in Syria is driven by several strategic, ideological, and geopolitical factors:

1. **Preserving the Axis of Resistance**: Iran's alliance with Syria is a critical component of its broader regional strategy, which seeks to confront Israeli and Western influence in the Middle East. Through its partnership with Syria, Iran has been able to support and supply **Hezbollah**, the Lebanese Shia militant group that serves as a major deterrent against Israeli aggression. The loss of Assad's regime would disrupt this supply line and weaken Iran's ability to exert influence in Lebanon and beyond.

2. **Countering Sunni Arab Rivals**: Iran has long viewed the Sunni-majority countries of the **Gulf Cooperation Council (GCC)**, particularly Saudi Arabia, as rivals for regional hegemony. The Syrian civil war, which pitted Assad's Alawite-led government against largely Sunni opposition forces, quickly became a proxy battle between Iran and Saudi Arabia. By supporting Assad, Iran sought to prevent Syria from falling into the hands of Sunni Islamist groups aligned with Saudi Arabia or Qatar, which would have diminished Iran's regional influence.

3. **Protecting Shia and Alawite Populations**: While Assad's government is secular, the ruling elite in Syria is dominated by members of the **Alawite sect**, a minority offshoot of **Shia Islam**. Iran's support for Assad is partly motivated by its desire to protect the Alawite community and other Shia minorities in Syria, who face existential threats from Sunni jihadist groups like **ISIS** and **Jabhat al-Nusra**. This aligns with Iran's broader role as the self-proclaimed protector of Shia Muslims throughout the region.

4. **Strategic Access to the Mediterranean**: Syria provides Iran with a strategic gateway to the **Mediterranean Sea**, which is critical for its regional ambitions. Through Syria, Iran can maintain a direct line of influence stretching from **Tehran** to the **Mediterranean coast**, passing through Iraq and Lebanon. This corridor, sometimes referred to as the **Shia Crescent**, allows Iran to project power in the Levant and establish a presence near Israel's borders.

2. Iran's Military and Financial Support for Assad

From the early stages of the Syrian civil war, Iran provided extensive military, financial, and logistical support to the Assad regime. While the exact extent of Iran's financial assistance to Syria remains difficult to quantify, estimates suggest that Iran has spent **billions of dollars** propping up Assad's government. This financial aid has been used to pay Syrian government salaries, support the economy, and fund military operations.

Militarily, Iran's involvement escalated as the conflict deepened. The **Islamic Revolutionary Guard Corps (IRGC)**, particularly its **Quds Force**, played a leading role in coordinating Iran's military strategy in Syria. The Quds Force, led by **General Qassem Soleimani** until his assassination by the U.S. in 2020, was responsible for orchestrating Iran's support for both Syrian government forces and a network of Shia militias that Tehran deployed to the battlefield.

Iran's strategy in Syria relied heavily on these **Shia militias**, which were drawn from various countries across the region. Notable among them were the **Hezbollah** fighters from Lebanon, who were instrumental in key battles such as the defense of **Damascus** and the recapture of **Aleppo**. In addition to Hezbollah, Iran also mobilized Shia militias from Iraq, Afghanistan, and Pakistan, sending thousands of fighters to Syria to bolster Assad's forces.

Iran's military involvement in Syria was not without its costs. The IRGC and its militia allies suffered significant casualties, and Iran's financial outlay in Syria placed a strain on its already beleaguered economy, especially in the face of **international sanctions**. Nonetheless, Tehran remained committed to Assad's survival, viewing the Syrian war as a critical front in its broader regional strategy.

3. The Role of Hezbollah in the Syrian Conflict

One of the most important elements of Iran's strategy in Syria was the deployment of **Hezbollah**, the Lebanese militant group that has long been a proxy for Iranian influence in the Levant. Hezbollah, which had previously focused its military efforts on fighting Israel, became a key player in the Syrian civil war, helping to tip the balance in Assad's favor at several critical junctures.

Hezbollah's involvement in Syria was motivated by both ideological and strategic considerations. The group's leader, **Hassan Nasrallah**, framed Hezbollah's intervention as part of the broader struggle to defend Shia Islam and protect Lebanon from the spread of jihadist groups like ISIS. Hezbollah also viewed the survival of Assad's regime as essential to maintaining its supply lines from Iran and safeguarding its base of operations in southern Lebanon.

Hezbollah forces played a decisive role in the **Battle of Qusayr** in **2013**, where they helped Syrian government forces retake a strategically important town near the Lebanese border that had been held by rebel groups. The victory at Qusayr marked a turning point in the war, bolstering the morale of Assad's forces and allowing them to regain the initiative on the battlefield.

Over the course of the war, Hezbollah deployed thousands of fighters to Syria, many of whom were seasoned veterans of the conflict with Israel. The group's experience in guerrilla warfare, combined with its close coordination with the IRGC and Syrian government forces, made it one of the most effective fighting forces on the pro-Assad side.

Russian Involvement in Syria

While Iran's involvement in Syria was driven by its regional ambitions and sectarian interests, **Russia's** decision to intervene in the conflict was motivated by a combination of geopolitical, strategic, and economic factors. Russia has long-standing ties to Syria, dating back to the Cold War when the Soviet Union provided military and economic support to **Hafez al-Assad's** government. In the decades since, Syria remained one of Russia's closest allies in the Middle East, and Moscow sought to protect this relationship as the Syrian civil war escalated.

1. Russia's Strategic Interests in Syria

Russia's involvement in Syria is rooted in several key strategic objectives:

1. **Preserving its Military Presence in the Mediterranean**: Syria is home to Russia's only naval base outside the former Soviet Union, located in the port city of **Tartus** on the Mediterranean coast. The base at Tartus provides Russia with a critical foothold in the Mediterranean and enables Moscow to project naval power in the region. Losing Syria to a hostile government or jihadist forces would jeopardize Russia's access to the Mediterranean and its influence in the Middle East.

2. **Countering Western Intervention**: Russia's intervention in Syria was also driven by its desire to prevent the United States and its Western allies from orchestrating regime change in Damascus. Russia viewed the 2011 **NATO intervention in Libya**, which led to the fall of **Muammar Gaddafi**, as a betrayal of an international consensus and sought to prevent a similar scenario from unfolding in Syria. By backing Assad, Russia positioned itself as a defender of state sovereignty and opposed what it viewed as Western attempts to impose regime change under the guise of humanitarian intervention.

3. **Demonstrating Russia's Global Power**: Russia's intervention in Syria was part of a broader effort by **President Vladimir Putin** to reassert Russia's role as a major global power. By intervening militarily in Syria, Russia aimed to demonstrate its ability to shape outcomes in the Middle East and challenge the dominance of the United States and its allies. Syria became a proving ground for Russia's military capabilities, particularly its **airpower** and **precision-guided munitions**.

4. **Preventing the Spread of Jihadist Extremism**: While Russia's primary motivation for supporting Assad was strategic, it also sought to prevent the spread of jihadist groups like ISIS and al-Qaeda, which posed a direct threat to Russian security. Thousands of foreign fighters from the **Caucasus** and **Central Asia** had traveled to Syria to join ISIS and other jihadist factions, and Russia feared that these fighters would return to Russia or its near abroad and carry out attacks. By targeting jihadist groups in Syria, Russia sought to degrade their capabilities and prevent their expansion into Russian territory.

2. Russia's Military Intervention: A Turning Point in the War

Russia's direct military intervention in Syria began in **September 2015**, when Russian aircraft launched airstrikes against rebel-held areas, marking a decisive turning point in the conflict. Prior to Russia's intervention, Assad's forces were struggling to hold onto key areas, and many observers believed the regime was on the verge of collapse. Russia's intervention helped to reverse these losses and allowed Assad to regain control over large parts of the country.

Russia's military campaign in Syria was characterized by the extensive use of **airpower**, with Russian jets carrying out thousands of airstrikes against opposition forces. While Moscow claimed that its air campaign was primarily aimed at ISIS and other jihadist groups, many of the strikes targeted **moderate opposition forces** backed by the West, particularly in areas around **Aleppo** and **Idlib**. The Russian air campaign was critical in enabling Assad's forces, along with Iranian and Hezbollah fighters, to recapture key cities and towns that had been held by the opposition.

In addition to airpower, Russia deployed **special forces**, **artillery**, and **advisers** to support Syrian government forces on the ground. Russian troops played a key role in the **siege of Aleppo**, which ended in December 2016 with the city's recapture by Assad's forces after months of heavy bombing and fighting. The fall of Aleppo marked a major victory for Assad and effectively ended the opposition's hopes of overthrowing the regime.

3. Russia's Geopolitical Gains and Long-Term Presence in Syria

Russia's intervention in Syria has been widely viewed as a success from Moscow's perspective. By saving Assad's regime from collapse, Russia has secured its military presence in the Mediterranean and reasserted itself as a key player in the Middle East. In 2017, Russia signed an agreement with Syria to expand its naval base at Tartus and maintain a long-term military presence at the **Hmeymim airbase**. These bases give Russia the ability to project power in the Eastern Mediterranean and beyond.

In addition to its military gains, Russia has positioned itself as an indispensable power broker in Syria. Through its role in the **Astana peace talks**, which brought together Iran, Turkey, and other regional actors, Russia has sought to shape the post-war settlement in Syria and ensure that Assad remains in power. Russia's involvement in Syria has also allowed it to deepen its relationships with regional powers such as **Turkey** and **Iran**, despite their sometimes conflicting interests in the conflict.

While Russia's intervention has helped Assad regain control of much of Syria, the war is far from over. Large parts of the country, particularly in the northeast and northwest, remain outside the regime's control, and Syria faces enormous challenges in rebuilding its war-ravaged infrastructure and economy. Nevertheless, Russia's involvement has ensured that Assad will remain in power for the foreseeable future, and Moscow is likely to remain a key player in Syria's future.

Broader Implications of Iranian and Russian Support for Assad

The involvement of Iran and Russia in the Syrian civil war

has had profound implications for the region and for global geopolitics. For Iran, its military and financial investment in Syria has cemented its role as a dominant regional power and allowed it to expand its influence across the Levant. However, Iran's involvement has also fueled sectarian tensions and exacerbated its rivalry with Saudi Arabia and other Sunni Arab states.

For Russia, its intervention in Syria has allowed it to reassert its role as a global power and challenge the dominance of the United States in the Middle East. Russia's success in Syria has emboldened Moscow to take a more assertive stance in other parts of the world, from Ukraine to Libya, where it has sought to expand its influence.

The survival of Assad's regime, thanks to Iranian and Russian support, has also reshaped the balance of power in the Middle East. While the conflict in Syria is far from resolved, it is clear that Assad's victory has strengthened the hand of authoritarian regimes across the region and demonstrated the limits of Western efforts to promote regime change and democracy in the Middle East.

The Syrian Refugee Crisis: A Humanitarian Crisis with Global Consequences

The **Syrian civil war** has not only devastated the country's infrastructure and economy but has also led to one of the largest humanitarian crises in modern history. The conflict displaced millions of Syrians, both internally and externally, leading to a massive refugee crisis that affected neighboring countries, the broader **Middle East**, and **Europe**. The scale and scope of this crisis are unparalleled in recent memory, with profound social, economic, and political ramifications for host countries and the international community.

This section explores the social and economic impacts of the

Syrian refugee crisis on neighboring countries like **Jordan**, **Turkey**, and **Lebanon**, as well as the broader implications for Europe, which faced its most significant influx of refugees since **World War II**. The humanitarian consequences of the war continue to reverberate, highlighting the complex relationship between armed conflict, migration, and regional stability.

Scale of the Refugee Crisis

The Syrian civil war has displaced more than **13 million people**, roughly half of the country's pre-war population. Of these, over **6.6 million** fled the country as refugees, while **6.7 million** remain internally displaced within Syria. The United Nations High Commissioner for Refugees (**UNHCR**) has called the Syrian crisis "the largest displacement crisis of our time." Syrians have sought refuge in neighboring countries, with **Turkey**, **Lebanon**, **Jordan**, and **Iraq** hosting the majority of refugees. Significant numbers of Syrians have also sought asylum in **Europe**, with a particular concentration in **Germany**, **Sweden**, and **Greece**.

The exodus of Syrians has placed an immense strain on host countries, many of which were already grappling with economic challenges and political instability. These countries have had to absorb millions of refugees, providing them with basic services such as housing, healthcare, and education, while also dealing with the broader social and economic impacts of such a large influx of people.

Jordan: Coping with the Refugee Influx

Jordan, with a population of approximately **10 million**, has long been a host for refugees, including **Palestinians** and **Iraqis**. However, the Syrian refugee crisis posed an unprecedented challenge for the small kingdom, which now hosts over **1.3 million** Syrians. While not all of these are registered as refugees, the impact of their presence is profound.

The largest concentration of Syrian refugees in Jordan is in the **Zaatari refugee camp**, located near the Syrian border. Originally established in 2012, Zaatari has grown into one of the world's largest refugee camps, housing over **80,000** people at its peak. While many refugees initially fled to camps like Zaatari, the majority of Syrians in Jordan now live in urban areas, where they face challenges in accessing housing, employment, and services.

The influx of refugees has placed significant pressure on Jordan's public services, particularly in healthcare and education. Hospitals and clinics have become overcrowded, and schools have struggled to accommodate the large number of Syrian children. Jordan's already limited resources have been stretched thin, leading to tensions between host communities and refugees. In some cases, local Jordanians perceive Syrians as competition for jobs and social services, contributing to a rise in anti-refugee sentiment.

Economically, Jordan has borne the brunt of the crisis. The country's economy, already weakened by regional instability, has struggled to provide opportunities for both its citizens and the growing refugee population. Unemployment remains high, particularly among youth, and refugees often work in the informal sector, where wages are low and labor protections are minimal. Despite significant international aid, Jordan's economic recovery has been slow, and the long-term presence of Syrian refugees continues to present challenges for the country's development.

Turkey: The Largest Host of Syrian Refugees

Turkey, which shares a long border with Syria, has become the largest host of Syrian refugees, with over **3.6 million** Syrians currently living in the country. The Turkish government initially adopted an open-door policy, welcoming Syrians fleeing the conflict, and providing them with temporary protection. However, as the war dragged on and the number of refugees swelled, Turkey's capacity to absorb them became strained.

The vast majority of Syrian refugees in Turkey live in urban areas, where they face significant challenges in accessing housing, employment, and social services. While the Turkish government has made efforts to integrate refugees, including providing access to healthcare and education, many Syrians remain marginalized and face difficulties in securing formal employment. The result has been the growth of a large informal economy in which Syrians often work in low-paying, exploitative conditions.

The presence of millions of Syrian refugees has also had political implications for Turkey. President **Recep Tayyip Erdoğan** initially used Turkey's role as a host nation to bolster his image domestically and internationally. However, as public opinion has shifted, particularly in economically disadvantaged regions, Erdoğan's government has faced increasing pressure to address the economic burden posed by the refugees. Anti-Syrian sentiment has grown, with some Turks blaming Syrians for rising unemployment and strained public services. In response, the Turkish government has taken steps to tighten its border and has encouraged refugees to return to northern Syria, where Turkish-backed forces control certain areas.

Turkey's role as a host nation has also affected its relationship with Europe. In **2016**, Turkey and the **European Union** struck a deal in which Turkey agreed to stem the flow of refugees into Europe in exchange for financial aid and other concessions. While this deal helped reduce the number of refugees reaching European shores, it also placed a significant burden on Turkey, which continues to host the largest refugee population in the world.

Lebanon: A Country Overwhelmed by the Crisis

Lebanon, with a population of just over **6 million**, has been disproportionately affected by the Syrian refugee crisis. The country hosts approximately **1.5 million** Syrians, making it the highest per capita recipient of refugees in the world. This has placed immense pressure on Lebanon's fragile political and economic systems, which were already under strain before the outbreak of the Syrian civil war.

Lebanon's political system is deeply divided along sectarian lines, and the influx of Syrian refugees has exacerbated these divisions. The refugees, most of whom are Sunni Muslims, have altered the country's delicate sectarian balance, fueling fears among some communities—particularly the **Christian** and **Shia** populations—that their influence will be diminished. This has led to tensions between Syrian refugees and Lebanese host communities, with refugees often facing discrimination and hostility.

Economically, Lebanon has struggled to cope with the refugee crisis. The country's infrastructure, including electricity, water, and waste management systems, was already inadequate before the crisis, and the arrival of hundreds of thousands of additional people has only worsened these problems. The Lebanese economy has stagnated, and unemployment remains high, particularly among the country's youth. Syrian refugees, who often work in low-wage sectors such as construction and agriculture, are seen by many Lebanese as competing for scarce jobs, further fueling resentment.

In recent years, Lebanon's government has taken steps to encourage the return of Syrian refugees, but these efforts have been complicated by the ongoing conflict in Syria and the reluctance of many refugees to return to a country that remains deeply unstable. The international community has provided significant aid to Lebanon to help it cope with the crisis, but the long-term presence of such a large refugee population remains a major challenge for the country's development and stability.

Impact of the Refugee Crisis on Europe

The Syrian civil war has also had a profound impact on **Europe**, which experienced a dramatic increase in the number of asylum seekers and refugees arriving on its shores between **2014** and **2016**. During this period, more than **1 million** refugees, primarily from Syria, Afghanistan, and Iraq, made the perilous journey across the **Mediterranean Sea** to reach Europe. The sheer scale of this migration triggered a political crisis across the continent, as governments struggled to manage the influx and provide for the needs of the refugees.

The vast majority of Syrian refugees initially sought asylum in **Germany**, **Sweden**, and **Greece**, with Germany, under **Chancellor Angela Merkel**, adopting an open-door policy. Merkel's decision to welcome hundreds of thousands of Syrians was praised by some as a humanitarian gesture but criticized by others as reckless and unsustainable. The arrival of so many refugees strained social services, housing, and healthcare systems in many European countries, leading to a backlash from both the public and political leaders.

In several European countries, the refugee crisis fueled the rise of **far-right** and **populist** political movements that exploited public fears about immigration, security, and cultural integration. Parties like the **Alternative for Germany (AfD)** and **Marine Le Pen's National Rally** in France gained significant political ground by opposing immigration and calling for stricter border controls. The refugee crisis also led to deep divisions within the **European Union (EU)**, as member states disagreed on how to share the burden of hosting refugees. While countries like Germany and Sweden welcomed refugees, others, particularly in Eastern Europe, refused to take in significant numbers.

In response to the crisis, the EU implemented measures to control the flow of refugees, including the **EU-Turkey agreement** of 2016, which aimed to reduce the number of migrants reaching Europe by returning them to Turkey. Additionally, several European countries tightened their borders, built fences, and increased security measures to stem the flow of refugees. While these efforts succeeded in reducing the number of arrivals, they also highlighted the EU's inability to create a unified and cohesive policy for dealing with asylum seekers.

Long-Term Impact of the Refugee Crisis

The long-term impact of the Syrian refugee crisis is still unfolding, both for the countries that have hosted refugees and for the refugees themselves. In many cases, refugees remain in a state of limbo, unable to return to Syria due to ongoing instability but also facing significant barriers to integration in their host countries. Many refugees continue to live in precarious conditions, with limited access to education, employment, and healthcare.

For host countries like Jordan, Turkey, and Lebanon, the presence of such large numbers of refugees has had both positive and negative effects. On the one hand, refugees have contributed to the local economy by participating in the labor force and starting small businesses. On the other hand, their presence has strained public services and exacerbated existing social and economic problems.

In Europe, the refugee crisis has reshaped political landscapes, fueling debates about immigration, national identity, and the future of the EU. While some countries have embraced multiculturalism and sought to integrate refugees, others have taken a more insular approach, raising concerns about the erosion of **European solidarity** and the rise of xenophobia.

The Syrian refugee crisis stands as a stark reminder of the human cost of conflict. The displacement of millions of people has reshaped the Middle East and Europe, presenting significant challenges for both host countries and the international community. As the war in Syria continues, the fate of millions of refugees remains uncertain, and the global response to the crisis will continue to have far-reaching implications for regional stability, international relations, and humanitarian policy.

PART IV: THE MIDDLE EAST IN CHAOS

CHAPTER 10 - THE LIBYAN CRISIS: GADDAFI'S OUSTER AND THE CHAOS LEFT BEHIND

"We came, we saw, he died."
Hillary Rodham Clinton,
Former U.S. Secretary of State

The **Libyan intervention** that led to the fall of **Muammar Gaddafi** in 2011 was one of the most significant and controversial examples of Western involvement in the Middle East and North Africa. To fully understand the chaos that followed Gaddafi's ouster, it's important to explore the broader historical context, especially Gaddafi's long-standing and complicated relationship with the **United States** and Western powers, his ambitions for **Pan-Africanism**, and his efforts to reshape the geopolitical landscape of Africa.

Gaddafi's rise to power in **1969** came at a time when Libya, a former Italian colony, was still adjusting to its newfound independence. The young **colonel**, inspired by **Arab nationalism** and the revolutionary zeal of figures like **Gamal Abdel Nasser** of Egypt, led a **bloodless coup** that ousted Libya's monarch, **King Idris**. Gaddafi soon positioned himself as a charismatic and defiant leader, determined to establish Libya as an independent and powerful force, free from Western influence. He nationalized the country's vast oil reserves, using the wealth to modernize Libya and to fund ambitious infrastructure projects. However, Gaddafi's rule was also marked by increasingly autocratic tendencies and violent repression of dissent.

From the outset, Gaddafi was deeply suspicious of Western intentions in the region, especially those of the United States and European powers like **France** and **Britain**. His defiant posture often put him at odds with the West, particularly because of his alignment with **anti-imperialist** and **revolutionary** causes. Over the course of his rule, Gaddafi supported numerous militant and insurgent groups across Africa and the Middle East, earning him the reputation of a **pariah** in Western eyes.

One of the key points of contention between Gaddafi and the West was his desire to reshape Africa's political landscape. Gaddafi envisioned himself as the champion of **Pan-Africanism**, a movement that sought to unify the continent under a single African identity, free from the legacy of **colonialism** and **Western exploitation**. He invested heavily in the creation of the **African Union**, hoping to position Libya as a leader in African affairs. Gaddafi's vision for Africa included a common currency, a unified military, and a continent-wide effort to resist Western influence. This ambition put him on a collision course with Western powers, who saw his rhetoric and influence in Africa as a threat to their strategic and economic interests on the continent.

Gaddafi's **Pan-Africanist** aspirations were deeply intertwined with his long history of **anti-Western** rhetoric and actions. During the **Cold War**, he forged close ties with the **Soviet Union**, and while he nominally pursued **non-alignment**, his financial and military support for anti-imperialist movements across the world—including in **Ireland**, **Palestine**, and **Southern Africa**—antagonized the United States and its allies. The West viewed Gaddafi as a destabilizing force in regions critical to its interests, particularly in terms of access to **oil** and **strategic resources**. Gaddafi's open support for groups the U.S. and Europe classified as **terrorist organizations**, such as the **Palestinian Liberation Organization (PLO)** and the **Irish Republican Army (IRA)**, made him a target for retaliation.

The most notable escalation in U.S.-Libyan tensions occurred in the 1980s, under **President Ronald Reagan**. Gaddafi's government was implicated in a series of attacks on American and European targets, most notably the **1986 bombing of a Berlin nightclub**, which killed two U.S. servicemen. In response, the U.S. launched **airstrikes** on Libya, targeting Gaddafi's residence in **Tripoli**. While Gaddafi survived the attack, the airstrikes significantly worsened relations between the two nations. Shortly thereafter, the **Lockerbie bombing** in 1988, which involved the destruction of **Pan Am Flight 103** over **Scotland**, was traced back to Libyan agents. The bombing killed 270 people, including 190 Americans, and led to international outrage, placing Gaddafi and his regime under intense global scrutiny.

The Lockerbie bombing marked a turning point in U.S.-

Libyan relations. For much of the 1990s, Libya remained under **international sanctions**, isolated diplomatically and economically. Gaddafi, once a vocal and flamboyant leader on the world stage, became more reclusive as his country's economy stagnated under the weight of these sanctions. However, in the early 2000s, as part of an effort to re-establish ties with the West, Gaddafi made a surprising pivot. He renounced **weapons of mass destruction**, agreed to compensate the victims of the Lockerbie bombing, and even began cooperating with Western nations in the fight against **al-Qaeda**. This move led to a thaw in relations between Libya and the West, with Gaddafi being rebranded, at least temporarily, as a "reformed" leader.

Despite this shift, Gaddafi's ambitions for Africa and his longstanding support for radical movements continued to make him a problematic figure for the U.S. and its allies. His desire to create a **United States of Africa**, complete with a single currency and a unified military, was seen as a direct challenge to the dominance of Western institutions like the **International Monetary Fund (IMF)** and **World Bank**, which played pivotal roles in shaping the economic policies of African nations. Moreover, Gaddafi's financial backing for African leaders and his efforts to position Libya as a key player in African affairs were viewed with suspicion by Western powers, who feared that he was using his influence to promote instability.

In 2011, as the Arab Spring swept across the region, Libya became the next target for regime change. Protests against Gaddafi's four-decade rule began in **Benghazi** before spreading to other cities. Gaddafi's harsh crackdown on the protests, which included the use of military force against civilians, triggered widespread condemnation from the international community. The **United Nations** authorized military intervention to protect civilians, leading to **NATO**'s involvement in Libya. While the intervention was framed as a humanitarian mission, it quickly evolved into an effort to remove Gaddafi from power.

The **U.S.-led NATO intervention** played a decisive role in the collapse of Gaddafi's regime. By August 2011, Gaddafi's forces had lost control of Tripoli, and within weeks, Gaddafi was captured and killed by rebel forces in his hometown of **Sirte**. While the fall of Gaddafi was hailed as a victory for democracy and human rights, the aftermath of his removal plunged Libya into chaos.

The power vacuum created by Gaddafi's ouster left Libya without a functioning central government, and rival militias, tribal groups, and jihadist factions quickly filled the void. What followed was a period of prolonged instability, with competing factions vying for control of the country's vast oil wealth and strategic assets. The absence of strong governance also allowed groups like **ISIS** to establish a foothold in Libya, further complicating efforts to restore peace and stability.

The **Western intervention** in Libya, though initially seen as a success, soon came to be viewed as another example of the unintended consequences of foreign intervention. Gaddafi's removal did not lead to a stable or democratic Libya but rather to a fractured, war-torn state that continues to struggle with violence and lawlessness. For the U.S. and its allies, the Libyan conflict served as a cautionary tale about the dangers of regime change without a clear plan for post-conflict governance.

Gaddafi's fall also left a lasting impact on the broader region. The collapse of Libya's government contributed to the proliferation of arms and fighters across North Africa, fueling conflicts in neighboring countries like **Mali** and exacerbating the rise of militant groups in the **Sahel** region. The instability in Libya, combined with the ongoing civil war in Syria, also contributed to the European **migrant crisis**, as hundreds of thousands of refugees and migrants used Libya's coast as a launching point to cross the Mediterranean into Europe.

In retrospect, Gaddafi's complex relationship with the U.S. and other Western nations, his ambitions for African unity, and his long history of defiance toward Western dominance help explain why his regime was targeted. However, the chaos that followed his removal underscores the importance of understanding the deeper historical and geopolitical dynamics that shaped Libya's trajectory. The downfall of Gaddafi serves as a stark reminder that regime change, even when justified on humanitarian grounds, can have far-reaching and destabilizing consequences for both the country in question and the broader international community.

U.S. Support for Libyan Rebels and NATO's Role in Toppling Gaddafi

The U.S. intervention in Libya in 2011, framed as part of a **NATO**-led coalition aimed at protecting civilians from the brutal crackdown of **Muammar Gaddafi's** regime, became one of the most controversial military actions of the decade. The initial goal of protecting Libyan civilians, under the guise of **Responsibility to Protect (R2P)**, quickly morphed into a regime-change operation that ended with Gaddafi's violent death and the subsequent collapse of Libya into chaos. The U.S. and NATO's backing of the **Libyan rebels** who opposed Gaddafi's rule mirrored earlier mistakes seen in Afghanistan, where U.S. support for **mujahideen** fighters during the **Soviet-Afghan War** ultimately led to long-term instability and the rise of extremist factions.

The intervention in Libya, which initially seemed like a success in its removal of a dictatorial regime, proved to have disastrous consequences, both for the Libyan people and for regional stability. This section explores how U.S. and NATO support for the rebels contributed to Libya's fragmentation and descent into warring factions.

The decision to intervene in Libya came against the backdrop of the **Arab Spring**, a wave of protests and uprisings that swept across the Middle East and North Africa. As demonstrations against Gaddafi's regime began in **Benghazi**, the Libyan government responded with overwhelming force, deploying military assets to crush the rebellion. Gaddafi's threats of mass violence against the rebels and their civilian supporters prompted widespread international condemnation and calls for action. The United Nations passed **UN Security Council Resolution 1973**, authorizing the use of "all necessary measures" to protect Libyan civilians, effectively giving NATO the green light for intervention.

From the outset, the U.S. played a critical role in building the international coalition that would eventually carry out the intervention. President **Barack Obama's** administration framed the action as part of a multilateral effort to prevent a humanitarian disaster, and **Secretary of State Hillary Clinton** was instrumental in garnering support for the operation. NATO, led by the U.S., **France**, and **Britain**, began a coordinated **air campaign** to enforce a **no-fly zone** over Libya and to target Gaddafi's military infrastructure.

Initially, the airstrikes were intended to prevent Gaddafi's forces from advancing on rebel-held areas like **Misrata** and **Benghazi**, where the regime had threatened to "show no mercy." However, as the campaign progressed, it became increasingly clear that NATO's involvement had shifted from protecting civilians to supporting the rebels in their bid to overthrow Gaddafi. Western forces provided not only air cover but also intelligence, logistical support, and weapons to the opposition, effectively turning the tide of the conflict in favor of the rebels.

The parallels between U.S. support for the Libyan rebels

and earlier interventions in **Afghanistan,** are striking. In Afghanistan, the U.S. had armed and trained local mujahideen fighters during the 1980s to resist the Soviet occupation, viewing them as a bulwark against communist expansion. However, after the Soviet withdrawal, these same factions turned against each other, and the country descended into civil war. The rise of extremist groups like the **Taliban** and **al-Qaeda** emerged in the power vacuum left behind, with long-term consequences for global security.

Similarly, in Libya, the U.S. and its NATO allies quickly armed and supported a patchwork of rebel factions with little consideration for the political and ideological differences between them. The coalition backing the rebellion against Gaddafi was fragmented from the start, composed of groups with vastly different visions for Libya's future. While some factions were relatively secular and aligned with Western democratic ideals, others were Islamist groups with ties to extremist ideologies. The lack of a unified opposition or a coherent post-Gaddafi plan for governance was a major flaw in the Western intervention.

The airstrikes, combined with the rebels 'ground advances, eventually led to the collapse of Gaddafi's regime. By August 2011, the capital city of **Tripoli** had fallen to rebel forces, and within weeks, Gaddafi himself was captured and killed in his hometown of **Sirte**. His death marked the end of over four decades of authoritarian rule in Libya, but it also marked the beginning of the country's descent into chaos.

Fragmentation of Libya into Warring Factions

The downfall of Gaddafi created a **power vacuum** in Libya, which quickly fragmented into a patchwork of competing factions and militias. Without a strong central government to fill the void, various groups—many of which had received Western backing during the rebellion—began to vie for control of the country's resources, particularly its vast oil wealth. This fragmentation was exacerbated by Libya's tribal structure and the absence of cohesive national institutions, leaving the country with little chance for stability in the immediate aftermath of Gaddafi's ouster.

The **National Transitional Council (NTC)**, which had been formed by the rebels to act as a provisional government, struggled to assert authority over the country. Many of the militias that had fought against Gaddafi refused to disarm, instead carving out their own territories and enforcing their own rules. The NTC's inability to provide security or basic services further weakened its legitimacy, and the hope for a quick transition to democracy evaporated as the situation deteriorated.

Libya's fragmentation into warring factions mirrored the post-Soviet experience in Afghanistan, where the withdrawal of a centralized government led to a prolonged and bloody civil war. In Libya, as in Afghanistan, the groups that had united against a common enemy were unable to form a stable post-conflict government. The absence of a plan for governance after the removal of Gaddafi proved catastrophic, as the competing factions began to fight for dominance.

Several key players emerged in the aftermath of Gaddafi's fall. The **Libyan Dawn** coalition, an Islamist group, took control of **Tripoli** and much of western Libya, while **General Khalifa Haftar**, a former Gaddafi loyalist turned rebel, led the **Libyan National Army (LNA)** in the east. Haftar, who had lived in exile in the United States for many years, positioned himself as a secular, anti-Islamist leader, and his forces quickly gained control over **Benghazi** and other eastern cities. The conflict between these two factions soon escalated into a full-blown civil war, with both sides receiving support from foreign powers.

The involvement of external actors further complicated

the situation in Libya. While the U.S. and most Western nations officially supported the NTC and the subsequent **Government of National Accord (GNA)**, Haftar received backing from countries like **Egypt** and the **United Arab Emirates**, which viewed him as a bulwark against the spread of Islamist influence. Meanwhile, **Turkey** and **Qatar** supported the Islamist factions, deepening the divisions between the warring sides.

The lack of a coherent Western strategy for post-Gaddafi Libya allowed these regional powers to exert their influence, turning Libya into a proxy battleground. The situation was further complicated by the rise of jihadist groups like **ISIS**, which took advantage of the chaos to establish a presence in the country. By 2015, ISIS had taken control of **Sirte**, Gaddafi's hometown, and used it as a base from which to launch attacks across Libya and the wider region. The presence of ISIS in Libya drew renewed international attention, but efforts to combat the group were hampered by the lack of a unified government capable of coordinating an effective response.

The parallels to Afghanistan's descent into civil war following the Soviet withdrawal are clear. In both cases, the absence of a central authority and the proliferation of armed factions led to prolonged instability and violence. In Libya, as in Afghanistan, the U.S. and its allies had focused primarily on regime change without adequately planning for the aftermath, leaving the country vulnerable to fragmentation and extremist influence.

Consequences of the Fragmentation

The fragmentation of Libya has had far-reaching consequences, both for the country itself and for the wider region. Internally, Libya has been plagued by ongoing violence and lawlessness. The lack of a central government has allowed human trafficking networks to flourish, turning Libya into a major transit point for migrants and refugees attempting to cross the **Mediterranean Sea** to reach Europe. The collapse of Libya's economy, combined with the widespread availability of weapons, has fueled crime and instability, making daily life perilous for many Libyans.

Regionally, the fall of Gaddafi has had destabilizing effects on **North Africa** and the **Sahel**. Weapons looted from Gaddafi's arsenals have spread across the region, fueling conflicts in countries like **Mali**, where Islamist insurgents seized control of the northern part of the country in 2012. The Libyan conflict has also contributed to the rise of jihadist groups across the Sahel, which continue to pose a serious threat to regional security.

For the United States and its NATO allies, the intervention in Libya has been a cautionary tale about the unintended consequences of military action without a clear post-conflict plan. While the removal of Gaddafi was initially seen as a success, the fragmentation of Libya into warring factions has shown that regime change is only the beginning of the challenge. As Libya continues to struggle with instability, the long-term consequences of the intervention remain a stark reminder of the limits of Western interventionism.

The Libyan intervention, like the earlier U.S. support for the mujahideen in Afghanistan, and the Syrian rebels demonstrates the dangers of arming rebel groups and pursuing regime change without fully considering the aftermath. In both cases, the short-term success of removing a regime gave way to long-term instability, creating a power vacuum that was filled by competing factions and extremist groups. The lessons learned from Libya are particularly relevant for future U.S. foreign policy, as they highlight the importance of a comprehensive strategy that includes not just military intervention but also a clear plan for governance and stability in the post-conflict period.

The Benghazi Attack: U.S. Destabilization of Libya and the Consequences of Creating Power Vacuums

The attack on the U.S. consulate in **Benghazi** on September 11, 2012, was a tragic and defining moment in the aftermath of the **Libyan intervention**, exposing the volatile and dangerous environment created by the power vacuum that followed the ousting of **Muammar Gaddafi**. The assault, which resulted in the deaths of U.S. Ambassador **Christopher Stevens** and three other American personnel, not only highlighted the instability of post-Gaddafi Libya but also underscored a recurring pattern in U.S. foreign policy—where efforts to destabilize regimes lead to unintended and often catastrophic consequences, including the empowerment of hostile forces that the U.S. initially supported or facilitated.

In the case of Libya, the U.S. and its **NATO** allies intervened with the primary goal of removing Gaddafi from power under the auspices of humanitarian protection. However, like many regime-change operations before it, the intervention neglected to plan for the aftermath of Gaddafi's downfall, resulting in a fractured and chaotic landscape that allowed extremist groups to flourish. The 2012 attack on the U.S. consulate in Benghazi was a direct consequence of this vacuum, an example of how the instability created by U.S. intervention can backfire, with the very forces the U.S. once sought to empower turning hostile.

The Power Vacuum in Post-Gaddafi Libya

Gaddafi's regime, for all its authoritarianism, had maintained a semblance of order in Libya through a combination of centralized power, tribal alliances, and the brutal repression of dissent. His overthrow in **2011**, facilitated by a U.S.-led NATO campaign that provided air support and logistical assistance to rebel forces, left the country without a clear governing authority. The **National Transitional Council (NTC)**, which was supposed to guide Libya toward democracy, lacked the institutional capacity and political legitimacy to unite the country. As a result, Libya quickly descended into a **power vacuum**, with various factions, militias, and extremist groups vying for control of territory, resources, and political influence.

The absence of a functioning central government created fertile ground for armed groups to proliferate. Many of these groups had been armed by the West during the uprising against Gaddafi, receiving weapons, training, and support to fight the regime. However, once Gaddafi was gone, these militias—often ideologically diverse and regionally based—turned their attention to consolidating power in the post-war landscape. Some aligned with local tribal interests, while others were motivated by Islamist ideology or criminal enterprises. The lack of disarmament and reintegration plans for these militias contributed to the fragmentation of the country.

In particular, **Benghazi**, Libya's second-largest city and the birthplace of the anti-Gaddafi revolution, became a focal point of instability. The city was home to a variety of militias, including **Ansar al-Sharia**, an Islamist group that would later be implicated in the attack on the U.S. consulate. As the central government in Tripoli struggled to assert control, Benghazi's militias effectively ran the city, establishing their own checkpoints, enforcing their own laws, and engaging in violent power struggles with rival factions. This anarchic environment was a direct result of the **lack of a coherent post-Gaddafi governance structure**, and it laid the groundwork for the violence that would erupt in 2012.

The U.S. Consulate in Benghazi: A Vulnerable Target

As the situation in Libya deteriorated, the U.S. maintained

a diplomatic presence in Benghazi, partly because of the city's symbolic importance as the heart of the revolution. **Ambassador Christopher Stevens**, who had been a strong advocate of the U.S. intervention in Libya, was stationed at the **Benghazi consulate** as part of an effort to stabilize the country and foster relationships with the various factions on the ground. Stevens had developed close ties with many of the Libyan rebel groups during the NATO intervention and believed that U.S. engagement was critical to supporting the country's fragile transition to democracy.

However, by 2012, the security situation in Benghazi had become increasingly perilous. The city was rife with lawlessness, and **militias**—some of which had once fought against Gaddafi with Western support—were now engaged in turf wars and power struggles. Extremist groups, including Ansar al-Sharia, had gained a foothold in the city, exploiting the absence of a strong central government to expand their influence. Despite the deteriorating security environment, the U.S. consulate in Benghazi remained **under-protected**, relying on local militia forces for security rather than U.S. military personnel.

This reliance on local militias for security proved to be a fatal mistake. Many of these militias had their own agendas, and their loyalty to the U.S. was tenuous at best. The consulate was seen by some as a symbol of Western interference in Libyan affairs, and extremist groups began to view it as a soft target. Ansar al-Sharia, in particular, had a growing animosity toward the U.S., fueled by the group's radical Islamist ideology and opposition to what it perceived as American imperialism in the region.

The Attack on the Consulate

On the night of September 11, 2012, a group of heavily armed militants launched a coordinated assault on the U.S. consulate in Benghazi. The attackers overwhelmed the lightly guarded compound, setting fires and firing rocket-propelled grenades. Ambassador Stevens and another American diplomat, **Sean Smith**, were killed in the initial attack, while two CIA contractors, **Tyrone Woods** and **Glen Doherty**, were killed in a subsequent assault on a nearby CIA annex.

The attack on the consulate was a shocking and tragic event that sent shockwaves through Washington and the international community. In the immediate aftermath, there was widespread confusion about the motives behind the attack and the identity of the perpetrators. While the assault was initially blamed on spontaneous protests sparked by an anti-Islamic video circulating online, it soon became clear that it was a premeditated attack carried out by extremist elements in Benghazi, likely led by Ansar al-Sharia.

The attack highlighted the dangers of the **power vacuum** that had emerged in Libya following Gaddafi's overthrow. The very forces that the U.S. and NATO had supported during the revolution had now turned hostile, either directly or indirectly contributing to the attack on the consulate. The U.S.'s reliance on local militias for security, many of which were ideologically opposed to Western influence, left American personnel vulnerable to the very groups they had once considered allies. The absence of a coherent and functional Libyan state, combined with the proliferation of extremist groups, created a chaotic environment in which the U.S. consulate became an easy and symbolic target.

The Recurring Cycle of Proxy Forces Turning Hostile

The Benghazi attack is a stark reminder of a recurring theme in U.S. foreign policy—where proxy forces, initially armed and supported by the U.S. to achieve short-term objectives, later turn hostile and contribute to long-term instability. This pattern can be traced back to the U.S.'s involvement in Afghanistan during the 1980s, when **mujahideen** fighters, armed and funded by the U.S. to resist the Soviet occupation, later gave rise to extremist groups like the **Taliban** and **al-Qaeda**. In Libya, a similar dynamic played out. The rebel groups and militias that had received U.S. and NATO backing during the uprising against Gaddafi were unable to form a cohesive and unified government after his fall, leading to infighting and the rise of radical factions.

The **fragmentation** of Libya into warring militias, some of which were ideologically aligned with jihadist movements, created an environment where U.S. interests became vulnerable. The weapons and support provided to the Libyan rebels, intended to liberate the country from Gaddafi's authoritarian rule, instead empowered militias that would later act in ways contrary to U.S. objectives. Ansar al-Sharia, which played a role in the Benghazi attack, was one of the many extremist groups that had taken advantage of the instability to gain power, using the post-revolution chaos to impose their radical vision on parts of the country.

This recurring cycle of proxy forces turning against their former backers is emblematic of a broader failure in U.S. interventionist policies. In the rush to achieve immediate military victories, the long-term consequences of arming and supporting non-state actors are often overlooked. Once the immediate objective is achieved—whether it be the ousting of the Soviets in Afghanistan or the removal of Gaddafi in Libya—the lack of a clear strategy for post-conflict stabilization allows for the rise of extremist forces, who often turn their weapons and influence against the very powers that once supported them.

Lessons for U.S. Foreign Policy

The attack on the U.S. consulate in Benghazi had far-reaching political and strategic consequences. In the United States, the incident sparked a bitter political debate, with critics accusing the Obama administration of failing to protect American personnel and misleading the public about the nature of the attack. Multiple congressional investigations were launched, focusing on the administration's handling of the crisis and the lack of adequate security at the consulate.

Beyond the immediate political fallout, the Benghazi attack also raised serious questions about the broader U.S. strategy in Libya and the Middle East. The intervention that had initially been celebrated as a victory for humanitarian interventionism was now viewed as a cautionary tale about the dangers of regime change without a clear plan for governance. The U.S. had removed Gaddafi but failed to help Libya build the institutions necessary to prevent the rise of extremist groups and militias.

For U.S. foreign policy, the Benghazi attack reinforced the need for a more comprehensive approach to post-conflict stabilization. The lesson was clear: **regime change**, by itself, is not enough. Without the infrastructure and institutions needed to fill the power vacuum, the forces unleashed by revolution can lead to even greater instability and violence. The attack also highlighted the risks of relying on proxy forces, many of which may have agendas that diverge from U.S. interests once the common enemy is gone.

The Benghazi attack serves as a grim reminder of the complexities and unintended consequences of foreign intervention. In the rush to oust Gaddafi and support the Libyan rebels, the U.S. and its allies failed to fully account for the long-term instability that would follow. The result was a fractured Libya, a power vacuum filled by extremist groups, and, ultimately, the loss of American lives in an attack that symbolized the perils of short-term strategic thinking in a region marked by deep-seated divisions and unresolved conflicts.

CHAPTER 11 - YEMEN: THE FORGOTTEN PROXY WAR

The conflict in **Yemen** is often referred to as the "**forgotten war**," overshadowed by higher-profile conflicts in the Middle East, such as the wars in **Syria** and **Iraq**. Yet, Yemen's civil war, which began in **2014**, has evolved into one of the most devastating humanitarian crises in modern history and a proxy battlefield where regional powers, particularly **Saudi Arabia** and **Iran**, have played significant roles. While initially seen as a local conflict between Yemeni factions, the war quickly escalated into a broader geopolitical struggle that has drawn in major players from across the region, turning Yemen into a theater of **sectarian** and **political rivalry**.

The roots of the Yemeni conflict stretch back decades, to the complex and often turbulent history of the country. Yemen has long been a nation divided along **sectarian**, **tribal**, and **regional** lines. The north of Yemen was ruled by the **Zaidi imams**, a branch of **Shia Islam**, until the 1960s, while the south was a British protectorate before gaining independence and briefly becoming a **Marxist state**. Yemen's reunification in **1990** did little to resolve the deep-seated divisions that have plagued the country. In fact, it exacerbated them, with years of political instability, economic challenges, and internal divisions creating fertile ground for conflict.

The **Houthi movement**, a group representing Yemen's Zaidi Shia minority, emerged as a significant force in northern Yemen in the early 2000s. Initially formed to resist marginalization and discrimination by the central government, the Houthis gradually evolved into a well-organized military force. Their relationship with **Iran**—a key point of contention in the ongoing proxy war—began to develop during this period, as Iran saw in the Houthis a potential ally to counterbalance Saudi influence in the Arabian Peninsula.

By the time the **Arab Spring** swept across the region in **2011**, Yemen was already on the brink of collapse. Longtime president **Ali Abdullah Saleh**, whose rule had been characterized by corruption and autocracy, was forced to step down amid protests. His successor, **Abdrabbuh Mansur Hadi**, struggled to consolidate power and faced growing discontent from various factions, including the Houthis. In 2014, the Houthis seized the capital, **Sana'a**, with support from Saleh, who had turned against Hadi. This marked the beginning of the current phase of the Yemeni civil war.

What began as a domestic power struggle soon transformed into a full-blown regional conflict. **Saudi Arabia**, alarmed by the Houthis' growing influence and their ties to Iran, launched a military intervention in **2015**, leading a coalition of Arab states to restore Hadi's government. For Saudi Arabia, the Houthis represented not just a domestic threat to Yemen but also a strategic challenge to its dominance in the region. The **Iranian** backing of the Houthis heightened Riyadh's fears of a **Shia** arc of influence stretching from **Tehran** through **Baghdad**, **Damascus**, and now Sana'a, positioning Iran as a rival for regional hegemony.

For **Iran**, Yemen became an opportunity to bleed Saudi

resources and keep its rival bogged down in a costly and protracted war. While Iranian support for the Houthis has been more indirect than its involvement in places like **Syria** and **Lebanon**, Tehran has provided weapons, training, and political backing, exploiting Saudi Arabia's fears to expand its influence in the Arabian Peninsula. This dynamic has turned Yemen into a **proxy battlefield**, mirroring the sectarian and geopolitical rivalry between the two regional powers.

The intervention by **Saudi Arabia**, supported by **U.S. intelligence**, logistical assistance, and arms sales, has only deepened the humanitarian disaster in Yemen. The coalition's relentless airstrikes, combined with a blockade that has restricted the flow of food, medicine, and other essential goods, have created what the **United Nations** calls the world's worst humanitarian crisis. Millions of Yemenis are on the brink of famine, and the war has left tens of thousands dead and millions more displaced.

Yet, despite the overwhelming human toll, Yemen remains a conflict often overlooked by the global community, particularly in the West, where it is treated as a side issue in the broader context of U.S.-Saudi relations and the fight against **al-Qaeda** and **ISIS** in the region. The U.S., in particular, has played a complex role in Yemen's war, providing military support to the Saudi-led coalition while also conducting **counterterrorism operations** against al-Qaeda in the Arabian Peninsula (**AQAP**), one of the most active and dangerous branches of the terrorist organization.

The Yemeni civil war, however, is not just a Saudi-Iranian proxy war. It is also a reflection of the deep fractures within Yemen itself, including regional, sectarian, and tribal divisions that have been exacerbated by decades of poor governance, economic mismanagement, and external interference. The war has seen multiple factions emerge, from southern separatists to Sunni Islamist groups like **al-Qaeda** and **ISIS**, each with their own goals and motivations. This fragmentation has made peace elusive, as even the Saudi and Iranian proxies have found it difficult to unify the country under any one authority.

As Yemen's war drags on, it has become a microcosm of the broader struggle for influence in the Middle East, with devastating consequences for its population. The conflict exemplifies how proxy wars, driven by external powers, can prolong and intensify civil strife, leaving nations in ruins. For the U.S. and its allies, the war in Yemen poses difficult questions about the cost of supporting authoritarian allies like Saudi Arabia, the ethics of arms sales in the context of human rights violations, and the long-term consequences of getting involved in proxy wars where the underlying causes are far more complex than mere sectarian rivalry.

In the pages that follow, we will examine how the Yemeni conflict became a battleground for regional dominance, analyze the role of external powers in perpetuating the war, and explore the devastating impact on the Yemeni people —while situating Yemen within the broader pattern of U.S. foreign policy missteps in the Middle East.

The U.S. Role in Arming Saudi Arabia and Its Coalition

The **U.S. role in arming Saudi Arabia** and supporting its coalition in the **Yemeni civil war** represents one of the most controversial aspects of U.S. foreign policy in the Middle East. As the conflict has dragged on since 2015, it has not only claimed tens of thousands of lives and plunged Yemen into a humanitarian catastrophe, but it has also exposed the United States' complex and often contradictory position in the region. On one hand, the U.S. has expressed concern over the humanitarian crisis and called for an end to hostilities, while on the other, it has continued to sell billions of dollars in weapons to **Saudi Arabia** and its allies, providing critical military support for the very operations that have exacerbated Yemen's suffering.

The U.S.'s involvement in arming Saudi Arabia is deeply rooted in its long-standing strategic partnership with the **Kingdom of Saudi Arabia**, a relationship that dates back to the 1940s. While this partnership has been primarily driven by economic and geopolitical interests—centered on Saudi Arabia's vast **oil reserves** and its role as a counterbalance to Iranian influence in the region—it has also shaped U.S. military policy in the Middle East. Over the decades, the U.S. has supplied Saudi Arabia with advanced military equipment and training, transforming the kingdom into one of the largest recipients of U.S. arms in the world. This military support has been crucial to Saudi Arabia's ability to project power in the region, particularly in its intervention in Yemen.

Beginning of Saudi Arabia's Intervention in Yemen

Saudi Arabia's military intervention in Yemen began in **March 2015**, after the **Houthi** rebel movement, which is aligned with Iran, seized control of the capital, **Sana'a**, and forced President **Abdrabbuh Mansur Hadi** to flee to Saudi Arabia. For the Saudis, the rise of the Houthis—a group from the Zaidi Shia sect—represented a direct threat to their influence on the Arabian Peninsula and a potential foothold for **Iran** just south of the kingdom's border. To counter this perceived threat, Saudi Arabia assembled a coalition of Arab states, including the **United Arab Emirates (UAE)**, **Egypt**, **Bahrain**, **Kuwait**, and **Jordan**, and launched a military campaign aimed at restoring Hadi to power and rolling back the Houthi gains.

From the outset, Saudi Arabia relied heavily on **U.S. military equipment** and logistical support to conduct its campaign in Yemen. The Saudis had been building up their military capabilities for decades, largely thanks to U.S. arms sales that included advanced fighter jets, bombs, missiles, and tanks. By the time the Yemen intervention began, Saudi Arabia's military was well-equipped with **American-made F-15 fighter jets**, **Patriot missile defense systems**, **Apache helicopters**, and **precision-guided munitions**.

The U.S. was not just a passive arms supplier in this conflict. In the early stages of the war, the U.S. provided crucial **logistical support**, including **in-flight refueling** for Saudi aircraft, allowing them to carry out sustained airstrikes deep into Yemen. The **Pentagon** also provided **intelligence** and **targeting assistance** to help the Saudi-led coalition identify and strike Houthi positions, though this assistance became controversial as reports of civilian casualties mounted.

Billions in Arms Sales

Between **2015** and **2020**, the U.S. sold more than **$60 billion** in arms to Saudi Arabia and its coalition partners, making the kingdom one of the top buyers of U.S. military equipment. These arms sales included advanced weapons systems, such as **F-15 fighter jets**, **precision-guided bombs**, **missile defense systems**, and other tools of modern warfare. The U.S. also sold Saudi Arabia and the UAE the technology needed to conduct sophisticated air campaigns, including **satellite-guided bombs** and **surveillance systems**.

One of the most controversial aspects of these arms sales was the provision of **precision-guided munitions (PGMs)**, which were touted by U.S. officials as tools that would allow the Saudi-led coalition to minimize civilian casualties by striking only military targets. However, as the war progressed, it became increasingly clear that the coalition's airstrikes were not as "precise" as advertised. Bombing campaigns hit **hospitals**, **schools**, **markets**, and other civilian infrastructure, leading to widespread condemnation from human rights organizations and the international community.

The **Obama administration**, which initially authorized the sale of these weapons, faced mounting criticism for its role in the conflict. While President Obama sought to distance the U.S. from direct involvement, he also viewed the arms sales as a way to reassure Saudi Arabia of U.S. support at a time when the kingdom was deeply concerned about the **Iran nuclear deal**. This balancing act—providing arms to Saudi Arabia while attempting to limit U.S. involvement—proved difficult to maintain, particularly as the human toll in Yemen escalated.

Impact of U.S.-Made Weapons in the War

The U.S.-supplied weapons played a central role in the Saudi-led coalition's air campaign, which has been responsible for some of the most devastating consequences of the war. The coalition's airstrikes have repeatedly struck civilian targets, including **weddings**, **funerals**, and **food markets**, leading to thousands of civilian deaths and injuries. A particularly infamous incident occurred in **August 2018**, when a Saudi airstrike hit a school bus in **Saada province**, killing **40 children** and wounding dozens more. The bomb used in the attack was later identified as a **U.S.-made laser-guided bomb**, manufactured by **Lockheed Martin**.

The use of U.S.-made weapons in such attacks has raised serious ethical and legal questions about America's role in the conflict. Human rights organizations, including **Amnesty International** and **Human Rights Watch**, have accused the U.S. of being complicit in potential war crimes by supplying weapons to a coalition that has repeatedly violated international humanitarian law. These groups have documented numerous instances where U.S.-made bombs were used in attacks that killed civilians, destroyed vital infrastructure, and contributed to the humanitarian disaster in Yemen.

The **United Nations** has also weighed in, with a report from a panel of UN experts concluding that both the Saudi-led coalition and the **Houthi rebels** may have committed war crimes during the conflict. The report cited the coalition's airstrikes as a major cause of civilian casualties and pointed to the U.S. and other arms suppliers as contributing to the continuation of the war by providing weapons that enabled the coalition to maintain its military campaign.

The Humanitarian Toll

The impact of the U.S.-backed Saudi air campaign on Yemen's civilian population has been catastrophic. The relentless airstrikes, combined with a **blockade** imposed by the coalition on **Yemeni ports**, have crippled the country's economy, leading to widespread **famine**, the **destruction of infrastructure**, and the collapse of basic services such as healthcare and education. The blockade, which was ostensibly aimed at preventing weapons from reaching the Houthis, has severely restricted the flow of food, medicine, and fuel into the country, exacerbating the suffering of millions of Yemenis.

As of **2021**, the war has killed an estimated **233,000 people**, with more than **100,000** of those deaths resulting from direct violence. However, the majority of the deaths—nearly **130,000**—have been caused by the secondary effects of the war, including **famine** and **disease**. Yemen has also suffered one of the worst **cholera outbreaks** in modern history, with over **2.5 million cases** reported since the start of the war. The UN has described the situation in Yemen as the world's worst humanitarian crisis, with **80% of the population**—about **24 million people**—in need of humanitarian assistance.

Shifting U.S. Policy under Trump and Biden

The U.S.'s role in the Yemen conflict evolved under **President Donald Trump**, who took a more aggressive stance in supporting Saudi Arabia. Trump's administration approved

massive arms sales to the kingdom, despite opposition from Congress and human rights organizations. In **2017**, Trump signed a **$110 billion** arms deal with Saudi Arabia during his first foreign trip as president, signaling his administration's willingness to continue backing the coalition despite the growing humanitarian toll.

Trump also vetoed multiple bipartisan efforts by Congress to end U.S. support for the Saudi-led war in Yemen, arguing that such moves would damage America's relationship with a key ally in the fight against **Iran** and **terrorism**. His administration continued to provide logistical support and intelligence to the coalition, even as reports of civilian casualties mounted.

The election of **President Joe Biden** in **2020** brought a shift in U.S. policy toward Yemen. Biden pledged to end U.S. support for offensive operations in the war and to prioritize diplomacy to resolve the conflict. In **February 2021**, the Biden administration announced the end of all U.S. support for Saudi **"offensive operations"** in Yemen, including the suspension of certain arms sales. Biden also appointed a special envoy to Yemen to pursue a diplomatic solution to the war.

However, the distinction between "offensive" and "defensive" operations has remained murky. The U.S. continues to provide **defensive weapons** to Saudi Arabia, including **Patriot missile systems**, to protect the kingdom from **Houthi missile and drone attacks**. Critics argue that this continued military support, even for defensive purposes, allows the Saudis to maintain their war effort and contributes to prolonging the conflict.

Consequences for U.S. Foreign Policy and Credibility

The U.S. role in arming Saudi Arabia and supporting the coalition in Yemen has damaged America's reputation as a promoter of human rights and international law. While U.S. officials have repeatedly called for an end to the war and a peaceful resolution to the conflict, the continued flow of arms to Saudi Arabia and the coalition has sent a contradictory message. The perception that the U.S. is complicit in the war crimes committed by the coalition has fueled anti-American sentiment in the region and weakened America's moral standing on the global stage.

The Yemen conflict also highlights the broader dilemmas faced by U.S. policymakers when balancing **strategic interests** with **humanitarian concerns**. Saudi Arabia is a key U.S. ally in the fight against **Iranian influence** in the region, and its cooperation is seen as vital to maintaining stability in the Arabian Peninsula. However, the cost of this partnership—both in terms of human lives and America's global image—has raised serious questions about the wisdom of continuing to arm an ally engaged in such a destructive war.

The conflict in Yemen is far from over, and the humanitarian crisis continues to worsen. As the U.S. reevaluates its role in the war and its broader relationship with Saudi Arabia, the legacy of its involvement in Yemen will likely continue to shape American foreign policy in the region for years to come.

How Iran's Support for the Houthis Turned Yemen into a Proxy Battleground

While the roots of the civil war in Yemen are deeply embedded in Yemen's internal political, tribal, and sectarian divisions, the conflict has been significantly influenced by external actors with competing interests. The rise of the **Houthi** movement in northern Yemen and Iran's increasing support for this group played a pivotal role in drawing the country into the broader geopolitical struggle between the **Sunni** and **Shia** powers of the region.

This section explores how **Iran's backing of the Houthis**—a Zaidi Shia movement—transformed Yemen into a flashpoint for the regional contest between **Tehran** and **Riyadh**. It also examines the strategic motivations behind Iran's involvement in Yemen, how this support has played out on the battlefield, and the broader implications for the region, which has witnessed a sharp escalation of sectarian tensions.

Rise of the Houthis

The **Houthi** movement, formally known as **Ansar Allah**, began as a relatively small, local insurgency in northern Yemen in the early 2000s. Its roots lie in the **Zaidi Shia** population of Yemen's **Saada** region, a historically marginalized group that often found itself at odds with Yemen's central government, which had long been dominated by Sunni elites. The Houthis, named after their leader **Hussein Badreddin al-Houthi**, initially rose in opposition to what they saw as economic neglect, political marginalization, and the spread of **Salafism** and **Wahhabism**—ultraconservative forms of Sunni Islam—supported by Saudi Arabia.

Iran's involvement with the Houthis began slowly and quietly in the early 2000s but became more pronounced as the group grew in strength and influence. While the **Zaidi Shia** branch practiced by the Houthis differs from the **Twelver Shia Islam** followed in Iran, Tehran saw in the Houthis a useful ally in its ongoing efforts to expand influence across the Arabian Peninsula and challenge Saudi hegemony. The Houthis provided Iran with an opportunity to establish a foothold in Yemen, a country of strategic importance due to its proximity to critical maritime routes, such as the **Bab el-Mandeb Strait**, and its border with Saudi Arabia.

For much of the early 2000s, Iran's support for the Houthis was primarily diplomatic and ideological, with limited material assistance. However, as the Houthis became embroiled in a series of conflicts with Yemen's central government, particularly during **Ali Abdullah Saleh's** presidency, Iranian support gradually increased. Tehran began providing the Houthis with **weapons, funding,** and **training**, though the full extent of this assistance remains a subject of debate.

The Houthi movement's fortunes dramatically changed during the **Arab Spring** in 2011, when long-standing political grievances in Yemen boiled over into widespread protests. The uprisings eventually forced President **Ali Abdullah Saleh** to step down after more than three decades in power, leading to the appointment of his vice president, **Abdrabbuh Mansur Hadi**, as a transitional leader. However, Hadi's government struggled to consolidate power, and Yemen's already fragile political system began to unravel as various factions jockeyed for control.

In 2014, the Houthis capitalized on the weakness of Hadi's government and seized control of **Sana'a**, Yemen's capital. By early 2015, they had forced Hadi to flee to **Aden** and later into exile in Saudi Arabia. The Houthis' sudden rise to power alarmed Saudi Arabia, which viewed the group as a **proxy for Iranian influence** on its southern border. Riyadh saw the Houthi takeover as part of a broader Iranian strategy to encircle the kingdom with Shia-dominated or Shia-aligned forces, including **Hezbollah** in **Lebanon**, **Shia militias** in **Iraq**, and **Assad's regime** in **Syria**.

It was at this point that Iran's support for the Houthis became more direct and visible. Iran, seeing an opportunity to extend its influence in the **Arabian Peninsula** and challenge Saudi Arabia's regional dominance, stepped up its backing of the Houthis. Iranian weapons shipments to the Houthis increased, despite a **UN arms embargo** imposed on the group in 2015. These shipments included **ballistic missiles, drones,** and **anti-ship missiles**, all of which significantly bolstered the Houthis' military capabilities. The **Islamic Revolutionary Guard Corps (IRGC)**, specifically its elite **Quds Force**, played a key role in providing the Houthis with technical expertise and training.

Iran's involvement in Yemen was not purely military. Tehran also sought to support the Houthis diplomatically, framing the group's struggle as part of a broader Shia resistance against **Western imperialism** and **Saudi tyranny**. Iranian media outlets portrayed the Houthis as freedom fighters resisting the aggression of Saudi Arabia and its Western backers. This narrative helped Tehran gain sympathy and support from Shia communities across the Middle East, further fueling sectarian tensions.

While Iranian support for the Houthis has never been on the same scale as its involvement in other regional conflicts, such as in Syria or Iraq, it has been enough to help the group sustain its military campaign against the Saudi-led coalition. Iran's provision of **ballistic missile technology** has allowed the Houthis to strike deep into Saudi territory, including attacks on **Riyadh** and critical infrastructure like **oil facilities**. These missile attacks have heightened tensions between Saudi Arabia and Iran, threatening to draw both countries deeper into direct confrontation.

Saudi Arabia's Response: Escalating the Proxy War

Saudi Arabia's response to the Houthi takeover of Sana'a was swift and forceful. In **March 2015**, Riyadh launched **Operation Decisive Storm**, a large-scale military intervention aimed at restoring Hadi to power and rolling back the Houthi gains. Saudi Arabia framed its intervention as a necessary measure to protect Yemen's legitimate government and prevent Iran from gaining a foothold in the Arabian Peninsula.

The Saudi-led coalition, which included **the United Arab Emirates**, **Bahrain**, **Kuwait**, **Egypt**, and other Arab states, launched an extensive **air campaign** against the Houthis, targeting military installations, supply lines, and Houthi-controlled cities. The coalition also imposed a **naval blockade** on Yemen, ostensibly to prevent Iranian weapons shipments from reaching the Houthis, though the blockade also contributed to the humanitarian disaster by restricting the flow of food, medicine, and fuel into the country.

For Saudi Arabia, the intervention in Yemen became a critical front in its broader rivalry with Iran. Riyadh viewed the Houthis 'rise to power as part of a wider Iranian strategy to undermine Saudi dominance in the region, and the war in Yemen became an existential battle for influence in the **Gulf**. The Saudis were determined to prevent Yemen from becoming another **Shia-dominated** state aligned with Iran, similar to **Iraq** or **Lebanon**.

However, as the war dragged on, it became increasingly clear that the Saudi-led coalition was facing significant challenges. Despite the coalition's overwhelming superiority in terms of **air power** and **military resources**, the Houthis proved remarkably resilient. Their knowledge of the local terrain, their use of **asymmetric warfare**, and their ability to sustain supply lines through covert channels enabled them to withstand the coalition's onslaught. Iran's support, while limited, provided the Houthis with the tools they needed to strike back at Saudi forces, prolonging the conflict and making a decisive Saudi victory elusive.

Broader Regional Implications of Iran's Involvement

Iran's support for the Houthis has had far-reaching consequences, both for Yemen and the broader region. The conflict has deepened the sectarian divide between Sunni and Shia Muslims, which has been a driving force behind much of the violence and instability in the Middle East. For many in the Sunni Arab world, the war in Yemen is seen as part of a broader struggle to contain Iranian influence, with the Houthis viewed as an extension of Iran's geopolitical ambitions.

The proxy nature of the conflict has also drawn in other regional and international players, further complicating efforts to reach a peaceful resolution. The **United States**, **France**, and **Britain** have provided military and logistical support to the Saudi-led coalition, while Iran has continued to back the Houthis, either directly or through **Hezbollah**, which has sent advisors to Yemen to assist the Houthis. The war has also become a testing ground for **Iranian missile technology**, with the Houthis using Iranian-supplied ballistic missiles and drones to target Saudi cities and oil infrastructure, including the high-profile attack on **Aramco** oil facilities in **2019**.

The conflict has also highlighted the limits of both Saudi Arabia's military capabilities and its ability to project power in the region. Despite the kingdom's vast military spending and its close ties with Western arms suppliers, the war in Yemen has dragged on for years without a clear resolution, exposing Saudi vulnerabilities and undermining its claims of regional leadership.

For Iran, its involvement in Yemen has served multiple strategic purposes. By supporting the Houthis, Tehran has been able to bleed Saudi resources, bogging the kingdom down in a costly and protracted conflict. Iran's support for the Houthis also allows it to project power in the **Arabian Peninsula** without committing significant resources or forces, thereby extending its influence in a region traditionally dominated by Saudi Arabia.

Furthermore, the war in Yemen has provided Iran with a means of showcasing its **asymmetric warfare** capabilities, particularly its ability to supply non-state actors with missile and drone technology. The success of the Houthis in targeting Saudi infrastructure has enhanced Iran's reputation as a regional power capable of defying the military might of both Saudi Arabia and its Western allies.

The Yemeni civil war transformed into a classic proxy conflict, driven by the regional rivalry between Saudi Arabia and Iran. Iran's support for the Houthis, while limited in scope compared to its involvement in Syria or Iraq, has been enough to sustain the group's military efforts and turn Yemen into a quagmire for Saudi Arabia. The war has underscored the deep-seated sectarian and geopolitical divides in the region, with the Houthis and their Iranian backers representing a growing challenge to Saudi dominance in the Gulf.

Wider Implications of the Yemeni Civil War and the Ensuing Humanitarian Crisis

The civil war in **Yemen**, now entering its ninth year, has left behind a devastating humanitarian crisis, one that ranks among the worst in modern history. The conflict, which began as a local struggle for political power, rapidly escalated into a **regional proxy war** involving **Saudi Arabia**, **Iran**, and a host of other regional actors. As military operations intensified and the political situation deteriorated, millions of Yemeni civilians found themselves caught in the crossfire, with the country's infrastructure crumbling and its people facing **famine**, **disease**, and widespread **displacement**.

The war has had a profound impact on Yemen's population, the wider Middle East, and the international community. Its effects are not confined to the battlefield; they extend far beyond Yemen's borders, influencing **migration patterns**, **regional security dynamics**, and **geopolitical relations**. This section explores the catastrophic humanitarian toll the war has taken on Yemen, the war's broader implications for the region, and the urgent need for a comprehensive international response to address both the human suffering and the long-term consequences of the conflict.

Scale of the Humanitarian Crisis

Since the start of the war in **2014**, Yemen has been plunged into a humanitarian catastrophe of epic proportions. The conflict has killed over **233,000 people**, according to **UN estimates**, with approximately **100,000** deaths resulting from direct violence, and the remainder due to **indirect causes** such as famine, disease, and the collapse of public services. What makes the situation in Yemen particularly dire is that the country was already one of the poorest in the Arab world prior to the conflict. Years of economic mismanagement, political corruption, and dependency on food imports left Yemen highly vulnerable to instability, and the outbreak of war further exacerbated these underlying conditions.

The ongoing conflict has shattered Yemen's infrastructure, with hospitals, schools, factories, and roads destroyed by airstrikes and ground fighting. In particular, the Saudi-led coalition's **blockade** on **Hodeidah Port**, a key entry point for food, fuel, and medical supplies, has worsened the humanitarian situation. As a result, over **80% of Yemen's population**—approximately **24 million people**—are now in need of humanitarian assistance. More than **17 million** Yemenis face food insecurity, with **5 million** on the brink of famine. Malnutrition, particularly among children, has reached alarming levels, with **2 million** children under the age of five suffering from severe acute malnutrition.

In addition to hunger, Yemen has been ravaged by preventable diseases, including the largest **cholera outbreak** in modern history. Since **2016**, over **2.5 million cases** of cholera have been reported, with more than **4,000 deaths**. The outbreak was made worse by the destruction of water and sanitation facilities, coupled with a lack of access to healthcare. With Yemen's healthcare system collapsing under the weight of the war, many people have been unable to access basic medical services, leading to a surge in deaths from otherwise treatable diseases such as **malaria**, **dengue fever**, and **diphtheria**.

The war has also displaced millions of people. An estimated **4.3 million** Yemenis have been forced to flee their homes since the start of the conflict, either seeking refuge in other parts of the country or attempting to cross borders into neighboring nations. Many live in **makeshift camps** with inadequate access to food, water, and shelter. These displaced populations are particularly vulnerable to violence, exploitation, and disease, and their plight has added further strain to Yemen's already overstretched resources.

Impact of the Blockade and Airstrikes

A significant factor contributing to Yemen's humanitarian crisis has been the **Saudi-led coalition's blockade** of major ports, most notably **Hodeidah**. The blockade, ostensibly intended to prevent **Iranian arms** from reaching the **Houthi rebels**, has had the unintended (or, in some cases, deliberate) effect of cutting off vital supplies from reaching the Yemeni population. Yemen relies heavily on imports, with up to **90%** of its food, fuel, and medicine coming from abroad. The blockade has drastically reduced the flow of goods into the country, leading to skyrocketing food prices and widespread shortages.

In addition to the blockade, the coalition's **airstrike campaign** has inflicted heavy damage on Yemen's civilian infrastructure. Hospitals, markets, factories, and schools have been repeatedly targeted, often with **U.S.-made precision-guided munitions**. These airstrikes have not only caused immediate casualties but have also contributed to the long-term degradation of essential services, leaving the population without access to healthcare, education, and clean water. For example, the repeated bombing of water treatment plants and sewage facilities has contributed directly to the cholera outbreak, while the destruction of food supply chains has exacerbated famine conditions.

The **UN** and various **human rights organizations** have accused both sides in the conflict, including the **Houthi rebels**, of violating **international humanitarian law**. The Houthis, for their part, have been accused of using **indiscriminate shelling** and planting **landmines** in civilian areas, further endangering the population. The Saudi-led coalition, however, has faced the brunt of international criticism due to its air campaign, which has repeatedly struck civilian targets in violation of the **laws of war**. Despite international outcry, the airstrikes have continued unabated, prolonging the suffering of millions of Yemenis.

Regional and Global Implications of the Yemen War

Beyond the borders of Yemen, the conflict has had profound implications for the wider **Middle East** and the international community. Yemen's strategic location along the **Bab el-Mandeb Strait**, a key maritime chokepoint for global trade, makes it a focal point for regional power dynamics. As the war has unfolded, it has deepened the sectarian divide between **Sunni Saudi Arabia** and **Shia Iran**, with both nations using Yemen as a proxy battleground for their broader geopolitical rivalry. This sectarian dimension has fueled instability across the region, contributing to tensions in countries like **Lebanon**, **Iraq**, and **Syria**.

The conflict has also strained relations between **Saudi Arabia** and its Western allies, particularly the **United States**. While the U.S. has provided military support to the Saudi-led coalition, including **arms sales**, **logistical assistance**, and **intelligence sharing**, the growing humanitarian toll has led to increasing opposition to the war in Western capitals. In **Washington**, bipartisan efforts in **Congress** have sought to end U.S. involvement in the conflict, citing the widespread civilian casualties and the **human rights violations** committed by the coalition. The U.S.'s support for Saudi Arabia, particularly under the **Trump administration**, has raised ethical and moral questions about America's role in fueling a war that has brought untold suffering to millions of

Yemenis.

At the same time, the war in Yemen has had a ripple effect on **migration** patterns, particularly as **displaced Yemenis** have sought refuge in neighboring countries. Nations like **Saudi Arabia**, **Oman**, and **Djibouti** have been forced to grapple with the influx of refugees, further complicating their domestic political and economic situations. Yemen's crisis has also contributed to the broader **refugee crisis** that has impacted Europe, as many Yemenis, alongside Syrians, Iraqis, and other displaced populations, have made perilous journeys across the Mediterranean in search of safety.

The **economic** consequences of the war extend far beyond Yemen's borders. The ongoing conflict has disrupted trade routes, particularly through the **Bab el-Mandeb Strait**, which connects the **Red Sea** to the **Gulf of Aden** and the **Indian Ocean**. This chokepoint is critical for the global oil supply and maritime commerce, and instability in the region threatens to disrupt international trade, potentially leading to higher energy prices and economic uncertainty. Several attacks on oil tankers near the strait, attributed to **Houthi forces**, have underscored the vulnerability of global shipping routes to the conflict.

Moreover, Yemen's war has emboldened extremist groups like **al-Qaeda in the Arabian Peninsula (AQAP)** and **ISIS**, which have taken advantage of the chaos to establish a foothold in the country. AQAP, in particular, has used Yemen's lawlessness to launch attacks against both Yemeni and Western targets, including an attempted bombing of a U.S.-bound airliner in **2009**. The proliferation of extremist groups in Yemen poses a significant security threat to both the region and the international community, as these groups are likely to use Yemen as a base for launching terrorist operations globally.

International Response and the Need for Humanitarian Aid

The international community's response to Yemen's humanitarian crisis has been slow and inadequate. Despite the overwhelming scale of the suffering, **humanitarian aid** efforts have been hampered by the ongoing fighting, the Saudi blockade, and logistical challenges. While **UN agencies** and **non-governmental organizations (NGOs)** have worked tirelessly to provide food, water, and medical care to Yemen's population, their efforts have been insufficient to meet the overwhelming needs. The **UN World Food Programme (WFP)**, for example, has repeatedly warned of funding shortfalls, with Yemen's humanitarian response plan chronically underfunded.

In addition to the logistical challenges, the politicization of aid has further complicated the situation. Both the **Saudi-led coalition** and the **Houthis** have been accused of diverting aid for their own purposes, preventing much-needed supplies from reaching those in need. The coalition's **airstrikes** have targeted warehouses and distribution centers, while the Houthis have reportedly blocked aid deliveries to certain areas as part of their broader military strategy. These tactics have contributed to the deterioration of the humanitarian situation, as millions of Yemenis remain without access to life-saving supplies.

In recent years, there have been growing calls for a comprehensive international response to address the humanitarian crisis in Yemen. Human rights organizations, aid groups, and certain political figures have urged the international community to prioritize **humanitarian assistance** over military engagement, emphasizing the need for a **ceasefire** and a negotiated peace settlement. Some progress has been made, particularly with the **2023 ceasefire negotiations** led by **China**, but much more remains to be done to alleviate the suffering of Yemen's population and ensure a lasting peace.

Urgent Need for Peace and Reconstruction

The humanitarian crisis in Yemen is a stark reminder of the devastating human cost of war, particularly when compounded by external involvement and geopolitical rivalries. As the conflict enters its ninth year, the prospects for a lasting peace remain uncertain, but the recent ceasefire talks offer a glimmer of hope. For Yemen's population, an end to the war would provide the opportunity to begin rebuilding their lives, but the scale of the destruction will require significant international support for **reconstruction, economic recovery**, and **political reconciliation**.

The war's wider implications—ranging from regional instability and migration to the proliferation of extremist groups—underscore the urgent need for a comprehensive solution that addresses both the humanitarian crisis and the underlying causes of the conflict. For the international community, the challenge is to shift from military engagement to **diplomacy** and **humanitarian assistance**, ensuring that Yemen's future is shaped by peace and stability rather than perpetual war. Only through sustained diplomatic efforts and robust humanitarian support can Yemen hope to recover from the devastation of the past decade.

China's Role in Brokering Peace in Yemen: A Testament to Waning U.S. Influence

As the war in **Yemen** appears to be approaching an end, a surprising new player has emerged as a potential peacemaker: **China**. For years, the conflict had raged on, driven by **Iranian-backed Houthis** and a **Saudi-led coalition** supported by the **United States**. But in recent developments, it is China's diplomacy—not U.S. military might—that has set the stage for a potential ceasefire and broader peace talks. These developments not only reflect the changing dynamics in the Middle East but also illustrate the shifting balance of global power, with the **United States** appearing increasingly sidelined as **China** steps into a role traditionally played by Washington.

For nearly a decade, the war in Yemen has been one of the most devastating humanitarian crises in the world. What began as a local conflict quickly escalated into a **proxy war**, with Iran backing the Houthis and Saudi Arabia leading a military campaign to restore the exiled Yemeni government. Throughout the conflict, the U.S. consistently supported Saudi Arabia through **arms sales**, **logistical support**, and **intelligence sharing**, making it a key player in the coalition's war efforts. Yet, despite this support, the war dragged on, leading to widespread civilian casualties, famine, and the collapse of Yemen's infrastructure.

Enter **China**, whose approach to diplomacy in the region has starkly contrasted with that of the U.S. In **2023**, reports began to emerge that a ceasefire agreement between the Saudi-led coalition and the Houthis had been brokered, with China playing a crucial role in facilitating the negotiations. According to sources, the **Saudi government** was preparing to engage in direct talks with the Houthis in **Sana'a** to discuss the terms of a permanent ceasefire. These discussions come as part of a broader regional rapprochement, facilitated by China, which also brokered a landmark agreement to restore diplomatic relations between **Saudi Arabia** and **Iran**.

The U.S. media initially reported the ceasefire with cautious optimism, noting denials from the Houthis and mixed signals about the deal's finality. However, subsequent reports from outlets like **Al Mayadeen** and **Reuters** confirmed that Saudi envoys were indeed preparing to engage with the Houthis. This marked a significant shift in the dynamics of the conflict, with Saudi Arabia appearing to capitulate to several Houthi demands, including opening key ports and lifting blockades that had exacerbated Yemen's humanitarian crisis.

China's Diplomatic Triumph: What Made the Ceasefire Possible

The role China has played in brokering this potential ceasefire is particularly noteworthy because it underscores Beijing's growing influence in the region. For decades, the U.S. had positioned itself as the primary power broker in the Middle East, often relying on **militarized interventions** and arms deals to maintain its influence. Yet, despite the U.S.'s promises—such as **President Joe Biden's** 2020 campaign pledge to end the war in Yemen—it was China's pragmatic diplomacy that appears to have laid the groundwork for peace.

"Biden promised to end the war in Yemen. Two years into his presidency, China may have delivered on that promise," said **Trita Parsi**, executive vice president of the **Quincy Institute for Responsible Statecraft**. This turn of events highlights how decades of U.S. foreign policy in the Middle East, which has been heavily reliant on military force and arms deals, have opened the door for China to present itself as a reasonable and constructive partner for peace. Rather than backing one side in the conflict or supplying arms, China focused on brokering negotiations between the warring parties, culminating in what may be the end of the war.

One key factor in China's success was its ability to extract significant concessions from Saudi Arabia. Reports indicate that the Saudis have agreed to several of the Houthis' primary demands, including lifting the blockade on **Hodeidah Port**, allowing flights into **Sana'a**, and giving Yemen's central government access to its currency to stabilize the economy and pay workers. These concessions are not only a testament to China's diplomatic efforts but also reflect **Saudi Arabia's shifting priorities**. The kingdom, under **Crown Prince Mohammed bin Salman**, has increasingly focused on economic development and regional stability at home, which is difficult to achieve while embroiled in an expensive and unpopular war.

"**The Saudi concessions—including a potential lifting of the blockade and exit from the war—demonstrate that their priority is to protect Saudi territory from attack and focus on economic development at home,**" said **Erik Sperling**, executive director of **Just Foreign Policy**. This strategic shift by Saudi Arabia marks a departure from the hardline approach that has been backed by many in Washington, who believed that continued military pressure could force the Houthis into ceding more power to the **U.S.-backed Yemeni government**.

China's involvement is further bolstered by the broader **Iran-Saudi rapprochement** that Beijing facilitated. This landmark agreement, which reinstates diplomatic relations between the two regional powers, is key to the Yemeni ceasefire negotiations. With **Saudi Arabia** and **Iran** agreeing to restore flights, reopen embassies, and expand commercial cooperation, tensions between the two countries have eased, creating a more favorable environment for the resolution of the Yemen conflict.

"**The full scope of this appears to have been unlikely without the Saudi-Iranian normalization brokered by China,**" Parsi said, emphasizing the broader significance of China's diplomatic engagement in the region. Although it remains unclear whether China directly intervened in the Yemeni peace talks, Beijing will undoubtedly receive credit for creating the conditions that made these talks possible.

The Waning Influence of the United States

China's growing role in Middle Eastern diplomacy comes at

a time when U.S. influence in the region is perceived to be declining. Washington's approach to the Yemen conflict has often been criticized for its reliance on military solutions, as well as its support for Saudi Arabia's aggressive actions. As the war escalated, the U.S. consistently backed Saudi Arabia with arms deals and intelligence support, turning a blind eye to the growing civilian toll and the humanitarian catastrophe that unfolded in Yemen.

In contrast, China's ability to remain neutral in the conflict, while offering economic incentives and political mediation, has allowed it to position itself as a more balanced and effective diplomatic player. The Biden administration, despite its initial rhetoric, has largely been absent from the recent diplomatic breakthroughs in the region, including the Saudi-Iran agreement. In fact, reports from **The Wall Street Journal** revealed that **CIA Director William Burns** expressed frustration during an unannounced visit to Saudi Arabia, reportedly feeling "blindsided" by Riyadh's rapprochement with both Iran and **Syria**, under the auspices of China.

This perceived absence of the U.S. in critical negotiations signals a broader decline in Washington's influence in the Middle East, where decades of military interventions and **saber-rattling** have alienated many regional powers. China, on the other hand, has offered a new approach—one rooted in diplomacy, economic cooperation, and respect for regional sovereignty. This shift is emblematic of Beijing's long-term strategy in the Middle East, where it seeks to replace the U.S. as a dominant force, not through military might but through diplomacy and economic engagement.

As **Hassan El-Tayyab**, legislative director for **Middle East policy at the Friends Committee on National Legislation**, noted, "**Now is the time for the United States to do everything it can to support these negotiations to finally end the war and support robust humanitarian funding to address**

the suffering of the Yemeni people." The U.S. still has a role to play, but its diminished standing in the region means that it must adopt a more cooperative approach to diplomacy, rather than obstructing initiatives led by other powers like China.

The Endgame for Yemen and the Challenge of Maintaining Peace

While the ceasefire talks between Saudi Arabia and the Houthis offer a glimmer of hope for an end to the Yemen conflict, the road to lasting peace will be fraught with challenges. The war has left Yemen deeply fragmented, with various factions—including **al-Qaeda in the Arabian Peninsula (AQAP)** and **ISIS**—still operating in the country. Additionally, some **Saudi-backed militants** may continue to resist a permanent peace agreement, leaving open the possibility of continued skirmishes and unrest.

For China, brokering peace is only the first step. Maintaining it will be an even greater challenge, as Yemen's complex web of tribal, sectarian, and political rivalries will require sustained diplomatic engagement and economic reconstruction efforts. However, Beijing's ability to remain an influential mediator between Riyadh and Tehran will be critical in ensuring that the ceasefire holds and that the region can move toward stability.

At the same time, the **United States** must carefully reconsider its approach to the Middle East. As El-Tayyab pointed out, "**If Washington rejects regional power-sharing and obstructs a world in which other nations have a vested interest in peace, it risks jeopardizing America's own economic and security interests and its international reputation.**" The rise of China as a diplomatic power in the region signals a shift in the global order—one where U.S. militarized foreign policy is giving way to more nuanced, multi-polar diplomacy.

Ultimately, the potential end of the Yemen war, driven by Chinese-led diplomacy, is a stark reminder of the changing landscape of global power. The U.S., long seen as the preeminent force in the Middle East, now finds itself on the sidelines, as Beijing's pragmatism and commitment to economic partnerships pave the way for peace. Whether or not China can maintain its role as a stabilizing force remains to be seen, but its ability to bring Saudi Arabia and Iran to the negotiating table offers a glimpse into the future of Middle Eastern diplomacy—a future where U.S. influence is no longer guaranteed.

CHAPTER 12 - RISE OF IRAN AS A REGIONAL POWER

The Domino Effect of U.S. Foreign Policy vis-à-vis Iran

The rise of **Iran** as a dominant regional power in the Middle East over the past few decades is one of the most significant geopolitical shifts in the region's modern history. Ironically, much of Iran's ascent to regional influence can be traced back to **U.S. interventions** and foreign policy decisions that were often intended to curb Tehran's power. Rather than containing Iran, these interventions—whether in **Iraq**, **Afghanistan**, **Lebanon**, **Syria**, or **Yemen**—have inadvertently created conditions that allowed Iran to expand its reach, both directly and through a network of **proxy forces**.

In the wake of U.S. interventions, power vacuums, weakened states, and destabilized regimes have provided Iran with opportunities to exert its influence, creating what many describe as a **"Shia Crescent"** stretching from **Tehran** to the Mediterranean. This chapter will explore how U.S. military actions and strategic miscalculations in the Middle East have played a significant role in strengthening Iran's regional clout, and how Tehran has skillfully leveraged these opportunities to bolster its position as a key player in Middle Eastern politics.

The 2003 Invasion of Iraq and the Power Vacuum that

Followed

One of the most consequential U.S. interventions that empowered Iran was the **2003 invasion of Iraq** and the subsequent removal of **Saddam Hussein**. Prior to the invasion, Iraq under Saddam served as a bulwark against Iranian influence in the region. As a **Sunni**-dominated, Baathist regime, Saddam's government was staunchly anti-Iranian, having fought a brutal eight-year war against Iran in the 1980s. Iraq was, in effect, a counterweight to Iran's regional ambitions, preventing Tehran from projecting power beyond its borders.

However, the U.S.-led invasion, which was justified by the Bush administration on the grounds of eliminating **weapons of mass destruction** (WMDs) and promoting democracy, had profound unintended consequences. The swift overthrow of Saddam's regime dismantled the Sunni-dominated government and military apparatus that had kept Iran's influence at bay. In the chaotic aftermath of Saddam's fall, Iraq became a deeply divided and fragile state, torn apart by sectarian violence and political instability.

As the U.S. struggled to stabilize post-Saddam Iraq, Iran seized the opportunity to fill the power vacuum. Iran's influence in Iraq expanded dramatically, largely through its support for **Shia political factions** and **militias**. Tehran backed powerful Shia parties such as the **Islamic Supreme Council of Iraq (ISCI)** and the **Dawa Party**, both of which had longstanding ties to Iran and played a dominant role in the new Iraqi government. Iranian influence extended into Iraq's political, military, and economic spheres, as Tehran cultivated relationships with key leaders and factions within the Shia-majority government.

At the same time, Iran supported and armed a number of **Shia militias**, including groups like **Kataib Hezbollah** and **Asaib Ahl al-Haq**, which operated under the umbrella of the

Popular Mobilization Forces (PMF). These militias became powerful players in Iraq's security landscape, often operating outside the control of the central government and acting as de facto Iranian proxies. Through these militias, Iran exerted direct influence over Iraq's internal security, ensuring that its interests were safeguarded in any post-Saddam political order.

In effect, the removal of Saddam Hussein, a key Iranian adversary, paved the way for Iran to emerge as one of the most influential actors in Iraq. U.S. intervention, intended to create a stable, democratic Iraq, instead resulted in a fractured state where Iran held significant sway. The irony of the U.S. invasion is that it effectively handed Iraq—once a fierce rival of Iran—into the hands of Shia parties and militias closely aligned with Tehran.

Iran's Role in Syria: From Ally to Lifeline of the Assad Regime

Another key example of how U.S. interventions have indirectly bolstered Iran's influence is the civil war in **Syria**. In the early stages of the war, which began in **2011** as part of the **Arab Spring** uprisings, the U.S. and its Western allies supported Syrian opposition forces seeking to overthrow the regime of **Bashar al-Assad**. Assad's government, which had been a long-standing ally of Tehran, was seen as a strategic partner by Iran, providing it with a crucial link to **Lebanon**, home of Iran's proxy group, **Hezbollah**.

As the conflict escalated and Assad's grip on power weakened, Iran stepped in as one of the regime's most important backers. Tehran provided **military**, **financial**, and **logistical support** to Assad's government, deploying members of the **IRGC**, including the elite **Quds Force**, to assist Syrian forces on the ground. Iran also mobilized **Hezbollah** fighters from Lebanon, who played a key role in turning the tide of the war in Assad's favor.

While the U.S. and its allies initially supported opposition groups fighting against Assad, the rise of extremist factions such as **ISIS** and **Jabhat al-Nusra** complicated the situation. The U.S. was forced to shift its focus to combating ISIS, particularly after the group seized large swathes of territory in Iraq and Syria. This shift allowed Iran to deepen its involvement in Syria, becoming the Assad regime's lifeline in its battle for survival. Tehran's commitment to Assad, alongside Russian military support, was instrumental in preventing the regime's collapse.

The result of Iran's intervention in Syria has been the solidification of its influence not just in Damascus but across the Levant. By propping up Assad, Iran has maintained its **land corridor** stretching from Tehran through Iraq and Syria to Lebanon. This so-called **Shia Crescent** has given Iran significant strategic depth, allowing it to project power into the eastern Mediterranean and bolster Hezbollah's position as a deterrent against Israel. The failure of U.S. efforts to oust Assad has, in effect, preserved Iran's dominance in Syria and entrenched its role as a key regional player.

Iran's Proxy Network: Hezbollah, the Houthis, and the Expansion of Regional Influence

Another critical dimension of Iran's rise as a regional power has been its cultivation of a network of **proxy forces** across the Middle East. These proxies, which include groups like **Hezbollah** in Lebanon, the **Houthis** in Yemen, and Shia militias in Iraq, have been instrumental in advancing Iran's regional ambitions, often allowing Tehran to exert influence in conflicts where it does not have a direct military presence. U.S. interventions in the region have inadvertently strengthened this proxy network by destabilizing states and creating conditions conducive to the rise of non-state actors.

Hezbollah, one of Iran's most successful proxy groups, has been a key player in Lebanon since its formation in the early 1980s, following Israel's invasion of southern Lebanon. Backed by Iran's **IRGC**, Hezbollah has developed into a formidable military and political force, effectively acting as a state within a state in Lebanon. The group's military capabilities, including its arsenal of **rockets and missiles**, have made it a powerful deterrent against Israel, while its political influence has allowed it to shape Lebanese politics in Iran's favor.

U.S. policies in the region, particularly in Iraq and Syria, have helped to create conditions that bolster Hezbollah's role. The destabilization of Syria, for example, gave Hezbollah an opportunity to expand its operational capabilities beyond Lebanon, as it deployed thousands of fighters to support Assad's regime. In turn, Iran's support for Hezbollah has enabled it to build a robust deterrent against Israel, reinforcing its position in the Levant and allowing it to influence regional politics in ways that align with Tehran's objectives.

In **Yemen**, the rise of the **Houthi movement**, which has strong ideological and material ties to Iran, has further extended Tehran's influence into the Arabian Peninsula. The Houthis, who belong to Yemen's Zaidi Shia minority, seized control of the capital, **Sana'a**, in 2014 and have since been embroiled in a civil war against a **Saudi-led coalition** that seeks to restore the internationally recognized government. While Iran's support for the Houthis has been more indirect than its backing of Hezbollah, Tehran has provided arms, training, and financial support to the group, allowing the Houthis to sustain their military campaign against Saudi forces.

The U.S.'s involvement in Yemen, through its support for Saudi Arabia's intervention, has done little to weaken Iran's position. Despite the coalition's overwhelming military superiority, the Houthis have proved remarkably resilient, even launching **missile attacks** and **drone strikes** deep into Saudi territory. This proxy conflict has allowed Iran to project power into the southern Arabian Peninsula, where it can challenge Saudi hegemony and bog down its regional rival in a costly and protracted war.

The Nuclear Issue: Aftermath of the U.S. Withdrawal from the JCPOA

Another U.S. policy decision that has inadvertently strengthened Iran's hand was the Trump administration's decision to withdraw from the **Joint Comprehensive Plan of Action (JCPOA)**, commonly known as the **Iran nuclear deal**, in **2018**. The deal, negotiated under President **Barack Obama** in 2015, had placed limits on Iran's nuclear program in exchange for sanctions relief. While far from perfect, the JCPOA had created a framework for managing Iran's nuclear ambitions and opened the door for potential diplomatic engagement.

The U.S. withdrawal from the deal and the subsequent reimposition of sanctions under the **"maximum pressure"** campaign severely undermined this framework. Rather than curbing Iran's regional activities or bringing Tehran to the negotiating table, the U.S.'s unilateral actions pushed Iran to ramp up its nuclear program, expand its influence through proxies, and retaliate through military means. By abandoning the JCPOA, the U.S. effectively removed a key lever of influence over Iran's nuclear activities, while emboldening hardliners in Tehran who were already skeptical of diplomacy with the West.

The U.S. withdrawal from the JCPOA also strained Washington's relationships with its European allies, who were committed to maintaining the agreement and continuing diplomatic engagement with Iran. In the absence of a coherent U.S. strategy to contain Iran, Tehran has pursued a more aggressive regional policy, including stepping up its support for militias in **Iraq**, **Syria**, and **Lebanon**, and conducting **attacks on Gulf oil infrastructure**. These actions have solidified Iran's position as a regional power capable of defying U.S. sanctions and asserting its interests in the face of Western pressure.

Unintended Consequences of U.S. Interventions

Throughout the past several decades, U.S. interventions in the Middle East—whether in Iraq, Syria, Lebanon, or Yemen—have inadvertently strengthened Iran's regional influence. Rather than curbing Tehran's ambitions, these interventions have often destabilized states, created power vacuums, and provided Iran with opportunities to expand its network of proxy forces. In the aftermath of U.S.-led military actions, Iran has emerged as a dominant power in the region, extending its influence through both direct military involvement and the cultivation of non-state actors that serve as its proxies.

As the U.S. continues to grapple with the consequences of its interventions, it faces the challenge of managing an increasingly assertive Iran, whose regional influence now stretches from the **Gulf** to the **Mediterranean**. Understanding how U.S. policies have contributed to this shift is critical for shaping future American strategy in the Middle East, as the region remains a key battleground for competing powers and interests.

Iran's Role in Shaping the Outcomes of Conflicts Across the Middle East

In the modern geopolitical landscape of the Middle East, **Iran** has become one of the most influential actors, shaping the outcomes of conflicts across the region through its sophisticated network of **proxy forces** and alliances. While the **United States** has historically employed its own interventions and strategic partnerships to influence the region, Iran has developed a parallel strategy, leveraging non-state actors and insurgent movements to expand its power and safeguard its interests. Over the past few decades, Tehran's ability to influence the outcomes of conflicts in **Iraq**, **Syria**, **Lebanon**, **Yemen**, and elsewhere has solidified its status as a formidable regional power.

This approach, often referred to as **proxy warfare**, allows Iran to exert influence without directly engaging in large-scale military conflict. Instead, Iran trains, arms, and funds militias and insurgent groups that can advance its objectives on the ground. These groups—whether it is **Hezbollah** in Lebanon, **the Houthis** in Yemen, or **Shia militias** in Iraq—have become essential instruments of Iran's foreign policy, enabling Tehran to project power beyond its borders. In doing so, Iran mirrors the **Cold War-era** tactics once employed by the U.S. and the Soviet Union, where superpowers backed insurgents and militias to influence conflicts indirectly. Today, Iran's proxy network spans the Middle East, aligning with the broader power struggle involving **Russia**, **China**, and Western nations.

The Hezbollah Model: Iran's Success in Lebanon

One of the earliest and most successful examples of Iran's use of proxy forces is **Hezbollah**, the powerful political and military organization in **Lebanon**. Formed in the 1980s during the Lebanese Civil War and the Israeli occupation of southern Lebanon, Hezbollah was created with the backing of Iran's **Islamic Revolutionary Guard Corps (IRGC)**. Over the years, Hezbollah has grown from a small militant group into a significant political force, controlling much of Lebanon's security and wielding enormous influence in the country's government.

Hezbollah serves as a key pillar of Iran's strategy to counterbalance **Israel** and maintain leverage in the **Levant**. Its military capabilities, which include a vast arsenal of **rockets** and **missiles**, have allowed Hezbollah to act as a deterrent against Israeli military actions. Beyond military strength, Hezbollah's political and social services network has also given Iran significant soft power in Lebanon, allowing Tehran to present itself as a protector of Shia communities and a counterweight to Western influence.

By supporting Hezbollah, Iran has also been able to influence the broader dynamics of the **Arab-Israeli conflict**. Hezbollah's military operations during conflicts such as the **2006 Lebanon War** demonstrated its resilience and capacity to stand up to Israeli forces, further emboldening Iran's position in the region. Hezbollah's role in the **Syrian Civil War**, where it fought alongside Iranian and Syrian forces to preserve the **Assad regime**, also highlighted its value as a proxy force capable of operating across borders. Through Hezbollah, Iran has successfully extended its influence across Lebanon, Syria, and into the broader Israeli-Palestinian conflict, positioning itself as a key player in any future regional peace negotiations.

Iran's Role in Iraq: Shia Militias and the Power Struggle Post-Saddam

In **Iraq**, Iran's influence is perhaps most visible through its backing of **Shia militias**, many of which operate under the umbrella of the **Popular Mobilization Forces (PMF)**. These militias were originally formed to combat **ISIS** during the group's rapid expansion across Iraq and Syria in **2014**, but they have since become powerful political and military actors in their own right. Many of these groups, including **Kataib Hezbollah**, **Asaib Ahl al-Haq**, and the **Badr Organization**, have long-standing ties to Iran's IRGC and receive funding, weapons, and training from Tehran.

Iran's support for these militias has allowed it to wield significant influence over Iraq's political and security landscape, particularly after the **U.S. invasion of Iraq** in 2003 and the subsequent collapse of the **Baathist regime**.

By backing militias aligned with Iraq's **Shia majority**, Iran has effectively positioned itself as a protector of Iraq's Shia population, allowing it to counterbalance the influence of **Sunni powers** like Saudi Arabia and Turkey. The Shia militias, in turn, have become key players in Iraq's internal power struggles, often operating with greater autonomy than the central government and challenging U.S. efforts to stabilize the country.

In the post-ISIS era, these militias have also been instrumental in shaping the political future of Iraq. Many of their leaders have entered Iraq's political system, running for office and securing positions of power in the government. This integration of Iranian-backed militias into the formal political structure of Iraq has cemented Tehran's influence in the country, ensuring that any future Iraqi government will likely remain closely aligned with Iranian interests.

However, Iran's role in Iraq has also fueled tensions with the United States, which continues to maintain a military presence in the country. Iranian-backed militias have frequently clashed with U.S. forces, particularly in the aftermath of the **assassination of Qassem Soleimani**, the head of the **IRGC-Quds Force**, in a U.S. drone strike in **2020**. This killing, along with the broader U.S.-Iran confrontation in Iraq, highlights the ongoing power struggle between Washington and Tehran, with Iraq often serving as the battleground for their proxy war.

The Houthis and the Yemen Conflict: Iran's Role in a Key Proxy War

In **Yemen**, Iran's support for the **Houthi** rebels transformed the country's civil war into another major proxy conflict in the Middle East. The Houthis, who belong to Yemen's Zaidi Shia minority, have long-standing grievances against Yemen's central government, but their rise to power in 2014—when they seized control of **Sana'a**, the capital—drew the attention of Saudi Arabia and its allies. Fearing that the Houthis represented a growing Iranian influence on its southern border, **Saudi Arabia** launched a military intervention in **2015**, backed by a coalition of Arab states and supported by the United States.

Iran's support for the Houthis has been strategic, allowing Tehran to bog down its chief rival, Saudi Arabia, in a costly and protracted war. While Iran's direct involvement in Yemen has been less overt than in places like Iraq or Lebanon, the **Houthi rebels** have received **weapons**, **financial support**, and **military training** from Tehran. Iranian weapons, including **ballistic missiles** and **drones**, have been used by the Houthis to strike targets deep inside Saudi territory, including **Riyadh** and critical oil infrastructure.

The war in Yemen has also drawn international attention to Iran's ability to use relatively small groups to challenge much larger and better-funded adversaries. Despite Saudi Arabia's overwhelming military superiority and the backing of Western powers, the Houthis have proven remarkably resilient, holding large swathes of territory in northern Yemen and continuing to launch cross-border attacks on Saudi Arabia. The conflict has become a focal point for the broader **Saudi-Iranian rivalry**, with Yemen serving as a battleground for regional hegemony.

In recent years, the Houthis have also increased their international profile, engaging in negotiations with **Saudi Arabia** and other regional actors to bring an end to the conflict. Iran's support for the group has thus given Tehran leverage in any future peace settlement, ensuring that Iran will have a say in Yemen's political future and maintaining its influence in the Arabian Peninsula. The war in Yemen, much like Iran's involvement in Iraq and Syria, demonstrates Tehran's ability to extend its reach through proxies, turning local conflicts into broader regional struggles.

Iran's Influence in Syria: Preserving the Assad Regime

The **Syrian Civil War** has been another key theater for Iran's projection of power through proxy forces. Since the onset of the war in 2011, **Iran** has been one of the most steadfast supporters of **Bashar al-Assad's** regime, seeing Assad's survival as critical to maintaining its influence in the **Levant**. Iran has provided military and financial support to Assad, deploying **IRGC forces**, **Hezbollah fighters**, and other Shia militias to assist in the fight against both Syrian opposition forces and extremist groups like **ISIS**.

Iran's role in Syria has been particularly important in preserving the **Shia Crescent**, a term used to describe Iran's network of influence stretching from **Tehran** through **Baghdad**, **Damascus**, and **Beirut**. By ensuring Assad's survival, Iran has maintained its critical land corridor through Syria, allowing it to transport weapons, fighters, and supplies to **Hezbollah** in Lebanon and maintain pressure on Israel.

At the same time, Iran's involvement in Syria has drawn it into a broader geopolitical struggle involving **Russia** and **Turkey**. While Russia has also backed Assad, the two powers have occasionally found themselves at odds over the future of the Syrian state. Similarly, Iran's influence in Syria has clashed with **Turkish interests**, particularly as Turkey has sought to establish its own sphere of influence in northern Syria through proxy forces. The complex dynamics of the Syrian conflict have thus created a multi-sided proxy war, with Iran playing a central role in shaping the outcome.

Russia, China, and the Global Power Struggle: Iran's Alignment with Non-Western Powers

Iran's role in shaping the outcomes of conflicts across the Middle East is not only a reflection of its rivalry with **Western**

powers, but also part of a broader alignment with **Russia** and **China**. Both of these powers have supported Iran in its regional ambitions, either directly or indirectly, and have sought to capitalize on the **U.S.'s declining influence** in the region.

Russia, in particular, has been a close ally of Iran in the **Syrian conflict**, with both countries working together to ensure Assad's survival and push back against Western-backed opposition forces. Russia's military intervention in Syria in **2015**, which included airstrikes and the deployment of Russian troops, complemented Iran's ground operations, creating a formidable coalition that turned the tide of the war in Assad's favor.

Meanwhile, **China** has taken a more indirect approach, focusing on **economic partnerships** and **diplomatic engagement** with Iran and its regional allies. China's **Belt and Road Initiative (BRI)** has brought significant investment to the Middle East, including infrastructure projects in Iran. In return, Iran has become a key partner for China's efforts to secure energy supplies and expand its influence in the region. China's role in brokering a rapprochement between **Iran and Saudi Arabia** in **2023** further underscores its growing influence as a mediator in Middle Eastern conflicts, positioning Beijing as a rising power that challenges the traditional U.S. role in the region.

Together, these alignments have created a new geopolitical dynamic in the Middle East, where Iran's influence is intertwined with the broader power struggles involving Russia and China. This new order, defined by proxy wars, regional rivalries, and shifting alliances, has reshaped the region's political landscape, with Iran firmly entrenched as a key player. As the U.S. continues to grapple with the unintended consequences of its interventions, Iran has leveraged its proxy network and alliances to advance its interests and shape the outcomes of conflicts across the Middle

JOSH LUBERISSE

East.

PART V: GLOBAL CONSEQUENCES

CHAPTER 13 - EXPANSION OF THE WAR ON TERROR: U.S. INTERVENTION IN SOMALIA, NIGER, AND BEYOND

In the aftermath of the **September 11, 2001**, terrorist attacks, the **United States** embarked on what would become a far-reaching and enduring global campaign known as the **War on Terror**. While the primary focus of this war initially centered on **Afghanistan** and later **Iraq**, the U.S. soon found itself expanding its counterterrorism efforts to regions beyond the Middle East, particularly in **Africa**. The U.S. interventions in countries like **Somalia** and **Niger**—along with broader military engagement in the **Sahel**, the **Horn of Africa**, and the **Maghreb**—highlight the evolving nature of America's global fight against terrorism and the complexities of military involvement in regions plagued by political instability, militant groups, and geopolitical rivalry.

This chapter provides a historical overview of U.S. intervention in Somalia and Niger, as well as a broader analysis of how American military involvement in Africa has expanded in the context of the War on Terror. The expansion of this campaign into these regions reflects not only the shifting geography of terrorism but also the increasingly interconnected nature of global security threats. Moreover, it illustrates the challenges the U.S. has faced in applying military solutions to deeply rooted political and social conflicts in fragile states.

Legacy of U.S. Intervention in Somalia

The U.S. military's involvement in **Somalia** is rooted in the chaotic aftermath of the country's **civil war**, which began in **1991**. Following the overthrow of Somali dictator **Siad Barre**, Somalia descended into lawlessness and factional violence as rival warlords vied for control of the capital, **Mogadishu**, and other key regions. The lack of a central government and the ensuing humanitarian crisis caught the attention of the international community, prompting the **United Nations** to launch a peacekeeping mission—**UNOSOM I**—in **1992**. This mission sought to restore order and provide humanitarian aid to a population ravaged by famine and conflict.

In **1993**, the U.S. joined the UN mission through **Operation Restore Hope**, which was intended to secure aid distribution routes and stabilize the country. However, the U.S. military soon became embroiled in local factional fighting, particularly with the forces loyal to warlord **Mohamed Farrah Aidid**. The infamous **Battle of Mogadishu**—also known as **Black Hawk Down**—in **October 1993** resulted in the deaths of 18 U.S. soldiers and marked a turning point in American involvement in Somalia. The brutal street fighting, captured on television screens around the world, shocked the American public and led to the U.S. withdrawing its forces from Somalia by **1994**.

For more than a decade, Somalia remained largely off the radar of U.S. military planners. However, following the 9/11 attacks, the **Horn of Africa** once again became a focus of U.S. counterterrorism efforts. Somalia, with its lawless, ungoverned spaces, provided fertile ground for extremist groups like **al-Qaeda** to operate. The emergence of **al-Shabaab**, an Islamist militant group with ties to al-Qaeda, in the mid-2000s drew the attention of the U.S. and its regional allies, including **Kenya** and **Ethiopia**. By **2006**, al-Shabaab had gained significant control over southern Somalia and parts of Mogadishu, imposing strict **Sharia law** and threatening to destabilize the region further.

In response, the U.S. began providing military and logistical support to **African Union Mission in Somalia (AMISOM)** troops, particularly those from **Kenya, Ethiopia, Burundi**, and **Uganda**, who were tasked with defeating al-Shabaab and restoring order in Somalia. The U.S. also conducted a series of **airstrikes** and **drone strikes** targeting al-Shabaab leaders and key operatives. These strikes, carried out by **U.S. Africa Command (AFRICOM)**, played a crucial role in degrading al-Shabaab's leadership, though the group has remained resilient, continuing to carry out attacks in Somalia and across the region, including high-profile bombings in **Nairobi** and **Kampala**.

While the U.S. has succeeded in eliminating key al-Shabaab leaders, the broader challenge of stabilizing Somalia remains daunting. Al-Shabaab continues to exploit Somalia's fragile political environment, benefiting from weak governance, clan divisions, and widespread poverty. The Somali government, though backed by the international community, struggles to assert control over large parts of the country. The U.S.'s military involvement in Somalia—focused on counterterrorism strikes and special operations missions—has become part of a broader international effort to build Somali security forces capable of defending the country against both al-Shabaab and other militant factions.

The U.S. Military's Growing Role in Niger and the Sahel

The U.S.'s expansion of the War on Terror into **West Africa**, particularly in **Niger**, underscores the broadening scope of American military engagement in the fight against terrorism. In contrast to Somalia's long history of political instability, Niger had been relatively stable until the early 2010s, when the broader **Sahel region** began to experience rising levels of violence due to the proliferation of **jihadist groups**. These groups, which include **al-Qaeda in the Islamic Maghreb (AQIM)**, **Boko Haram**, and **ISIS-West Africa**, have taken advantage of weak governance and porous borders to operate across several countries in the Sahel, including **Mali, Burkina Faso**, and Niger.

Niger's strategic location at the crossroads of the **Sahara Desert** and the Sahel has made it a key focus of U.S. military efforts to counter terrorism in the region. The country has become a base for U.S. drone operations, intelligence gathering, and special forces missions aimed at disrupting jihadist networks. The establishment of **Air Base 201** in **Agadez**, which became operational in **2019**, has allowed the U.S. to expand its surveillance and strike capabilities across the Sahel. The base, one of the largest U.S. military installations in Africa, houses **Reaper drones** and serves as a launchpad for counterterrorism missions targeting militants in Niger, Mali, and surrounding countries.

The U.S.'s involvement in Niger came into sharp focus following the **2017 ambush** in the **Tongo Tongo** region, where four U.S. soldiers were killed in a firefight with ISIS-affiliated militants. The incident, which drew widespread media attention in the U.S., highlighted the extent of American military operations in Niger and the challenges faced by U.S. troops operating in remote and hostile environments. The ambush also raised questions about the scope of the U.S. mission in Niger and the effectiveness of U.S. strategy in the region.

Niger, like many of its neighbors, is grappling with multiple insurgencies and security threats, compounded by political instability and the effects of climate change. The U.S.'s approach to Niger has been to provide military assistance to the Nigerien government while working closely with **French** forces, who have taken the lead in the region through **Operation Barkhane**, an anti-terrorism campaign focused on the Sahel. However, despite these efforts, jihadist groups have continued to gain ground, exploiting local grievances and weak state institutions to recruit fighters and expand their influence.

Broader Expansion of U.S. Military Engagement in Africa

The expansion of U.S. military engagement in **Africa** as part of the War on Terror extends beyond Somalia and Niger to other parts of the continent, including **Mali**, **Chad**, **Burkina Faso**, **Libya**, and the **Maghreb**. This broader engagement is a reflection of the evolving nature of global terrorism, as jihadist groups have shifted their operations from traditional conflict zones in the **Middle East** to the more ungoverned spaces of Africa.

The U.S. military's growing role in Africa has been driven in part by the increasing activities of **al-Qaeda** and **ISIS** affiliates, as well as homegrown extremist movements. Groups such as **AQIM**, **Boko Haram**, and **ISIS-West Africa** have become key targets of U.S. counterterrorism operations, particularly as these groups have demonstrated their ability to carry out attacks beyond their local environments, threatening U.S. interests and regional stability. For example, **Boko Haram**, which operates primarily in **Nigeria**, **Chad**, and **Cameroon**, has engaged in cross-border attacks and kidnappings, including the infamous abduction of over 200 schoolgirls in **Chibok, Nigeria**, in 2014.

In addition to direct military operations, the U.S. has

focused on **capacity-building efforts** aimed at strengthening the security forces of African nations. Programs like the **Trans-Sahara Counterterrorism Partnership (TSCTP)** and the **Africa Command (AFRICOM)** initiatives have provided training, equipment, and intelligence support to African militaries, helping them combat terrorism within their borders. However, these efforts have often been hampered by corruption, political instability, and the challenges of coordinating multi-national security efforts across vast, poorly governed regions.

The expansion of the War on Terror into Africa has also brought the U.S. into direct competition with other global powers, particularly **Russia** and **China**. Both nations have sought to expand their influence in Africa through military, economic, and diplomatic means. Russia, for example, has supported various governments in the Sahel with arms sales and mercenaries, most notably through the **Wagner Group**, a private military contractor linked to the Kremlin. China, while not directly involved in counterterrorism efforts, has expanded its economic footprint in Africa through investments in infrastructure and natural resources, building stronger ties with governments across the continent.

The **geopolitical rivalry** between the U.S., Russia, and China in Africa reflects the broader competition for influence in key regions of the world, with African nations often caught in the middle of this great-power struggle. The rise of terrorism in Africa, particularly in the Sahel and the Horn of Africa, has given external powers an opportunity to intervene under the guise of counterterrorism, but these interventions have also raised concerns about neocolonialism and the militarization of development aid.

Challenges and Consequences of U.S. Military Engagement in Africa

Despite the U.S. military's expanded role in Africa, the War on Terror has produced mixed results on the continent. In some areas, such as Somalia, U.S.-backed operations have succeeded in weakening militant groups like al-Shabaab, although these groups have proven resilient, continuing to launch attacks both domestically and across borders. In other regions, such as the Sahel, the security situation has deteriorated despite years of U.S. and French intervention, with jihadist groups expanding their reach and recruiting new fighters.

One of the key challenges facing the U.S. in Africa is the difficulty of applying military solutions to what are often deeply rooted political, economic, and social conflicts. Many of the insurgencies in Africa are driven by local grievances, including poverty, corruption, ethnic marginalization, and the lack of government presence in remote areas. While military operations can target and eliminate terrorist leaders, they often fail to address the underlying causes of extremism, leaving these regions vulnerable to continued violence and instability.

Additionally, U.S. military involvement in Africa has sometimes been perceived as **neocolonialism**, with local populations skeptical of foreign interventions, particularly those led by Western powers. The reliance on airstrikes, drone warfare, and special operations missions has also raised concerns about civilian casualties and the long-term impact of military engagements that often lack clear exit strategies.

U.S. Involvement in Counterterrorism Operations Across Africa

U.S. involvement in counterterrorism operations across Africa has steadily expanded in response to the growing threat posed by militant groups like **al-Qaeda**, **ISIS**, **Boko Haram**, and various regional affiliates. While U.S. engagement in the region initially began with a limited focus on intelligence gathering and support for local governments, over the past two decades, it has evolved into a broader and more proactive military campaign. Africa has become a critical front in the global War on Terror, with U.S. operations now spanning across multiple countries in the **Sahel**, the **Horn of Africa**, and **North Africa**, where terrorist networks have increasingly established a foothold.

In the Sahel, a region stretching from the Atlantic coast of West Africa to the Red Sea, the spread of jihadist insurgencies has drawn considerable U.S. attention. The region has long been plagued by instability, with weak central governments, vast ungoverned spaces, and porous borders creating an ideal environment for militant groups to operate. The rise of **al-Qaeda in the Islamic Maghreb (AQIM)** and splinter factions such as **Jamaat Nusrat al-Islam wal-Muslimin (JNIM)** and **ISIS-West Africa** prompted the U.S. to engage in counterterrorism operations aimed at disrupting these networks and preventing them from launching attacks beyond the region.

The U.S. military's presence in the Sahel has centered on providing support to **French** forces, which have been leading the anti-terrorism campaign under **Operation Barkhane**. The U.S. has contributed through the provision of **intelligence**, **logistical support**, and **airlift capabilities** for French troops, as well as training local security forces in Niger, Mali, and Burkina Faso. In addition, U.S. forces have conducted joint operations with these nations 'militaries to combat extremist groups. Despite these efforts, however, militant activity has continued to grow, with jihadists increasingly exploiting ethnic tensions and weak state institutions to recruit new members and carry out attacks on military and civilian targets.

One of the key areas where the U.S. has focused its attention is **Niger**, a country that has emerged as a major hub for American military operations in West Africa. The construction of **Air Base 201** in **Agadez**, which became operational in 2019, has allowed the U.S. to deploy **drones** for surveillance and airstrikes across the Sahel. The base, strategically located in the heart of the desert, serves as a crucial launchpad for counterterrorism missions targeting militant networks in Niger, Mali, and Libya. U.S. special forces have also been active in Niger, conducting joint patrols and advising local forces in their fight against jihadist insurgents.

The ambush in **Tongo Tongo** in **2017**, in which four U.S. soldiers were killed by militants affiliated with ISIS, brought increased scrutiny to the U.S. military's role in Niger. The incident underscored the risks faced by U.S. personnel operating in remote and hostile environments, as well as the growing sophistication of the militant groups they were fighting. While the U.S. presence in Niger has been primarily focused on counterterrorism, the broader goal has been to stabilize the region and prevent it from becoming a safe haven for terrorist organizations capable of launching global attacks.

In addition to the Sahel, the U.S. has maintained a significant military presence in the **Horn of Africa**, with **Somalia** being a primary focus of counterterrorism efforts. Since the mid-2000s, the U.S. has been engaged in efforts to degrade **al-Shabaab**, an Islamist militant group linked to al-Qaeda that controls large swathes of territory in southern Somalia. Al-Shabaab has carried out numerous high-profile attacks in Somalia, as well as cross-border attacks in **Kenya** and **Uganda**, targeting civilians, government officials, and security forces.

The U.S. has relied heavily on **airstrikes** and **drone strikes** to target al-Shabaab's leadership and operational capabilities, with **AFRICOM** conducting dozens of such strikes annually. These air campaigns have been complemented by special operations missions aimed at providing training and support to **Somali National Army** (SNA) forces, as well as African

Union peacekeepers operating under the **African Union Mission in Somalia (AMISOM)**. The U.S. has also provided assistance in building the capacity of the Somali government to fight extremism and restore stability, though progress has been slow due to ongoing political divisions and clan-based rivalries.

In **East Africa, Djibouti** plays a critical role as a base of operations for U.S. counterterrorism activities. **Camp Lemonnier**, the largest U.S. military installation in Africa, is home to thousands of U.S. personnel and serves as a forward base for operations throughout the region. From Djibouti, U.S. forces launch surveillance and strike missions against targets in Somalia, Yemen, and across the Red Sea corridor. The strategic location of Djibouti makes it an essential hub for monitoring extremist activities and securing maritime routes through the **Bab el-Mandeb Strait**, a critical chokepoint for global oil shipments.

Further north, in **Libya**, the U.S. has conducted limited counterterrorism operations aimed at curbing the rise of ISIS and other jihadist groups that took advantage of the chaos following the fall of **Muammar Gaddafi** in 2011. After the NATO-backed intervention that toppled Gaddafi, Libya descended into civil war, creating a vacuum that was quickly filled by extremist factions. ISIS established a stronghold in the coastal city of **Sirte**, using the instability to recruit fighters and plan attacks across the region.

In response, the U.S. launched **Operation Odyssey Lightning** in **2016**, a campaign of airstrikes aimed at dislodging ISIS from Sirte. Working in coordination with local militias loyal to the **Government of National Accord (GNA)**, U.S. forces played a key role in retaking the city. However, the broader conflict in Libya has continued, with rival governments and militias vying for control of the country's oil resources and territory, making counterterrorism efforts even more challenging.

Despite the success of Operation Odyssey Lightning, ISIS and other jihadist groups continue to operate in parts of southern Libya, where the lack of a central authority has allowed them to flourish.

In the **Maghreb**, particularly in **Algeria**, **Morocco**, and **Tunisia**, U.S. involvement in counterterrorism has focused on intelligence sharing, capacity building, and regional cooperation. The **Trans-Sahara Counterterrorism Partnership (TSCTP)**, established in 2005, aims to strengthen the ability of North African and Sahelian countries to combat terrorism through joint military training, law enforcement cooperation, and border security initiatives. The U.S. has also provided financial and technical support to these nations to help them address the root causes of extremism, including poverty, unemployment, and political marginalization.

While the U.S. military footprint in the Maghreb is smaller compared to regions like the Sahel and the Horn of Africa, the threat of jihadist violence remains a significant concern. **Al-Qaeda in the Islamic Maghreb (AQIM)**, based in Algeria, continues to operate in the region, launching attacks and engaging in smuggling and kidnapping activities. Tunisia, in particular, has seen a surge in ISIS-affiliated recruitment, with thousands of Tunisian nationals joining jihadist groups in Syria, Iraq, and Libya. The U.S. has worked closely with the Tunisian government to combat radicalization and prevent terrorist cells from gaining a foothold in the country.

The expanding U.S. involvement in counterterrorism operations across Africa has raised important questions about the effectiveness of military solutions in addressing the complex and multifaceted nature of extremism on the continent. While the U.S. has succeeded in eliminating key terrorist leaders and disrupting militant networks, the long-term stability of the regions where these operations take place remains fragile. Militant groups continue to adapt and evolve, often exploiting local grievances and the absence of effective governance to gain recruits and carry out attacks.

U.S. policymakers have emphasized the need for a holistic approach to counterterrorism in Africa, one that combines military action with diplomacy, economic development, and efforts to address the root causes of extremism. However, the reliance on drone strikes, air campaigns, and special operations missions has often overshadowed these broader initiatives, raising concerns about the sustainability of U.S. involvement in Africa's counterterrorism efforts.

The War on Terror in Africa has also highlighted the challenges of working with local governments and security forces that are often plagued by corruption, human rights abuses, and inefficiency. Despite years of training and support, many African militaries remain ill-equipped to confront the rising tide of extremism, and U.S. assistance has at times been undermined by political instability and governance failures. These challenges complicate U.S. efforts to achieve lasting security and stability across the continent, as extremist groups continue to exploit the vacuum left by weak state institutions and widespread poverty.

Unintended Consequences of U.S. Interventions Across Africa

U.S. interventions across various regions, particularly in **Africa**, have often been driven by the imperative to counter terrorism, promote stability, and safeguard American interests. However, the consequences of these interventions have frequently produced results that are far more complex and unpredictable than initially envisioned. The persistence of **instability** in regions such as the **Sahel**, the **Horn of Africa**, and **North Africa** serves as a stark reminder of the broader unintended consequences of U.S. military actions. These areas, once seen as secondary in the global War on Terror, have become crucial theaters of prolonged conflict, where weak governance, insurgencies, and extremist ideologies intersect to create conditions that are difficult to resolve through military means alone.

The U.S. strategy of deploying military forces, providing arms, and training local security forces to combat extremist groups has often had the opposite effect—fueling violence, exacerbating local conflicts, and creating power vacuums that militant groups eagerly exploit. These interventions also underscore the limits of a counterterrorism approach that focuses heavily on short-term military gains while neglecting the underlying social, economic, and political factors that contribute to long-term instability. As these regions struggle to recover from the cycles of conflict, displacement, and state failure, the broader consequences of U.S. interventions become evident, not just for the countries themselves, but for the wider region and international security.

Fragility of State Institutions and the Limits of Military Solutions

One of the most prominent consequences of U.S. interventions in Africa has been the exacerbation of weak state institutions. Countries such as **Mali**, **Niger**, **Somalia**, and **Libya** were already fragile and politically unstable prior to U.S. involvement. However, the influx of military aid, training, and direct intervention in these regions has, in many cases, weakened rather than strengthened their ability to govern effectively. The fragility of state institutions in these countries is not merely a byproduct of war but is deeply tied to issues such as corruption, the inability of governments to provide basic services, and the absence of effective security and law enforcement mechanisms in rural and underserved areas.

In places like **Somalia**, for example, U.S. efforts to support the Somali government and **African Union forces** in their fight against **al-Shabaab** have not resulted in the restoration of a strong, functioning state. While U.S. airstrikes and drone campaigns have successfully eliminated several high-ranking al-Shabaab leaders, the group remains deeply embedded in Somalia's social and political fabric. Al-Shabaab continues to operate as a parallel authority in areas where the central government has little to no presence, collecting taxes, providing services, and enforcing its interpretation of Sharia law. The Somali government, despite years of international support, remains highly dependent on external assistance, and its legitimacy is contested by a range of local actors, including clans and regional warlords. The U.S. strategy in Somalia has focused heavily on military solutions without sufficiently addressing the underlying issues of governance, political reconciliation, and economic development that fuel extremism.

Similarly, in the **Sahel**, U.S. interventions have been primarily focused on bolstering the military capabilities of local governments to fight insurgent groups such as **AQIM** and **ISIS-West Africa**. However, the reliance on militarized approaches has often had the unintended consequence of further destabilizing already fragile states. In **Mali**, for instance, the U.S. supported the government in its fight against northern separatist groups and jihadist insurgents following a military coup in 2012. Yet the subsequent deployment of U.S. and French forces, as well as the creation of local militias to combat these groups, did little to restore stability. Instead, the proliferation of armed groups, both state-sponsored and non-state actors, deepened Mali's internal divisions and contributed to the spread of violence across the Sahel.

One of the key problems with these interventions is that they have failed to address the root causes of insurgencies and extremism. In the Sahel, for example, jihadist groups have successfully exploited local grievances, such as ethnic tensions, land disputes, and the marginalization of rural populations by central governments. These groups have positioned themselves as protectors of local communities, offering an alternative to corrupt or ineffective state authorities. The U.S.'s emphasis on military solutions has often been perceived as foreign intervention that favors central governments at the expense of local autonomy, further alienating populations in areas like northern Mali, **Burkina Faso**, and **Niger**.

Rise of Militant Groups and the Proliferation of Weapons

Another major consequence of U.S. interventions has been the unintended empowerment of militant groups, both through the **proliferation of weapons** and the creation of power vacuums in the wake of military operations. In **Libya**, for instance, the 2011 NATO-backed intervention that led to the fall of **Muammar Gaddafi** was initially seen as a success in terms of removing a longstanding dictator. However, the collapse of Gaddafi's regime left a dangerous power vacuum, which was quickly filled by militias, jihadist groups, and rival political factions. The vast quantities of arms that flooded the region following Gaddafi's fall, much of which came from the looting of Libyan weapons stockpiles, found their way into the hands of insurgent groups not only in Libya but across the Sahel and North Africa.

Jihadist groups, including **AQIM** and **Boko Haram**, have taken advantage of the post-Gaddafi chaos to arm themselves and expand their operations. Weapons from Libyan stockpiles have been traced to conflicts as far afield as **Mali**, **Chad**, **Sudan**, and **Nigeria**, where they have been used by various insurgent and terrorist groups. The U.S. intervention in Libya, although it successfully removed a dictator, had the unintended effect of transforming Libya into a hub for weapons smuggling and a breeding ground for jihadist groups that now operate across the region.

In addition to the proliferation of weapons, U.S. interventions have also contributed to the rise of **local militias** and warlords, who have filled the security vacuum left by weak or absent central governments. In Somalia, for example, the U.S.-backed military operations against al-Shabaab have led to the emergence of local warlords and militias who exert control over territories outside of Mogadishu. These militias, often aligned with specific clans, have further fragmented Somalia's political landscape, making it even more difficult for the central government to assert its authority and rebuild the country.

In Libya, the absence of a unified national government has led to the rise of competing militias that control different regions of the country. These militias, some of which are backed by foreign powers such as **Turkey**, **Russia**, and **the UAE**, continue to engage in violent power struggles, preventing any meaningful progress toward national reconciliation or the reestablishment of state institutions. The U.S. role in Libya, particularly in terms of its involvement in the NATO-led intervention, has been criticized for failing to plan for the post-Gaddafi political landscape, which has since devolved into a protracted and multifaceted civil war.

Displacement and Humanitarian Crises

One of the most tragic consequences of U.S. interventions in Africa has been the large-scale **displacement** of civilian populations and the resulting **humanitarian crises**. In countries like Somalia, Mali, and Libya, years of conflict, insurgency, and state failure have led to the displacement of millions of people, both internally and across borders. These displaced populations face dire conditions in refugee camps, where access to food, clean water, and healthcare is often limited. The protracted nature of these conflicts means that many of these displaced communities remain in limbo, unable to return to their homes and with few prospects for long-term resettlement or integration.

In **Somalia**, decades of civil war and insurgency have displaced nearly **2.9 million** people, with many fleeing to refugee camps in **Kenya, Ethiopia**, and **Djibouti**. These camps, such as **Dadaab** in Kenya, have become semi-permanent settlements where generations of Somalis have grown up without ever knowing peace. The ongoing conflict with al-Shabaab, compounded by the lack of a functioning central government, has made it nearly impossible for displaced Somalis to return to their homes or rebuild their lives.

The situation is similarly dire in the **Sahel**, where the rise of jihadist insurgencies and intercommunal violence has displaced millions of people across **Mali, Niger**, and **Burkina Faso**. In addition to those displaced by conflict, the region is also experiencing severe **food insecurity** and **climate change**-related disasters, which have further exacerbated the humanitarian crisis. U.S. military interventions, while aimed at countering terrorism, have often failed to address the humanitarian needs of these displaced populations, leaving international aid organizations to fill the gap.

In **Libya**, the civil war has displaced hundreds of thousands of people, both within the country and across the **Mediterranean**. The collapse of state institutions and the proliferation of armed groups have made it dangerous for Libyans to return to their homes, while the war-torn economy has made it difficult for those who remain to access basic services. Libya has also become a major transit point for **migrants** and **refugees** from sub-Saharan Africa, many of whom attempt the perilous journey across the Mediterranean to reach Europe. The instability in Libya, fueled by the 2011 intervention and its aftermath, has turned the country into a major flashpoint for the broader European migration crisis.

Internationalization of Local Conflicts

One of the broader consequences of U.S. interventions in Africa has been the **internationalization** of local conflicts. What began as insurgencies or civil wars within individual countries have often evolved into regional conflicts that draw in a range of external actors, including **foreign powers**, **international organizations**, and **multinational corporations**. In Libya, for example, the civil war has become a battleground for competing foreign interests, with **Turkey**, **Russia**, **France**, and **the UAE** backing different factions. This external involvement has complicated efforts to resolve the conflict, as each foreign power pursues its own strategic objectives, often at the expense of peace and stability.

Similarly, in the Sahel, the rise of transnational jihadist networks has turned what were once localized conflicts into a regional crisis. Groups like **AQIM** and **ISIS-West Africa** have used the porous borders of the Sahel to establish cross-border networks of fighters, weapons, and funding. These groups operate across **Mali**, **Niger**, **Burkina Faso**, and even into **Chad** and **Algeria**, making it difficult for any single country to combat them effectively. The U.S. has sought to address this transnational threat through joint military exercises, intelligence sharing, and support for regional initiatives like the **G5 Sahel Joint Force**, but the broader internationalization of the conflict has made it difficult to contain.

In Somalia, al-Shabaab has also expanded its operations beyond the country's borders, launching attacks in **Kenya** and **Uganda** in retaliation for their involvement in AMISOM. These cross-border attacks have drawn additional countries into the conflict, further complicating efforts to stabilize Somalia and defeat al-Shabaab. The U.S., through its drone strikes and special operations missions, has targeted al-Shabaab leaders in Somalia and neighboring countries, but the group's ability to operate across borders has made it difficult to eliminate completely.

The internationalization of these conflicts highlights the interconnectedness of security challenges in Africa and the limitations of U.S. interventions that focus primarily on military solutions. In many cases, U.S. actions have contributed to the escalation of local conflicts into broader regional crises, with far-reaching consequences for stability, governance, and development.

CHAPTER 14 - ROLE OF RUSSIA AND CHINA: NEW POWER PLAYERS IN THE MIDDLE EAST

The geopolitical landscape of the **Middle East** has been defined for much of the modern era by Western, particularly **U.S.**, influence. For decades, the United States held sway over the region through its strategic alliances, military interventions, and economic investments, often seen as a stabilizing force against the Soviet Union during the Cold War and later as the dominant power in a post-Cold War unipolar world. However, as global power dynamics have shifted in the 21st century, the role of other major powers, particularly **Russia** and **China**, in the Middle East has expanded significantly. These nations have adopted new strategies that challenge U.S. dominance in the region and offer alternative models of engagement, both economic and military, with Middle Eastern states.

Russia and China's growing presence in the Middle East reflects broader global trends, including their efforts to position themselves as **counterweights** to U.S. influence and their desire to project power on a global scale. For Russia, its involvement in the Middle East represents a reassertion of its role as a global power after years of geopolitical retreat following the collapse of the **Soviet Union**. For China, the Middle East offers vast opportunities for **energy security**, **economic partnerships**, and the expansion of its global infrastructure initiative, the **Belt and Road Initiative (BRI)**.

While both Russia and China share an interest in reducing U.S. influence in the Middle East, their approaches to the region are distinct. Russia has focused primarily on **military engagement** and **political alliances**, often intervening directly in regional conflicts, most notably in **Syria**. China, on the other hand, has adopted a more cautious, **economically driven** strategy, preferring diplomacy and investment to military involvement. Together, these two nations have created new dynamics in the Middle East, reshaping regional alliances, altering the balance of power, and complicating the traditional U.S.-led order.

Russia's Return to the Middle East: Military Engagement and Political Influence

Russia's re-entry into the Middle East as a key player began in earnest with its **2015 intervention in Syria**, a decisive move that transformed the course of the Syrian Civil War and re-established Moscow as a critical power broker in the region. For much of the post-Cold War era, Russia had been largely absent from the Middle Eastern geopolitical landscape, its influence overshadowed by the dominance of the United States and its European allies. However, Russia's intervention in Syria—motivated by a combination of strategic, political, and economic factors—signaled a resurgence of Russian power in the Middle East.

The collapse of the **Soviet Union** in 1991 had left Russia in a diminished position on the global stage, including in the Middle East, where it had once maintained close ties with countries like **Syria**, **Iraq**, and **Egypt**. Throughout the 1990s and early 2000s, Russia's foreign policy was inwardly focused, as it dealt with the economic and political turmoil of the post-Soviet period. Meanwhile, the U.S. expanded its influence in the Middle East through a series of military interventions, including the **Gulf War** in 1991 and the invasions of **Afghanistan** and **Iraq** in the early 2000s.

However, as the **Putin administration** consolidated power in Russia and sought to reassert Moscow's role as a global power, the Middle East became a key arena for this resurgence. By the mid-2000s, Russia began to re-engage with countries in the region through arms deals, economic cooperation, and diplomatic outreach. The turning point in Russia's Middle East strategy came in 2015, when it intervened militarily in the Syrian Civil War to support the regime of **Bashar al-Assad**. This intervention, which involved Russian **airstrikes**, **military advisors**, and the deployment of **naval** and **ground forces**, marked the first time Russia had directly intervened in a Middle Eastern conflict since the Soviet era.

Russia's support for Assad was driven by several factors. First, Syria had been one of Russia's last remaining allies in the Arab world, and Assad's fall would have represented a significant loss of influence for Moscow. Second, Syria provided Russia with strategic access to the **Mediterranean Sea**, through its naval base in **Tartus**, and a foothold in the wider Levant region. Third, the intervention allowed Russia to position itself as a counterweight to U.S. and Western influence in the region, portraying itself as a reliable partner for governments facing insurgencies or Western pressure. Finally, Russia's intervention in Syria allowed Putin to demonstrate Russia's military capabilities and project strength on the global stage.

Russia's military intervention in Syria proved to be highly effective in turning the tide of the war in Assad's favor. By 2017, Assad's forces, bolstered by Russian airpower and **Iranian-backed militias**, had recaptured key territories from opposition forces and extremist groups such as **ISIS** and **Jabhat al-Nusra**. In the process, Russia established itself as the dominant foreign power in Syria and positioned itself as a mediator in the broader conflict, hosting peace talks in **Astana** and **Sochi** alongside Iran and Turkey. Moscow's role in shaping the outcome of the Syrian Civil War demonstrated its ability to influence regional conflicts and presented Russia as a credible alternative to U.S. leadership in the Middle East.

Beyond Syria, Russia has also expanded its political and military influence in other parts of the region. Russia has strengthened its ties with **Iran**, with both countries sharing common interests in supporting Assad's regime and countering U.S. influence in the region. Moscow has also cultivated relationships with **Turkey**, despite their differences over Syria, and has positioned itself as a mediator in conflicts involving Turkey, Iran, and Arab states. Russia's arms sales to countries like **Egypt**, **Saudi Arabia**, and the **United Arab Emirates** have further solidified its position as a key player in the region's defense sector, offering Middle Eastern governments an alternative to U.S. weapons systems and military aid.

China's Expanding Role: Economic Engagement and Energy Security

While Russia's reassertion of power in the Middle East has largely been driven by military and political considerations, **China** has taken a different path, focusing on **economic engagement** and **energy security** as the cornerstone of its Middle East strategy. China's interest in the Middle East has grown in tandem with its rise as a global economic power, as the region plays a critical role in meeting China's massive energy demands and facilitating its broader geopolitical ambitions through the **Belt and Road Initiative (BRI)**.

China's relationship with the Middle East is primarily defined by its dependence on the region for oil and gas imports. As the world's largest importer of crude oil, China relies heavily on Middle Eastern producers, particularly **Saudi Arabia**, **Iran**, and **Iraq**, to meet its energy needs. In **2019**, more than **40%** of China's oil imports came from the Middle East, making the region an essential component of China's energy security strategy. To safeguard these vital energy supplies, China has sought to establish stable relationships with all major oil-producing states in the region, regardless of their political alignments or involvement in regional conflicts.

China's energy interests have driven its **diplomatic engagement** with the region, as Beijing seeks to position itself as a neutral and non-interventionist power. Unlike the U.S. and Russia, China has largely avoided direct involvement in Middle Eastern conflicts, preferring to maintain friendly relations with all parties. This approach has allowed China to act as a broker between rival states, such as **Saudi Arabia** and **Iran**, and to expand its influence without becoming entangled in the region's complex political and sectarian rivalries.

The Belt and Road Initiative (BRI) has become a key vehicle for China's growing presence in the Middle East. Launched in 2013, the BRI aims to build a global network of infrastructure, trade routes, and investment partnerships that connect Asia, Europe, and Africa. The Middle East, as a crossroads between these regions, is central to China's BRI ambitions. China has invested heavily in infrastructure projects in the region, including ports, railways, and energy facilities, as part of its broader effort to enhance connectivity and facilitate trade.

One of the key aspects of China's involvement in the Middle East has been its deepening economic relationship with **Iran**. Despite U.S. sanctions, China has continued to engage with Iran, purchasing Iranian oil and investing in infrastructure projects. In **2021**, the two countries signed a **25-year strategic cooperation agreement** that encompasses a wide range of economic, military, and infrastructure initiatives. This agreement, which includes investments in Iranian energy infrastructure and the development of **joint military cooperation**, signals China's commitment to deepening its ties with Iran, even in the face of U.S. opposition.

China has also expanded its economic ties with **Saudi Arabia**, one of its largest oil suppliers and a key partner in the BRI. In recent years, China has increased its investments in Saudi infrastructure projects, including the construction of refineries and the development of **smart cities** like **NEOM**. At the same time, Saudi Arabia has sought to diversify its economy away from oil through its **Vision 2030** initiative, and China has emerged as a critical partner in this effort, providing investment and expertise in sectors such as **renewable energy**, **technology**, and **infrastructure**.

While China's strategy in the Middle East has largely focused on economic engagement, it has also begun to expand its **military footprint** in the region. In **2017**, China opened its first overseas military base in **Djibouti**, strategically located near the **Bab el-Mandeb Strait**, a key maritime chokepoint through which much of the world's oil passes. The base in Djibouti allows China to protect its shipping routes in the **Red Sea** and **Gulf of Aden** and to project power in the region. China has also increased its participation in **multilateral security initiatives**, such as anti-piracy operations off the coast of **Somalia** and peacekeeping missions in the region.

The Russia-China Dynamic: A Cooperative and Competitive Relationship

The simultaneous rise of Russia and China as power players in the Middle East has introduced a new dynamic to the region, with both countries seeking to expand their influence while maintaining a delicate balance of cooperation and competition. Although Russia and China share common goals in reducing U.S. influence in the Middle East, their strategies and interests are not always aligned.

Russia's focus on military engagement and political alliances has often put it at odds with China's more cautious, economically driven approach. For example, while Russia has invested heavily in supporting the Assad regime in Syria, China has been far less involved in the Syrian conflict, preferring to focus on economic investments and infrastructure development in the wider region. Nevertheless, the two countries have found common ground in their opposition to U.S. unilateralism and their shared interest in promoting **multipolarity** in the global order.

In many ways, Russia and China have complemented each other's efforts in the Middle East, with Russia taking the lead in military matters and China providing economic support. This division of labor has allowed both countries to expand their influence without directly competing for dominance in the region. For example, while Russia has worked to establish itself as the primary military power in Syria, China has focused on expanding its investments in Iraq, Iran, and the Gulf states.

At the same time, the growing presence of Russia and China in the Middle East has raised questions about the future of U.S. influence in the region. As both countries continue to strengthen their ties with key Middle Eastern states, they are increasingly seen as viable alternatives to the U.S., offering political and economic partnerships without the same conditions and demands that often accompany U.S. engagement. This shift has significant implications for the regional balance of power, as traditional U.S. allies like **Saudi Arabia**, **Egypt**, and **the UAE** explore closer ties with Russia and China while maintaining their relationships with Washington.

The growing role of Russia and China in the Middle East represents a major shift in the region's geopolitical landscape.

As both countries expand their military and economic engagement with Middle Eastern states, they are increasingly shaping the outcomes of conflicts, influencing political alliances, and challenging the long-standing dominance of the U.S. While the U.S. remains a key player in the region, particularly in terms of military presence and security partnerships, the rise of Russia and China signals a new era of multipolarity in the Middle East, where multiple powers vie for influence and control over the region's resources and strategic locations. As this competition unfolds, the future of the Middle East will be shaped by the complex interplay between these global powers, with far-reaching consequences for regional stability and global security.

How Russia Capitalized on U.S. Failures in Syria and Libya

Russia's growing presence and influence in the **Middle East** are largely the result of its ability to exploit the power vacuums and instability left behind by U.S. interventions and foreign policy missteps, particularly in **Syria** and **Libya**. These two nations, both ravaged by civil wars and insurgencies, have become critical theaters for Russia to project its power, assert its geopolitical ambitions, and challenge U.S. influence in the region. Through a combination of military intervention, diplomatic maneuvering, and strategic alliances, Russia has capitalized on U.S. failures to not only stabilize these nations but also to position itself as an indispensable power broker in the Middle East.

Syria: Russia's Reentry as a Regional Power

Russia's intervention in **Syria** in **2015** was a turning point in the country's civil war and a defining moment for Moscow's resurgence as a major player in Middle Eastern geopolitics. The U.S.'s approach to the Syrian conflict, which began in

2011 as part of the **Arab Spring** uprisings, was marked by indecision, a lack of clear strategy, and failed attempts to balance supporting opposition forces with combating extremist groups like **ISIS** and **Jabhat al-Nusra**. As the war dragged on, the **Obama administration** hesitated to intervene directly, despite calls to support moderate rebel groups and enforce **red lines** following the Assad regime's use of **chemical weapons**.

This reluctance and strategic ambiguity on the part of the U.S. created an opportunity for Russia to step in decisively. **Vladimir Putin's** government, a longtime ally of **Bashar al-Assad**, viewed the survival of the Assad regime as critical to maintaining Russia's foothold in the Middle East and its access to the **Tartus** naval base, its only Mediterranean port. By the time Russia intervened, Syria was on the brink of collapse, with Assad's forces losing ground to a combination of rebel factions, Kurdish forces, and ISIS fighters. The U.S., preoccupied with its efforts to defeat ISIS and skeptical of deep involvement in another Middle Eastern war, was reluctant to fully engage in the complexities of Syria's civil conflict, allowing Russia to fill the vacuum.

Russia's military involvement, which began with **airstrikes** in support of Assad's forces, was initially framed as part of the global fight against terrorism, particularly against ISIS. However, it soon became clear that Russia's primary goal was to shore up Assad's regime by targeting not only ISIS but also Western-backed rebel groups that posed a threat to the Syrian government. Russian airpower, combined with ground support from **Iranian** militias and **Hezbollah**, played a decisive role in reversing the momentum of the war. The recapture of key cities, including **Aleppo**, marked significant victories for the Assad regime and cemented Russia's role as the dominant external power in Syria.

While the U.S. had focused much of its attention on the fight against ISIS in northern Syria, particularly through its support of **Kurdish-led forces** in the **Syrian Democratic Forces (SDF)**, Russia positioned itself as the protector of the Syrian state. This stark contrast between U.S. and Russian objectives in Syria—Washington's focus on terrorism and Moscow's emphasis on regime preservation—allowed Russia to present itself as a more reliable ally to Assad, and by extension, to other regimes in the region that feared regime change and Western intervention.

Russia also capitalized on the fragmented nature of the Syrian opposition, which was deeply divided between secular nationalist forces, Islamist groups, and Kurdish factions. The U.S. struggled to navigate these divisions, often finding itself supporting groups that were either ineffective or entangled with jihadist factions. Russia, on the other hand, maintained a clear and consistent strategy: backing Assad at all costs, while using its military and diplomatic leverage to marginalize opposition groups. This approach culminated in Moscow's leadership of the **Astana peace talks**, which excluded the U.S. and elevated Russia, along with **Turkey** and **Iran**, as the key arbiters of Syria's future.

The U.S.'s failure to establish a coherent long-term strategy in Syria, particularly after the fall of **Raqqa**, the de facto capital of ISIS, left a power vacuum that Russia eagerly filled. The withdrawal of U.S. troops from northeastern Syria in **2019** under the **Trump administration** further weakened Washington's influence in the region, alienating the **Kurds**, who had been pivotal in the fight against ISIS. This withdrawal, which was widely seen as an abandonment of America's Kurdish allies, not only allowed Turkish forces to invade Kurdish-controlled areas but also gave Russia and the Assad regime an opportunity to reassert control over parts of northern Syria.

By positioning itself as the primary foreign power capable

of securing Assad's regime and brokering peace, Russia effectively sidelined the U.S. in the resolution of the Syrian conflict. Moscow's diplomatic efforts in Syria, which included hosting multiple rounds of negotiations with Turkey and Iran, further solidified its role as a regional power broker. Russia's success in Syria demonstrated its ability to achieve military and diplomatic victories where the U.S. had faltered, presenting itself as a stable and decisive ally to other authoritarian regimes in the Middle East.

Libya: Russia's Strategic Maneuvering in a Fractured State

Libya, like Syria, became a focal point of Russia's efforts to capitalize on U.S. failures and extend its influence in the Middle East and **North Africa**. The **2011 NATO intervention** in Libya, which led to the overthrow of **Muammar Gaddafi**, was initially hailed as a success in terms of regime change. However, the aftermath of Gaddafi's fall quickly descended into chaos, as rival militias, Islamist groups, and tribal factions vied for control of the country. The U.S., which had played a key role in the NATO intervention, failed to provide the necessary support to stabilize Libya in the post-Gaddafi era, leaving the country fragmented and vulnerable to external influence.

The vacuum created by the collapse of the **Libyan state** was further exacerbated by the **Benghazi attack** in 2012, which highlighted the inability of the U.S. to maintain a secure presence in the country. As Libya descended into civil war, the U.S. became increasingly disengaged, focusing its attention on other regional conflicts. This disengagement provided Russia with an opportunity to reassert itself in Libya, a country that had long been within the Soviet sphere of influence during Gaddafi's rule.

Russia's strategy in Libya has been both pragmatic and opportunistic. Rather than backing any one faction unconditionally, Moscow has maintained contacts with a range of actors, including the **Government of National Accord (GNA)** in **Tripoli** and the forces loyal to **General Khalifa Haftar** in the east. Russia's primary military involvement has been through the deployment of **mercenaries** from the **Wagner Group**, a private military contractor with close ties to the Kremlin. These mercenaries have provided Haftar's forces with crucial support, particularly in their campaign to capture Tripoli in **2019** and **2020**.

Russia's backing of Haftar, who controls much of eastern Libya and its vast oil resources, has been driven by several strategic interests. First, Haftar's control of the **Libyan National Army (LNA)** and his influence over key oil-producing regions provide Russia with leverage over Libya's energy sector. Second, Haftar's strongman leadership aligns with Russia's broader strategy of supporting authoritarian figures who can provide stability, as opposed to the U.S. proclaimed emphasis on democratic transitions. Finally, Libya's geographic location at the crossroads of **Europe**, **Africa**, and the **Mediterranean** makes it a critical hub for controlling migration routes, energy supplies, and trade corridors.

By supporting Haftar, Russia has positioned itself as a key player in Libya's fractured political landscape. Moscow has provided Haftar's forces with arms, logistical support, and intelligence, while also engaging in diplomatic outreach to other factions. This multifaceted approach has allowed Russia to maintain flexibility in Libya, ensuring that it retains influence regardless of the outcome of the civil war. At the same time, Russia's involvement has complicated efforts by the **United Nations** and Western powers to broker a lasting peace settlement in Libya.

Russia's military and economic activities in Libya have also drawn it into competition with other foreign powers, particularly **Turkey**, which supports the GNA. The two countries, while aligned in Syria through the **Astana process**, have found themselves on opposite sides of the Libyan conflict. However, both Russia and Turkey have demonstrated a willingness to negotiate and de-escalate tensions in Libya, recognizing that their mutual interests in the region would be better served through cooperation rather than direct confrontation.

The U.S.'s absence from the Libyan peace process has allowed Russia to fill a critical diplomatic void, offering itself as a mediator between Haftar's forces and the GNA. This has been particularly evident in **Berlin**, where Russia has taken part in international peace talks aimed at stabilizing Libya. By participating in these talks and positioning itself as a power capable of influencing both sides of the conflict, Russia has further entrenched its role as a key player in determining Libya's future.

Broader Implications for U.S. Policy in the Region

Russia's ability to capitalize on U.S. failures in Syria and Libya has broader implications for American policy in the Middle East. Moscow's success in these two conflict zones highlights the dangers of U.S. disengagement and the challenges of maintaining influence in a region where authoritarian regimes, fragile states, and proxy wars are the norm. Russia has effectively used its military and diplomatic tools to fill the gaps left by U.S. indecision and missteps, positioning itself as a reliable partner for regimes seeking stability and security without the constraints of Western demands for democracy or human rights.

By expanding its influence in Syria and Libya, Russia has not only bolstered its standing in the Middle East but also enhanced its broader global strategy of challenging Western dominance. Moscow's actions in these countries demonstrate its willingness to act decisively when opportunities arise, even in the face of Western sanctions or diplomatic isolation. As the U.S. continues to navigate the complexities of its Middle Eastern policy, it must contend with the reality that Russia has become a formidable rival, capable of reshaping the geopolitical landscape of the region in ways that challenge U.S. interests and influence.

China's Growing Influence in the Middle East through Economic and Military Partnerships

China's influence in the **Middle East** has steadily grown over the past two decades, driven by a combination of **economic**, **diplomatic**, and **military** engagements that reflect its broader ambitions to establish itself as a global power. Unlike Russia, whose resurgence in the region has been marked by military interventions and direct involvement in conflicts, China has pursued a more measured approach, focusing primarily on **economic partnerships** and **infrastructure development**. This strategy has allowed China to expand its influence without becoming entangled in the political and sectarian complexities that often characterize Middle Eastern conflicts.

However, as China's presence in the Middle East deepens, it is beginning to play a more active role in regional security and diplomacy. Beijing's ability to broker a **ceasefire in the Yemeni civil war**, along with its growing military cooperation with Middle Eastern states, signals a shift in its role from a purely economic partner to a key player in the region's geopolitics. By leveraging its economic clout and positioning itself as a neutral, non-interventionist power, China has managed to build strategic relationships with states across the political spectrum—from **Saudi Arabia** and **Iran** to **Israel** and the **United Arab Emirates (UAE)**—without aligning itself too closely with any one faction.

China's influence in the Middle East, though often understated, is reshaping the region's dynamics. As the U.S. recalibrates its presence and Russia asserts itself through military means, China is steadily gaining ground by offering what many Middle Eastern states see as a more attractive model of engagement: one that is focused on mutual economic benefit, infrastructure development, and respect for sovereignty without the conditions often attached to Western partnerships, such as human rights and democratic reforms.

Economic Partnerships and the Belt and Road Initiative (BRI)

China's primary tool for expanding its influence in the Middle East has been the **Belt and Road Initiative (BRI)**, launched in **2013** by **President Xi Jinping**. The BRI is a vast infrastructure and investment program designed to enhance global trade routes and economic connectivity by building roads, railways, ports, and energy infrastructure that link **Asia**, **Europe**, and **Africa**. The Middle East is a critical region for the BRI, serving as both a geographic crossroads and a major source of **energy** for China's rapidly growing economy.

Through the BRI, China has invested billions of dollars in infrastructure projects across the Middle East, creating new trade corridors and strengthening its economic ties with key regional players. **Saudi Arabia**, **Iran**, **Iraq**, the UAE, and **Egypt** have all become important partners in China's BRI vision. These investments have focused on sectors such as **energy**, **transportation**, **technology**, and **logistics**, which are crucial for China's long-term energy security and economic growth.

In **Saudi Arabia**, China has played a central role in supporting the kingdom's ambitious **Vision 2030** development plan, which aims to diversify the Saudi economy away from oil dependence. Chinese companies have invested heavily in Saudi infrastructure projects, including the construction of **refineries**, **power plants**, and the development of the futuristic city of **NEOM**. In return, Saudi Arabia has become one of China's largest oil suppliers, with energy trade between the two nations forming the backbone of their economic relationship.

China's growing economic ties with **Iran** have also been a key component of its Middle East strategy. Despite U.S. sanctions, China has continued to purchase Iranian oil and invest in Iranian infrastructure, including ports, railways, and energy facilities. In **2021**, China and Iran signed a **25-year cooperation agreement** that includes commitments for Chinese investments in Iran's energy, infrastructure, and technology sectors. This agreement has allowed Iran to bypass some of the economic isolation imposed by U.S. sanctions while providing China with access to critical energy resources and strategic influence in the region.

Beyond its energy partnerships, China has also invested in **technology** and **telecommunications** infrastructure in the Middle East. Chinese tech giants like **Huawei** and **ZTE** have become major players in the region, building **5G networks** and providing **smart city** technologies to countries such as Saudi Arabia and the UAE. These investments are part of China's broader strategy to dominate the digital economy and position itself as a leader in the technology-driven future of the Middle East.

Diplomatic Engagement and China's Role as a Mediator

While China's economic partnerships in the Middle East are well-established, its diplomatic role in the region has traditionally been more restrained. Beijing has long adhered to a policy of **non-interference** in the internal affairs of other nations, preferring to maintain neutrality in regional conflicts and avoid taking sides in the complex sectarian and political rivalries that define the Middle East. This approach has allowed China to maintain good relations with rival powers such as **Saudi Arabia** and **Iran**, and it has positioned China as a neutral actor that can engage with all parties.

However, in recent years, China has begun to play a more active diplomatic role, particularly in efforts to resolve regional conflicts. One of the most significant examples of this shift came in **2023**, when China brokered a **ceasefire** in the **Yemeni Civil War**, a conflict that had been raging since **2015** between the **Iran-backed Houthi rebels** and the **Saudi-led coalition**. The war in Yemen had created one of the world's worst humanitarian crises, with millions displaced and thousands killed, and neither side had been able to achieve a decisive victory.

China's involvement in brokering the ceasefire in Yemen demonstrated its growing influence in Middle Eastern diplomacy and its ability to act as a mediator between rival powers. The ceasefire negotiations were facilitated by China's broader diplomatic efforts to improve relations between **Saudi Arabia** and **Iran**, two of the key actors in the Yemeni conflict. In **March 2023**, China successfully brokered a rapprochement between Riyadh and Tehran, which had long been at odds over their competing interests in Yemen, Syria, Iraq, and Lebanon.

The Chinese-brokered deal between **Saudi Arabia** and **Iran** involved a series of concessions from both sides, including the lifting of the Saudi blockade on Yemen's main port and the resumption of flights into **Sana'a**, the Houthi-controlled capital. These concessions, coupled with China's diplomatic pressure on both parties, paved the way for ceasefire talks and a potential end to the conflict. While the ceasefire has not yet fully ended the war, it represents a significant step toward de-escalation and underscores China's emerging role as a peacemaker in the region.

China's ability to broker peace in Yemen, a conflict in which the U.S. had long backed Saudi Arabia and opposed the Houthis, highlights a key difference in diplomatic approaches.

Whereas the U.S. has often relied on **military interventions** and **sanctions** to achieve its objectives in the Middle East, China has positioned itself as a neutral power focused on diplomacy, economic cooperation, and stability. This approach has won China considerable goodwill among regional leaders, who see Beijing as a reliable partner with no ulterior political or ideological agenda.

The **Yemen ceasefire** is not the only example of China's expanding diplomatic role in the Middle East. China has also been involved in efforts to mediate disputes between **Israel** and **Palestine**, calling for dialogue and a two-state solution. Although China's influence in the **Israeli-Palestinian conflict** remains limited compared to that of the U.S., Beijing's willingness to engage in diplomacy reflects its broader ambitions to be seen as a responsible global power capable of resolving international conflicts.

Military Partnerships and Arms Sales

While China's primary focus in the Middle East has been on economic partnerships, it has also expanded its **military presence** and **defense partnerships** in the region. Unlike Russia and the U.S., which have established large military bases and conducted extensive combat operations in the Middle East, China's military footprint remains relatively small. However, China's **strategic military base in Djibouti**, located at the southern entrance to the **Red Sea**, is a significant part of its broader security strategy in the region.

Opened in **2017**, the Djibouti base is China's first overseas military installation and serves as a key hub for **anti-piracy operations**, **peacekeeping missions**, and **maritime security** in the **Gulf of Aden** and the **Indian Ocean**. The base allows China to protect its shipping routes, secure its energy supplies, and project military power in a region critical to global trade. While the Djibouti base is relatively small compared to U.S. and

French military installations in the area, it symbolizes China's growing military ambitions beyond its borders.

In addition to establishing military infrastructure, China has also become an increasingly important player in **arms sales** to Middle Eastern states. Chinese arms manufacturers, including **Norinco** and **AVIC**, have supplied a range of weapons systems to countries such as Saudi Arabia, the UAE, and Egypt. These sales include **drones**, **missile systems**, and **armored vehicles**, which have been used by Gulf states in their military operations in Yemen and elsewhere.

China's arms sales in the Middle East are part of its broader strategy to diversify its defense partnerships and reduce the region's reliance on U.S. and European weapons systems. By providing affordable and reliable military hardware without the political strings often attached to Western arms deals, China has positioned itself as an attractive partner for states seeking to bolster their defense capabilities.

The Shifting Balance of Power in the Middle East

The **Middle East**, long characterized by its strategic importance and political volatility, is undergoing a significant shift in the balance of power. For much of the 20th century and into the early 21st century, the United States has been the dominant external force in the region, shaping its political landscape through military interventions, economic aid, and alliances with key regional players. However, in recent years, the region has seen a recalibration of power dynamics, driven by both the rise of external actors like **Russia** and **China**, and internal developments such as the **Arab Spring**, the **Iran nuclear deal**, and the **fall of authoritarian regimes**. This shifting balance of power is transforming the geopolitical landscape, as traditional alliances are tested, and new coalitions emerge.

Several factors contribute to this shift, including the **waning influence of the U.S.**, the growing involvement of Russia and China, the changing ambitions of regional powers like **Saudi Arabia**, **Iran**, **Turkey**, and **Israel**, and the broader geopolitical realignment following U.S. military withdrawals from the region. As the balance of power shifts, regional actors are recalibrating their strategies, forging new alliances, and exploring alternative sources of military, economic, and diplomatic support.

Waning US Influence in the Middle East

For decades, the U.S. has been the key player in the Middle East, securing its influence through a combination of military interventions, economic aid, and strategic alliances with countries like **Saudi Arabia**, **Israel**, **Egypt**, and **Jordan**. Washington's dominance was cemented by its military presence in the region, its involvement in key conflicts like the **Gulf War**, and its central role in brokering peace agreements, most notably the **Camp David Accords** and the **Oslo Accords**.

However, the U.S.'s influence in the Middle East has been declining steadily over the past decade. The withdrawal of American forces from **Iraq** in **2011**, followed by the decision to pull troops out of **Afghanistan** in **2021**, marked significant moments in the U.S.'s disengagement from direct military involvement in the region. These withdrawals, coupled with the **Obama administration's" pivot to Asia"** and the **Trump administration's" America First"** foreign policy, signaled a shift away from the traditional U.S. focus on the Middle East as a primary theater of global geopolitics.

One of the most consequential events contributing to the perception of U.S. decline in the region was the **Syrian Civil War**. The U.S.'s failure to enforce its **red line** on the use of chemical weapons by the Assad regime, coupled with a lack of clear strategy in supporting Syrian rebel groups, allowed **Russia** to step in and fill the void. By 2015, Russia's military intervention in Syria, which included airstrikes and ground support for the Assad regime, demonstrated Moscow's willingness to assert itself as a decisive power in the Middle East, while the U.S. appeared increasingly reluctant to engage.

The U.S.'s failure to prevent the resurgence of **Iran** and its proxy forces, particularly in **Iraq**, **Syria**, and **Lebanon**, further contributed to the perception of declining American influence. While Washington has maintained sanctions and diplomatic pressure on Iran, its efforts to contain Tehran's influence have been complicated by Iran's ability to leverage proxy groups like **Hezbollah**, the **Houthis**, and **Shia militias** in Iraq to expand its regional footprint. The **Iran nuclear deal (JCPOA)**, negotiated under the **Obama administration** and abandoned by the **Trump administration**, has also been a point of contention, as it highlighted divisions within the U.S. foreign policy establishment and contributed to uncertainty among U.S. allies in the region.

In contrast to the U.S., **Russia** and **China** have capitalized on this period of American retrenchment, offering themselves as reliable alternatives to Middle Eastern regimes seeking military support, investment, and diplomatic backing.

Russia's Military Intervention and Political Influence

Russia's role in the Middle East has undergone a dramatic resurgence, particularly in the aftermath of its **2015 intervention in Syria**. The Kremlin's military support for **Bashar al-Assad** turned the tide of the civil war in Assad's favor, solidifying Russia's position as a key power broker in the region. By providing **air support**, **weapons**, and **diplomatic backing**, Russia ensured the survival of the Assad regime while marginalizing Western-backed rebel groups. Russia's intervention in Syria not only reestablished Moscow as a military power in the Middle East but also allowed it to showcase its ability to shape outcomes in regional conflicts.

In addition to its military role in Syria, Russia has expanded its political influence across the region by forging relationships with key actors on both sides of the region's political and sectarian divides. Russia has maintained strong ties with **Iran**, aligning with Tehran in their mutual support for Assad and their opposition to U.S. influence in the region. At the same time, Russia has cultivated relationships with traditional U.S. allies like **Israel** and **Saudi Arabia**. In **2017**, Saudi King **Salman** made a historic visit to **Moscow**, signaling a shift in Saudi Arabia's foreign policy and an acknowledgment of Russia's growing importance in the region.

Russia's ability to maintain relationships with opposing forces—whether between Iran and Saudi Arabia, or Israel and Syria—has positioned Moscow as a versatile mediator capable of navigating the region's complex dynamics. This has been particularly evident in Russia's role in the **Astana peace talks** for Syria, where Russia, alongside **Turkey** and Iran, has taken the lead in shaping the future of post-conflict Syria. By inserting itself as a central player in these negotiations, Russia has sidelined the U.S. and European powers, further enhancing its role as a key power broker in the region.

In **Libya**, Russia has also played a significant role in shaping the outcome of the country's civil war. Through its support for **General Khalifa Haftar** and the **Libyan National Army (LNA)**, Russia has backed Haftar's bid for control over eastern Libya. While Haftar's offensive to capture **Tripoli** ultimately failed, Russia's involvement in the conflict—primarily through **Wagner Group** mercenaries and military support—has given Moscow considerable influence over Libya's future.

Russia's strategy in the Middle East is rooted in **pragmatism** and **opportunism**, using military interventions, arms sales, and diplomatic mediation to advance its interests. While the U.S. remains preoccupied with broader geopolitical issues, such as its rivalry with China and the ongoing conflict in Ukraine, Russia has exploited the power vacuums left by U.S. disengagement to entrench itself in the Middle East, particularly in areas where the U.S. has faltered.

China's Economic Engagement and Diplomatic Influence

China's approach to the Middle East differs significantly from Russia's, focusing more on **economic partnerships** and **diplomatic engagement** than direct military involvement. Through its ambitious **Belt and Road Initiative (BRI)**, China has sought to integrate the Middle East into its global infrastructure and trade network, investing billions of dollars in ports, railways, energy infrastructure, and technology projects across the region.

China's growing economic presence in the Middle East is perhaps best exemplified by its partnerships with energy-rich states like **Saudi Arabia**, **Iran**, and **Iraq**. As the world's largest importer of oil, China relies heavily on Middle Eastern producers to meet its energy needs. This economic interdependence has driven China's engagement with the region, as Beijing seeks to secure stable energy supplies while expanding its influence through investment and trade.

China's **neutrality** and **non-interference** policy in Middle Eastern conflicts has also allowed it to maintain positive relationships with rival powers, such as **Saudi Arabia** and **Iran**. This neutrality has positioned China as a potential mediator in regional disputes, as evidenced by its role in brokering the **2023 rapprochement** between Saudi Arabia and Iran, which paved the way for ceasefire talks in **Yemen**. China's success in facilitating this agreement demonstrated its growing diplomatic clout and its ability to challenge the traditional U.S. role as a mediator in Middle Eastern conflicts.

China's military presence in the region, while more limited than that of the U.S. or Russia, is also expanding. In **2017**,

China established its first overseas military base in **Djibouti**, giving it a strategic foothold near key maritime chokepoints in the **Red Sea** and the **Indian Ocean**. The base allows China to protect its shipping routes and support its growing role in international peacekeeping and anti-piracy operations in the **Gulf of Aden**.

China's strategy in the Middle East is rooted in its long-term economic and geopolitical interests. While it has been careful to avoid becoming directly involved in the region's military conflicts, its growing investments and diplomatic engagement have made it an increasingly important actor in shaping the region's future.

Assertiveness of Regional Powers: Saudi Arabia, Iran, and Turkey

The shifting balance of power in the Middle East is not only driven by external actors like Russia and China but also by the changing ambitions of regional powers such as **Saudi Arabia**, **Iran**, and **Turkey**. These nations have been key players in shaping the region's politics, and as external powers reposition themselves, so too are these regional actors recalibrating their strategies to align with the new geopolitical realities.

Saudi Arabia, long a cornerstone of U.S. influence in the region, has begun to diversify its foreign policy, engaging more actively with Russia and China. The kingdom's desire to move away from oil dependency, as outlined in its **Vision 2030** plan, has driven its search for new economic partners and investments, leading to closer ties with China in areas such as **technology**, **energy**, and **infrastructure**. At the same time, Saudi Arabia's relationship with Russia has deepened, particularly in the context of **OPEC+** agreements to manage global oil production and prices.

Iran, meanwhile, has been able to withstand years of

U.S. sanctions and diplomatic isolation by strengthening its relationships with Russia and China. The **Iran-China 25-year cooperation agreement**, signed in 2021, signaled a deepening economic and strategic partnership between the two countries. For Tehran, the agreement represents an opportunity to bypass U.S. sanctions, secure foreign investment, and strengthen its hand in regional conflicts where it remains heavily involved through proxy forces.

Turkey, under the leadership of **Recep Tayyip Erdoğan**, has pursued an increasingly independent foreign policy, engaging in regional conflicts in **Syria**, **Libya**, and the **Eastern Mediterranean**. Turkey's relationship with Russia has been complex, as the two nations have found themselves on opposite sides of several conflicts, but they have also cooperated on issues such as Syria and energy. Turkey's desire to position itself as a regional power, capable of balancing relationships with both Western and Eastern powers, reflects its broader ambitions to play a leading role in the shifting geopolitical order of the Middle East.

As the Middle East continues to undergo these changes, the balance of power is likely to remain fluid. Russia's military interventions and China's economic diplomacy are reshaping the region, creating new opportunities for regional actors to forge alliances and assert their influence. At the same time, the U.S. must contend with the reality that its dominance in the region is no longer assured, as Middle Eastern states explore alternative partnerships and realign their foreign policies in response to the new geopolitical dynamics.

CHAPTER 15 -. REFLECTIONS ON U.S. FOREIGN POLICY: LESSONS LEARNED AND THE PATH FORWARD

Long-term Consequences of U.S. interventions in the Middle East

As we reflect on the trajectory of U.S. foreign policy, particularly in the **Middle East**, the record of interventions, while grounded in various strategic interests, leaves behind a trail of significant, often unintended, consequences. From the coup in Iran in **1953**, the invasion of **Iraq** in **2003**, to the more recent **withdrawal from Afghanistan**, the outcomes of American military, economic, and political actions have frequently diverged from the initial goals set by U.S. policymakers. Each of these interventions, framed in the language of protecting national security, promoting democracy, or containing adversaries, has led to profound shifts in regional dynamics, often undermining U.S. influence and credibility over time.

When we analyze these foreign policy decisions, it becomes evident that while U.S. interventions often sought to secure short-term objectives—whether they were tied to **oil**, **counterterrorism**, or **geopolitical dominance**—the long-term consequences were frequently counterproductive. As a result, what emerges is a complex and deeply paradoxical narrative of American involvement in the Middle East: interventions that were initially intended to stabilize the region have, more often than not, contributed to its fragmentation, sowing the seeds of future conflict and insecurity.

In examining these long-term consequences, it is essential to understand that the U.S. approach to the Middle East has been marked by a recurring pattern of **short-termism**—an inability or unwillingness to account for the deeper political, social, and cultural dynamics at play within the region. This failure to consider the broader implications of intervention has not only led to the unintended strengthening of adversaries, such as **Iran** and **Russia**, but has also contributed to the rise of non-state actors like **ISIS** and **al-Qaeda**, whose influence and impact continue to reverberate across the region and beyond.

The invasion of Iraq in 2003 serves as one of the most illustrative examples of how U.S. foreign policy, driven by a desire to oust **Saddam Hussein** and eliminate the perceived threat of **weapons of mass destruction**, ultimately created a **power vacuum** that destabilized the entire region. The toppling of Saddam's regime did not bring about the democratic transformation that U.S. leaders had envisioned. Instead, it triggered a sectarian conflict that engulfed the country, leading to a protracted civil war and the rise of **ISIS**. By dismantling Iraq's state apparatus and marginalizing its **Sunni** population, the U.S. inadvertently fostered the conditions for extremism to flourish, empowering jihadist groups that had once been contained.

The lessons from Iraq were stark, yet the U.S. approach to

intervention seemed to repeat many of the same mistakes in subsequent conflicts. In **Libya**, for instance, the **NATO-backed intervention** that led to the overthrow of **Muammar Gaddafi** was celebrated in the West as a triumph of humanitarian intervention. Yet, like in Iraq, the removal of a dictator without a clear plan for post-regime stabilization left the country fractured and in chaos. Libya soon descended into civil war, becoming a battleground for rival militias, extremist groups, and foreign powers vying for control. The instability that followed Gaddafi's ouster not only destabilized Libya but also contributed to the broader regional crisis, with arms and fighters flowing across borders into **Mali**, **Syria**, and **Yemen**, exacerbating conflicts in these countries.

The **Syrian civil war** further highlights the long-term consequences of U.S. interventions—or, in this case, the consequences of both intervention and non-intervention. When the Syrian uprising began in 2011, the U.S. found itself in a dilemma: how to support the opposition to **Bashar al-Assad** without becoming embroiled in another Middle Eastern conflict. The result was a piecemeal approach that saw the U.S. provide limited support to moderate rebel groups while avoiding direct confrontation with Assad's forces. This hesitancy allowed **Russia** to step in decisively in 2015, shifting the balance of power in Assad's favor and securing Moscow's foothold in the region. Meanwhile, extremist factions like **Jabhat al-Nusra** and **ISIS** filled the vacuum left by the collapse of state authority, prolonging the conflict and further destabilizing the region.

One of the most significant consequences of these interventions has been the **erosion of U.S. credibility** and the rise of alternative powers—most notably **Russia** and **China**—in the Middle East. The U.S.'s inability to secure lasting peace or stability in the countries where it intervened has led many regional actors to seek out new alliances, often turning to Moscow and Beijing as alternative patrons. Russia's decisive military intervention in Syria, coupled with its diplomatic efforts in **Libya** and **Egypt**, has allowed it to reassert itself as a major power in the region. China, meanwhile, has pursued a more subtle strategy, expanding its economic influence through **infrastructure investments** and **energy partnerships** while avoiding the political entanglements that have plagued U.S. policy.

China's role in **brokering a ceasefire** in the **Yemeni civil war**—an outcome the U.S. had been unable to achieve despite years of support for the **Saudi-led coalition**—further demonstrates how Beijing has capitalized on U.S. missteps. By positioning itself as a neutral, non-interventionist power, China has been able to engage with both Saudi Arabia and Iran, mediating conflicts and building long-term economic ties without the burden of military involvement. This shift underscores a broader trend in the region: as the U.S. grapples with the legacy of its interventions, other powers are stepping in to fill the void, often with more pragmatic, less ideologically driven approaches.

The long-term consequences of U.S. interventions are not limited to the rise of new powers and the proliferation of non-state actors. They also include the **humanitarian crises** that have followed in the wake of these conflicts. The wars in Iraq, Afghanistan, Syria, Libya, and Yemen have collectively displaced millions of people, creating one of the largest refugee crises in modern history. The U.S.'s failure to anticipate or mitigate the social and economic impact of these interventions has left the region in a state of perpetual crisis, with refugees and internally displaced persons (IDPs) facing dire conditions in camps across **Jordan**, **Lebanon**, **Turkey**, and Europe.

At the heart of these issues is a fundamental problem with U.S. foreign policy: the tendency to prioritize **military solutions** over **diplomatic engagement** and **long-term development**.

While military force has been effective in achieving short-term objectives, such as the removal of dictators or the defeat of terrorist groups, it has rarely succeeded in creating the conditions for lasting peace. In many cases, U.S. interventions have failed to address the underlying political, economic, and social grievances that give rise to conflict in the first place. The focus on counterterrorism and regime change, without a corresponding emphasis on state-building and governance reform, has led to a cycle of intervention, withdrawal, and re-intervention that has left the region more unstable than before.

As the U.S. looks toward the future, there are important lessons to be learned from the mistakes of the past. First, there is a need for greater **humility** in recognizing the limits of American power, particularly in regions as complex and volatile as the Middle East. The idea that the U.S. can reshape the political landscape of other nations through military force or economic pressure has proven to be a fallacy. Instead, U.S. policymakers must adopt a more nuanced approach that emphasizes diplomacy, multilateralism, and the importance of regional actors in shaping their own futures.

Second, the U.S. must shift away from a purely **counterterrorism**-driven foreign policy in the Middle East. While the threat of terrorism remains a significant concern, the focus on eliminating terrorist groups has often obscured the larger issues of governance, economic development, and social justice that are essential to long-term stability. A more holistic approach, one that addresses the root causes of extremism—such as poverty, corruption, and political disenfranchisement—will be necessary if the U.S. hopes to prevent the rise of future insurgencies and extremist movements.

Finally, the U.S. must recognize the importance of **sustained engagement** and **diplomatic leadership** in the region. The withdrawal of U.S. forces from Iraq and Afghanistan, while necessary to end long-standing wars, has left a vacuum that other powers have quickly moved to fill. If the U.S. is to maintain any influence in the Middle East, it must remain actively involved in the region's diplomatic processes, supporting peace negotiations, facilitating economic development, and working with both allies and adversaries to create a more stable and secure future.

The path forward for U.S. foreign policy in the Middle East will not be easy, and it will require a fundamental rethinking of how the U.S. engages with the region. The legacy of past interventions, from the coup in Iran to the wars in Iraq and Afghanistan, offers a cautionary tale about the dangers of overreach and the limits of military power. But it also provides valuable lessons about the importance of diplomacy, patience, and pragmatism in navigating the complex and ever-evolving dynamics of the Middle East.

Potential Strategies for Future Engagement in the Middle East and Beyond

As the U.S. contemplates its future role in the **Middle East** and the broader geopolitical landscape, it faces a region that is vastly different from the one it dominated for much of the late 20th and early 21st centuries. The challenges of the past —such as counterterrorism, regime change, and oil security —have not disappeared, but they have evolved in the context of a shifting global order. The rise of regional powers like **Iran**, the growing influence of non-Western actors such as **China** and **Russia**, and the changing nature of conflicts, which increasingly involve **non-state actors** and **proxy forces**, have created a complex web of political, economic, and security concerns that will require new strategies for U.S. engagement.

For the U.S., the days of unilateral military interventions, large-scale nation-building projects, and regime-change policies are largely behind it. The experiences in **Iraq**, **Afghanistan**, **Libya**, and **Syria** have demonstrated the limitations of such approaches. What is needed now is a more nuanced, long-term strategy that prioritizes **diplomacy**, **multilateralism**, and the **stabilization** of fragile states, while also addressing the root causes of conflict and extremism. This shift will involve rethinking not just how the U.S. engages with the Middle East but how it approaches global engagement in a multipolar world where its influence is increasingly challenged by rising powers and regional dynamics.

1. Emphasizing Diplomacy and Multilateralism

A key lesson from the U.S.'s past interventions is the necessity of **diplomatic engagement** over military solutions. While military force may be required in specific instances, such as fighting terrorism or protecting U.S. interests, the long-term success of U.S. foreign policy in the Middle East will depend on its ability to facilitate and participate in diplomatic processes that promote **peace**, **cooperation**, and **regional stability**.

One potential strategy for future engagement is a renewed commitment to **multilateralism**. This means working with **regional organizations** such as the **Arab League**, the **Gulf Cooperation Council (GCC)**, and **African Union**, as well as with global institutions like the **United Nations** and **NATO**, to build consensus and coordinate responses to regional crises. Multilateral diplomacy should also include partnerships with non-Western actors like China and Russia, recognizing that these powers now play a central role in shaping the Middle East's future.

Multilateral approaches to conflicts such as the ongoing **civil war in Yemen** have shown promise, especially in light of recent efforts by China to broker a ceasefire between **Saudi Arabia** and the **Houthi rebels**. The U.S. must be prepared to engage constructively with these new dynamics, supporting peace efforts and encouraging regional actors to take the lead in resolving their own conflicts. This will require a shift from the traditional U.S. posture of dominance to one of partnership, where the U.S. plays a supportive rather than directive role in regional diplomacy.

Additionally, the U.S. should prioritize **track two diplomacy** —informal, behind-the-scenes engagement with non-governmental actors, civil society, and opposition groups. This type of diplomacy can help build trust and lay the groundwork for more formal negotiations. Engaging with a wide array of stakeholders, particularly in countries with fragile political systems like **Lebanon**, **Iraq**, and **Libya**, is crucial for fostering inclusive peace processes that address the needs and grievances of marginalized populations.

2. Addressing Economic Stability and Development

Another critical aspect of future U.S. engagement must focus on promoting **economic stability** and **development** in the Middle East. Many of the region's conflicts are fueled by **economic inequality**, **unemployment**, and the failure of governments to provide basic services to their populations. Extremist groups, such as **ISIS** and **al-Qaeda**, have been able to exploit these economic grievances, offering disenfranchised individuals an alternative source of income and purpose.

The U.S. can play a pivotal role in fostering economic development by promoting **public-private partnerships** that encourage investment in infrastructure, technology, and education. Rather than focusing exclusively on military aid, the U.S. should direct its resources toward **human development** initiatives that empower local economies, particularly in post-conflict countries like Iraq and Syria. The **Marshall Plan**, which helped rebuild Europe after World War II, could serve as a model for a similar initiative in the Middle

East, where rebuilding war-torn economies and infrastructure is essential to achieving long-term stability.

One avenue for U.S. engagement could be supporting **regional trade agreements** and **economic integration** initiatives that promote cooperation among Middle Eastern countries. For instance, encouraging greater economic ties between **Gulf states**, **North Africa**, and **South Asia** could create new opportunities for trade and investment, reducing the region's dependence on oil exports and diversifying its economies. The U.S. could also play a key role in facilitating **green energy projects** and **renewable energy** initiatives, which align with global efforts to combat climate change while offering Middle Eastern economies a path toward diversification.

By investing in **education** and **skills training** for the region's youth, the U.S. can also address one of the root causes of instability: the high rates of unemployment and lack of opportunities for young people. Providing technical assistance and promoting **entrepreneurship** can empower local populations, reducing their vulnerability to extremist ideologies.

3. Counterterrorism with a Focus on Governance and Human Security

While counterterrorism will remain a critical component of U.S. foreign policy in the Middle East, it is essential that the U.S. adopt a more **comprehensive** and **holistic** approach to combating extremism. The traditional counterterrorism strategy—centered around military operations, drone strikes, and intelligence gathering—has often been effective in eliminating specific threats, but it has not addressed the underlying conditions that allow extremism to flourish.

Future U.S. counterterrorism efforts should focus more on **strengthening governance**, improving **rule of law**, and promoting **human security**. This means working with regional governments to build institutions that are capable of providing security, justice, and economic opportunities to their populations. Countries like **Somalia** and **Mali**, which have struggled with weak governance and lawlessness, need sustained support in building the capacities of their governments to combat extremism without relying on foreign intervention.

Security sector reform is also a crucial element of future counterterrorism strategy. In many Middle Eastern countries, the security forces themselves have contributed to instability through corruption, abuse, and human rights violations. The U.S. should use its leverage as a key provider of military aid to promote reforms that make security forces more accountable to civilian authorities, more respectful of human rights, and better equipped to protect their populations from both internal and external threats.

In the fight against non-state actors like **ISIS** and **al-Qaeda**, the U.S. should emphasize **counter-messaging** and **de-radicalization** efforts that challenge extremist ideologies. Working with local governments, civil society, and religious leaders, the U.S. can help develop narratives that counter the appeal of jihadist movements, focusing on positive alternatives that emphasize education, employment, and community engagement. By addressing the ideological and psychological dimensions of extremism, the U.S. can play a role in preventing the next generation of jihadists from emerging.

4. Supporting Political Reforms and Inclusive Governance

One of the most significant lessons from U.S. interventions in the Middle East is the importance of supporting **political reforms** and **inclusive governance**. Many of the region's conflicts have been driven by political exclusion, authoritarianism, and the failure of governments to represent their populations. Extremist groups have thrived in environments where citizens feel disenfranchised and alienated from the political process.

The U.S. must balance its strategic interests with the promotion of **democratic principles** and **human rights**. While the U.S. has often prioritized security and counterterrorism over political reform, this approach has sometimes contributed to the very instability it seeks to prevent. Supporting autocratic regimes at the expense of political openness can create resentment, fuel opposition movements, and increase the likelihood of future conflict.

To avoid these outcomes, the U.S. should adopt a more consistent approach to promoting **good governance** and **political inclusivity** in the Middle East. This does not mean imposing Western-style democracy, but rather supporting local efforts to build more accountable and transparent political systems. The U.S. should work with regional governments, civil society, and international organizations to promote **electoral reforms**, strengthen **judicial independence**, and encourage **freedom of the press**. It should also be willing to hold its allies accountable when they engage in repressive tactics, such as cracking down on opposition movements or curtailing civil liberties.

In countries where transitions to democracy are already underway—such as **Tunisia** and **Lebanon**—the U.S. should provide technical assistance and financial support to help these transitions succeed. In more authoritarian states, such as **Egypt** and **Saudi Arabia**, the U.S. should engage in quiet diplomacy, encouraging incremental reforms that expand political participation and human rights.

5. Engaging with Regional Powers: Iran, Turkey, and Saudi Arabia

Another critical component of future U.S. strategy in the

Middle East will involve managing its relationships with **regional powers**—particularly **Iran**, **Turkey**, and **Saudi Arabia**—which will continue to shape the region's political and security dynamics.

With **Iran**, the U.S. faces one of its most complex and enduring foreign policy challenges. The **nuclear issue**, Iran's support for proxy forces, and its regional ambitions have long placed Tehran at odds with Washington. However, the U.S. must also recognize that isolation and sanctions alone are unlikely to achieve a sustainable solution. A more balanced approach, involving diplomacy and engagement, could provide an opportunity to address Iran's security concerns while reducing its destabilizing activities in the region.

In the case of **Turkey**, the U.S. must navigate the complex relationship with a **NATO** ally that has increasingly pursued an independent foreign policy. Turkey's involvement in conflicts in **Syria**, **Libya**, and the **Eastern Mediterranean**—along with its growing ties to **Russia**—requires careful management. While the U.S. should maintain its alliance with Turkey, it must also encourage Ankara to pursue a more cooperative regional role, particularly in resolving the conflict in Syria and addressing the Kurdish issue.

Saudi Arabia remains a key U.S. ally, but the relationship has become more complicated in recent years due to issues like the **Yemeni civil war**. The U.S. should continue to work closely with Saudi Arabia on issues of mutual interest, such as counterterrorism and energy security, while also pushing for reforms that improve human rights and reduce the kingdom's reliance on military solutions in conflicts like Yemen.

By adopting a more **balanced** and **long-term** approach to its relationships with these regional powers, the U.S. can promote greater stability and cooperation in the Middle East.

The future of U.S. foreign policy in the Middle East—

and beyond—will require a **holistic** approach that balances military strength with **diplomacy, economic development**, and **good governance**. As the U.S. shifts away from large-scale interventions, it must embrace a strategy that emphasizes regional partnerships, multilateral cooperation, and a commitment to addressing the root causes of conflict. This path forward will not be easy, but with careful planning, the U.S. can play a constructive role in shaping a more stable, prosperous, and peaceful Middle East.

Understanding Historical Context to Avoid Repeating Past Mistakes

Understanding the **historical context** of U.S. interventions in the Middle East and beyond is crucial for developing a more effective and sustainable foreign policy. The past is replete with examples where the failure to grasp the intricate political, social, and cultural dynamics of a region has led to unintended consequences, many of which continue to reverberate through the present. From the overthrow of **Mohammad Mosaddegh** in Iran in **1953** to the invasion of **Iraq** in **2003**, U.S. foreign policy has often been shaped by immediate strategic or geopolitical goals, without fully accounting for the long-term implications of its actions. This lack of understanding, or in some cases willful disregard of historical and regional complexities, has frequently led to the very instability that U.S. interventions sought to prevent.

The importance of historical context becomes clear when examining the motivations and consequences of key interventions. Take, for example, the **1953 coup in Iran**, where the U.S., driven by Cold War anxieties and economic interests in Iranian oil, helped orchestrate the overthrow of a democratically elected government. The immediate goal—securing a pro-Western regime in Tehran—was achieved, but the longer-term consequences were far more damaging. The coup set the stage for decades of authoritarian rule under the Shah, fueling anti-Western sentiment and contributing to the **1979 Islamic Revolution**, which fundamentally transformed Iran into a theocratic state deeply hostile to U.S. interests. By failing to anticipate how its actions would alienate the Iranian population and radicalize opposition movements, the U.S. inadvertently helped create one of its most enduring adversaries in the region.

Similarly, the U.S. intervention in Iraq in 2003, which aimed to remove **Saddam Hussein** and promote democracy, ignored the profound sectarian divisions within the country and the delicate balance of power that had kept those tensions in check. The removal of Saddam's regime not only unleashed a brutal **sectarian civil war** but also created a **power vacuum** that allowed **ISIS** to emerge as a potent force, destabilizing Iraq and the broader region. By overlooking Iraq's historical complexities and internal divisions, U.S. policymakers repeated many of the same mistakes that had been made in earlier interventions, such as the failure to plan for the post-conflict reconstruction of Afghanistan.

The recurring theme in these interventions is a short-term focus on achieving immediate objectives—whether countering communism during the Cold War or eliminating a perceived security threat in the post-9/11 era—without adequately considering the long-term effects of U.S. actions on the political and social fabric of the countries involved. This pattern has been driven, in part, by a belief in the universality of Western political and economic models, and a corresponding assumption that the removal of authoritarian leaders will naturally lead to democratic transitions and stable governance. In reality, however, the imposition of external models has often clashed with local realities, leading to instability, resistance, and the rise of insurgent or extremist movements.

Historical context is also essential when assessing the role of **proxy forces** in U.S. foreign policy. The U.S. has repeatedly armed and supported local groups—whether in **Afghanistan**, **Libya**, or **Syria**—in the belief that these proxies would serve American interests by fighting against common enemies. Yet time and again, these groups have either turned against the U.S. or contributed to further destabilization. The support for the **mujahideen** in Afghanistan during the **Soviet-Afghan War** is a classic example. While the U.S. succeeded in its short-term objective of weakening the Soviet Union, it failed to foresee how the very forces it empowered would later evolve into **al-Qaeda** and the **Taliban**, leading to decades of conflict that culminated in the **9/11 attacks**.

Another clear case of the failure to account for historical context is found in the **Libyan intervention** in **2011**, which led to the fall of **Muammar Gaddafi**. The intervention, justified on humanitarian grounds, resulted in the overthrow of a long-standing dictator but also plunged Libya into chaos. The absence of a clear plan for post-Gaddafi Libya, combined with the country's complex tribal dynamics and lack of strong institutions, resulted in a fractured state, with competing militias and extremist groups vying for control. The U.S. and its NATO allies, by ignoring the lessons of Iraq and Afghanistan, repeated the mistake of removing a dictator without adequately preparing for the aftermath.

A deep understanding of historical context would also have shaped the U.S.'s approach to **Syria**, where the civil war that began in 2011 presented a complex and deeply entrenched conflict. U.S. support for moderate rebel factions, while part of a broader strategy to weaken **Bashar al-Assad** and counter ISIS, failed to account for the historical role of sectarianism and external powers in Syria's internal politics. The fragmented nature of the opposition, the influence of jihadist groups, and the involvement of **Russia** and **Iran** all made a simple solution to the conflict impossible.

Without understanding these dynamics, U.S. policymakers found themselves entangled in a conflict that spiraled out of control, resulting in a humanitarian disaster and further strengthening Assad's regime.

Beyond the Middle East, historical context is crucial for understanding how U.S. actions can have global repercussions. The legacy of U.S. interventions has not only affected the countries directly involved but also reshaped the broader international order. The war in Iraq, for example, not only destabilized the Middle East but also contributed to the rise of anti-American sentiment worldwide, particularly in Europe, where many countries opposed the invasion. This shift in global public opinion weakened U.S. alliances and provided opportunities for rising powers like **China** and **Russia** to expand their influence, offering alternative models of governance and economic development to countries disillusioned with the Western liberal order.

One of the key lessons from this history is that U.S. foreign policy must move beyond the **one-size-fits-all** approach to intervention and adopt a more nuanced, context-specific strategy that recognizes the diversity of political, cultural, and social conditions in different regions. This means investing in **diplomatic expertise**, **cultural knowledge**, and long-term **engagement** with local actors, rather than relying solely on military solutions or short-term political gains. It also requires a deeper understanding of the historical grievances and aspirations of the populations involved, many of whom view U.S. actions through the lens of colonialism, imperialism, or foreign domination.

A more historically informed U.S. foreign policy would also recognize the importance of **regional actors** and **multilateral frameworks** in addressing conflicts. In many cases, the U.S. has acted unilaterally or with limited international support, often sidelining regional powers or institutions that could play a stabilizing role. By engaging more deeply with organizations such as the **Arab League**, the **African Union**, or the **Gulf Cooperation Council**, the U.S. could help build regional solutions to regional problems, rather than imposing external solutions that may not align with local realities.

Understanding the historical context of U.S. interventions is not just an academic exercise—it is a critical tool for avoiding the mistakes of the past and crafting more effective, sustainable policies for the future. The world has changed dramatically since the early days of American interventionism, and the rise of new powers, the proliferation of non-state actors, and the increasing complexity of global conflicts demand a more thoughtful, historically grounded approach. By learning from its past, the U.S. can build a foreign policy that is not only more effective but also more attuned to the needs and aspirations of the people it seeks to help. This requires a shift away from short-term thinking and a renewed commitment to diplomacy, multilateralism, and a deep understanding of the historical forces shaping today's global challenges.

Additional Thoughts

To provide a deeper understanding of the flaws in U.S. foreign policy and underscore the lessons to be drawn from history, incorporating insights from **military officials**, **foreign policy experts**, and **regional analysts** is crucial. Their firsthand experiences and professional analyses lend both credibility and nuance to this discussion, offering perspectives that highlight the recurring missteps and their long-term consequences.

General David Petraeus, who oversaw U.S. operations in **Iraq** and **Afghanistan**, often reflects on the complexity of these conflicts. In interviews, Petraeus has noted that while tactical victories were frequently achieved—such as the **surge in Iraq**

in 2007 that temporarily stabilized the security situation—the absence of a broader, strategic framework for political reconciliation, governance reform, and economic stability meant that these victories were not sustainable. Petraeus has pointed out that military solutions alone cannot solve what are fundamentally political problems, a recurring flaw in U.S. strategy that often prioritizes immediate military success over long-term political stability.

Similarly, **John Nagl**, a former Army officer and expert on **counterinsurgency**, has critiqued the U.S.'s failure to engage in comprehensive **nation-building efforts** after regime changes in countries like Iraq and Afghanistan. In interviews, Nagl highlights that U.S. policymakers often misunderstood the importance of **winning hearts and minds**, assuming that removing a dictator would be enough to foster democracy. Nagl's reflections remind us that successful counterinsurgency and post-conflict reconstruction require much more than military force; they require a deep understanding of local cultures, economies, and power structures. His argument is particularly relevant when considering the power vacuums that emerged after the fall of **Saddam Hussein** in Iraq or the collapse of the **Taliban** in 2001.

In addition to military perspectives, experts in **foreign policy** and **regional studies** have also underscored the recurring strategic failures of U.S. interventions. **Andrew Bacevich**, a former U.S. Army colonel and professor of international relations, has been a vocal critic of the U.S.'s post-Cold War interventionist policies. Bacevich argues that the U.S. has consistently overestimated its ability to reshape foreign societies in its image, particularly in regions with vastly different political and cultural contexts. According to Bacevich, the interventions in **Vietnam**, Iraq, and **Afghanistan** all share a common thread: a failure to grasp the limits of American power and the complex realities on the ground.

In his analysis, Bacevich points out that U.S. leaders have repeatedly fallen into the trap of viewing foreign conflicts through the lens of American ideological values—freedom, democracy, and market capitalism—without recognizing that these ideals may not align with the political realities in regions like the Middle East. This ideological rigidity, combined with a lack of historical awareness, has often led the U.S. to intervene in conflicts it does not fully understand, with disastrous long-term consequences. Bacevich's critique of the **Iraq War** is particularly poignant, as he argues that the U.S.'s belief in **democracy promotion** was based on a flawed understanding of Iraq's sectarian divisions and the lack of institutions necessary to support democratic governance.

Vali Nasr, a prominent expert on **Middle Eastern politics** and former senior advisor to **Richard Holbrooke**, has also weighed in on the recurring errors in U.S. strategy. In particular, Nasr has emphasized how the U.S.'s focus on **military interventions** and **counterterrorism** has often come at the expense of engaging with regional powers through diplomacy. Nasr argues that in conflicts like those in **Syria** and **Yemen**, the U.S. failed to leverage diplomatic channels with key players like **Iran** and **Russia**, allowing those powers to shape the outcomes of these conflicts to their advantage. Nasr's analysis also touches on the long-term effects of U.S. sanctions and military pressure on Iran, which have strengthened Tehran's resolve to pursue its regional ambitions through proxy forces in **Iraq**, **Syria**, and **Lebanon**.

The insights from these military officials and foreign policy experts reveal a recurring pattern of strategic shortsightedness in U.S. interventions. Time and again, the U.S. has prioritized short-term military objectives over the more difficult task of building political and economic stability. For instance, **Gary Berntsen**, a former **CIA officer** who led the U.S. mission at **Tora Bora**, has spoken about the missed opportunity to capture **Osama bin Laden** in the early stages of the **War on Terror**. Berntsen's recounting of how bureaucratic indecision and a lack of coordination allowed bin Laden to escape provides a telling example of how tactical errors can have far-reaching consequences, prolonging conflict and contributing to future instability.

In the same vein, interviews with **Lawrence Wilkerson**, former chief of staff to **Secretary of State Colin Powell**, have revealed the extent to which the **Iraq War** was based on faulty intelligence and miscalculations. Wilkerson has been a staunch critic of the decision to invade Iraq, arguing that U.S. leaders failed to fully grasp the geopolitical consequences of dismantling Saddam's regime. According to Wilkerson, the invasion fractured Iraq's social fabric, empowering **Iran** and paving the way for the rise of extremist groups like **ISIS**. His reflections align with those of other critics who contend that the U.S.'s pursuit of regime change, without a clear plan for what would follow, has led to chaos and conflict across the region.

One of the most poignant reflections on U.S. foreign policy comes from **General Stanley McChrystal**, who led U.S. and NATO forces in **Afghanistan**. McChrystal has spoken about the limitations of using overwhelming military force to achieve political goals, particularly in countries with deeply entrenched insurgencies. He has pointed out that while the U.S. was able to defeat the **Taliban** militarily in the early stages of the Afghanistan War, it failed to provide a viable political and economic framework for the country's future. As a result, the Taliban was able to regroup and eventually regain power after the U.S. withdrawal in 2021, in what many analysts have described as a tragic example of history repeating itself.

By weaving together these expert perspectives, it becomes clear that U.S. foreign policy has been plagued by recurring strategic flaws. **Short-term victories**, such as the toppling of authoritarian regimes or the elimination of terrorist leaders, often come at the expense of **long-term stability**. The absence of a clear post-conflict strategy, the failure to understand the local political landscape, and the over-reliance on military solutions have left countries like Iraq, Afghanistan, Libya, and Syria mired in violence and instability.

These voices from the military and foreign policy communities provide valuable lessons for the U.S. moving forward. The U.S. must learn to approach future interventions with a more holistic, historically informed strategy that prioritizes **diplomacy**, **local partnerships**, and **sustainable development** over quick military victories. The long-term success of U.S. foreign policy will depend on its ability to address the underlying political, social, and economic factors that give rise to conflict, rather than relying solely on force to impose order.

By reflecting on these lessons from the past, the U.S. can avoid repeating the same mistakes and craft a more effective, sustainable approach to its engagement with the world. The incorporation of expert insights into the broader analysis of historical failures demonstrates the importance of **nuance**, **foresight**, and **context** in shaping future U.S. foreign policy, both in the Middle East and beyond.

APPENDICES

CHRONOLOGY OF U.S. INTERVENTIONS IN THE MIDDLE EAST

The story of U.S. intervention in the Middle East spans several decades, with its origins rooted in the geopolitical and economic imperatives of the post-World War II era. Each major intervention—from covert operations during the Cold War to large-scale military invasions in the 21st century—has left a profound impact on the region and shaped its future in ways often unforeseen by U.S. policymakers. To understand the scope of these interventions and their consequences, it is useful to trace a chronological path through the most significant episodes of American involvement in the Middle East.

This **chronology** of U.S. interventions in the Middle East offers a window into the complex and often contradictory nature of American foreign policy in the region. While each intervention was driven by a combination of **strategic interests**, **ideological beliefs**, and **security concerns**, the long-term consequences have frequently been destabilizing, contributing to the ongoing volatility that defines the Middle East today. Understanding this history is essential for crafting a more thoughtful and sustainable U.S. foreign policy moving forward

1947: U.S. Support for the Partition of Palestine

One of the earliest American engagements in the Middle East

involved its support for the **United Nations Partition Plan for Palestine**, which proposed the creation of separate Jewish and Arab states. The U.S. backed the plan as part of its broader policy of supporting the establishment of Israel, a move driven by a combination of moral and strategic considerations, including the need for a pro-Western foothold in the region. While the partition was accepted by Jewish leaders, it was vehemently opposed by Arab nations, setting the stage for decades of conflict and tension.

1953: Operation Ajax and the Overthrow of Mohammad Mosaddegh in Iran

In 1953, the CIA, working with British intelligence, orchestrated the **overthrow of Iranian Prime Minister Mohammad Mosaddegh**. Known as **Operation Ajax**, this covert operation was a response to Mosaddegh's decision to nationalize the **Anglo-Iranian Oil Company**, which had previously controlled Iran's oil industry. Fearing that Mosaddegh's government could align with the **Soviet Union** during the Cold War, the U.S. and Britain conspired to replace him with the pro-Western **Shah Mohammad Reza Pahlavi**.

The immediate outcome of the coup was the installation of the Shah's authoritarian regime, which aligned itself closely with Western powers and undertook a series of rapid modernization efforts. However, the long-term consequences were far more damaging. The coup deeply alienated the Iranian population, particularly among religious and nationalist groups, and sowed the seeds of the **1979 Iranian Revolution**, which replaced the Shah with the **Islamic Republic** led by **Ayatollah Khomeini**. The 1953 coup remains a pivotal event in the history of U.S.-Iran relations and is frequently cited by Iranian leaders as a justification for their anti-Western stance.

1958: U.S. Intervention in Lebanon

The U.S. intervention in **Lebanon** in 1958, known as **Operation Blue Bat**, marked the first deployment of American troops in the Middle East during the Cold War. President **Dwight D. Eisenhower** ordered the military intervention in response to a request from Lebanese President **Camille Chamoun**, who feared that growing sectarian tensions and the influence of **Nasserism** (inspired by Egyptian President **Gamal Abdel Nasser**) would lead to a pro-Soviet government in Lebanon.

Although the intervention was relatively short-lived, it underscored the U.S.'s commitment to containing Soviet influence in the Middle East. The U.S. quickly withdrew its forces after the crisis was resolved, but the intervention demonstrated the lengths to which America was willing to go to maintain a balance of power favorable to Western interests in the region.

1967: Six-Day War and U.S. Support for Israel

The **Six-Day War** in 1967 was a pivotal moment in U.S.-Middle East relations, during which Israel fought against Egypt, Jordan, and Syria. The war resulted in a stunning Israeli victory and the capture of the **Gaza Strip**, **Sinai Peninsula**, **West Bank**, and **Golan Heights**. While the U.S. was not directly involved in the conflict, its diplomatic and military support for Israel became more pronounced after the war.

The U.S. saw Israel as a key ally in the Middle East, providing military aid and diplomatic backing in subsequent decades. The Six-Day War also deepened the Arab-Israeli conflict, contributing to ongoing tensions in the region, including the **Yom Kippur War** of 1973 and the Palestinian struggle for statehood.

1973: Yom Kippur War and the Arab Oil Embargo

In October 1973, Egypt and Syria launched a surprise attack on Israel during the Jewish holiday of **Yom Kippur**, triggering a major conflict. The U.S. provided massive military aid to Israel, which helped it turn the tide of the war. In retaliation, the **Organization of Arab Petroleum Exporting Countries (OAPEC)** imposed an **oil embargo** on the U.S. and other Western nations, leading to a global energy crisis.

The Yom Kippur War and the ensuing oil embargo highlighted the strategic importance of Middle Eastern oil to the global economy and demonstrated the power of Arab nations to use oil as a political weapon. The U.S. responded by intensifying its efforts to secure energy supplies and broker peace agreements, culminating in the **Camp David Accords** in 1978, which led to a peace treaty between Israel and Egypt.

1979: Iranian Revolution and the Hostage Crisis

The **Iranian Revolution** of 1979, which overthrew the U.S.-backed Shah and established the **Islamic Republic** under **Ayatollah Khomeini**, was a turning point in U.S.-Middle East relations. The revolution was driven by widespread discontent with the Shah's authoritarian rule, his alignment with the West, and his attempts to modernize and secularize Iranian society. Khomeini's rise to power marked the beginning of a virulently anti-American regime that sought to export its revolutionary ideology throughout the region.

Later that year, the U.S. Embassy in **Tehran** was stormed by Iranian militants, who took **52 American diplomats** and citizens hostage. The **Iran hostage crisis**, which lasted for 444 days, profoundly affected U.S. public opinion and strained relations between Washington and Tehran. The U.S.'s inability to secure the release of the hostages through diplomatic means, combined with the failure of a military rescue mission, highlighted the limits of American power in the face of a determined revolutionary movement.

1980-1988: U.S. Involvement in the Iran-Iraq War

The **Iran-Iraq War**, which lasted from 1980 to 1988, was one of the bloodiest conflicts in the Middle East, with devastating consequences for both nations. The U.S. officially adopted a position of neutrality in the war but gradually tilted toward **Iraq** under **Saddam Hussein** as it sought to prevent the spread of Iran's revolutionary ideology. The U.S. provided intelligence and military support to Iraq, while also engaging in covert operations, such as **Operation Staunch**, to prevent arms sales to Iran.

The U.S.'s involvement in the conflict culminated in the **1988 downing of Iran Air Flight 655** by the U.S. Navy, which killed 290 civilians. The incident further soured relations between the U.S. and Iran, although it also contributed to Iran's decision to accept a ceasefire, ending the war.

1983: U.S. Intervention in Lebanon and the Beirut Bombings

In 1983, as part of a multinational peacekeeping force, U.S. Marines were deployed to **Lebanon** during its ongoing civil war. The mission was intended to stabilize the country and prevent further escalation of the conflict. However, the intervention took a tragic turn when a suicide bombing at the U.S. Marine barracks in **Beirut** killed **241 American servicemen**. The attack, attributed to the **Iranian-backed Hezbollah**, led to the withdrawal of U.S. forces from Lebanon.

The Beirut bombings demonstrated the risks of U.S. military involvement in the complex and deeply sectarian conflicts of the Middle East. It also highlighted the growing influence of Iranian proxy forces in the region, a trend that would continue to shape U.S. policy in subsequent decades.

1991: Gulf War and Operation Desert Storm

The **Gulf War** in 1991 was a major military intervention by the U.S. and its allies to expel Iraqi forces from **Kuwait**, which had been invaded by Iraq under **Saddam Hussein** in 1990. The U.S.-led coalition, operating under the banner of **Operation Desert Storm**, launched a massive military campaign that quickly liberated Kuwait and inflicted significant damage on Iraq's military infrastructure.

While the Gulf War was hailed as a decisive military victory, its aftermath left unresolved tensions. The U.S. established **no-fly zones** in northern and southern Iraq to protect **Kurdish** and **Shia** populations from Saddam's reprisals, while also imposing economic sanctions on Iraq. The decision not to pursue regime change in Baghdad at the time allowed Saddam Hussein to remain in power, setting the stage for further conflict a decade later.

2001: War in Afghanistan and the Global War on Terror

In response to the **September 11, 2001 attacks**, the U.S. launched **Operation Enduring Freedom**, a military campaign aimed at dismantling the **Taliban** regime in **Afghanistan** and eliminating the **al-Qaeda** network responsible for the attacks. The war in Afghanistan marked the beginning of the **Global War on Terror**, which would dominate U.S. foreign policy for the next two decades.

The initial phase of the war was successful in ousting the Taliban from power, but the conflict soon devolved into a protracted insurgency. The U.S. and its NATO allies struggled to build a stable Afghan government, while the Taliban regrouped in neighboring **Pakistan** and continued to wage a guerrilla war. The U.S.'s eventual withdrawal from Afghanistan in 2021, and the Taliban's swift return to power, raised serious questions about the long-term effectiveness of the intervention.

2003: Invasion of Iraq and the Fall of Saddam Hussein

In 2003, the U.S. invaded **Iraq** under the pretext that **Saddam Hussein** possessed **weapons of mass destruction (WMDs)** and had links to **terrorist groups**. The invasion quickly toppled Saddam's regime, but no WMDs were ever found, and the war soon turned into a brutal insurgency. The U.S.'s decision to disband the Iraqi military and remove the **Ba'ath Party** from power contributed to the rise of **sectarian violence** and the emergence of extremist groups like **al-Qaeda in Iraq**.

The Iraq War became one of the most controversial U.S. interventions in the Middle East, leading to significant loss of life, widespread instability, and the eventual rise of **ISIS**. The war also strained U.S. alliances, both in the region and globally, and raised profound questions about the wisdom of regime change as a foreign policy tool.

2011: Intervention in Libya and the Fall of Muammar Gaddafi

The U.S., along with **NATO** allies, intervened in **Libya** in 2011 in support of rebel forces seeking to overthrow **Muammar Gaddafi**. The intervention, framed as a humanitarian mission to prevent mass atrocities, resulted in Gaddafi's ouster and death. However, Libya soon descended into chaos as rival factions vied for control, and extremist groups, including **ISIS**, gained a foothold in the country.

The Libyan intervention highlighted the dangers of regime change without a clear post-conflict plan for stabilization. The power vacuum left by Gaddafi's removal contributed to Libya's fragmentation, with rival governments and militias continuing to fight for dominance.

2014: U.S. Campaign Against ISIS

In response to the rapid territorial gains made by **ISIS** in **Iraq** and **Syria**, the U.S. launched a military campaign in 2014 to degrade and ultimately destroy the group. Known as

Operation Inherent Resolve, the campaign involved airstrikes, special operations forces, and support for local ground forces, including the **Kurdish Peshmerga** and the **Syrian Democratic Forces (SDF)**.

While the U.S.-led coalition successfully rolled back ISIS's territorial control, the group's ideology and network of fighters continued to pose a threat in the region and beyond. The campaign against ISIS also deepened the U.S.'s involvement in Syria's civil war and highlighted the complexities of navigating a conflict with multiple factions and foreign powers involved.

2015: U.S. Support for Saudi-Led Intervention in Yemen

In 2015, the U.S. provided logistical and intelligence support to the **Saudi-led coalition** fighting **Houthi rebels** in **Yemen**. The conflict, which quickly escalated into a humanitarian catastrophe, has led to widespread famine, civilian casualties, and the displacement of millions of Yemenis. The U.S.'s involvement in the war, particularly its support for Saudi airstrikes, has drawn criticism from human rights organizations and lawmakers.

The war in Yemen has also been seen as a **proxy conflict** between **Saudi Arabia** and **Iran**, with the Houthis receiving support from Tehran. The U.S.'s backing of Saudi Arabia in this conflict has further complicated its relations with Iran and has raised questions about the long-term implications of its involvement in regional power struggles.

2021: U.S. Withdrawal from Afghanistan

After nearly two decades of military involvement, the U.S. completed its withdrawal from **Afghanistan** in August 2021. The withdrawal, which was chaotic and marked by the rapid collapse of the Afghan government, allowed the **Taliban** to regain control of the country. The fall of Kabul and the subsequent evacuation of U.S. personnel and Afghan allies raised serious questions about the effectiveness of the U.S.'s mission in Afghanistan and the broader strategy of nation-building.

The U.S.'s exit from Afghanistan, while ending its longest war, left a legacy of unresolved conflict and a humanitarian crisis. It also signaled a broader shift in U.S. foreign policy, as Washington seeks to pivot away from military interventions in the Middle East and focus on emerging challenges in **Asia** and **Europe**.

KEY PLAYERS IN PROXY WARS: A REFERENCE GUIDE

Proxy wars have been a recurring feature in global geopolitics, particularly in the **Middle East**, where regional and global powers use local factions, militant groups, and governments to advance their interests without direct confrontation. The following is a reference guide to some of the **key players** involved in these proxy conflicts, focusing on the major state actors and non-state actors who have shaped the outcomes of wars in **Syria, Yemen, Libya**, and beyond.

This reference guide highlights the complex web of **state actors** and **non-state actors** involved in Middle Eastern proxy wars. The interactions between these players shape the region's conflicts, with each pursuing its own agenda while aligning with global powers like the **U.S., Iran, Saudi Arabia, Russia**, and **Turkey**. These proxy wars have created enduring instability, fueled by both regional rivalries and international competition for influence. Understanding the key players is essential for analyzing the broader geopolitical dynamics that drive these conflicts and shape the future of the Middle East.

1. Iran

Role: Regional Power
Primary Proxy Forces: Hezbollah, Houthis (Ansar Allah), Shia Militias in Iraq, Syrian Regime
Conflict Zones: Syria, Yemen, Iraq, Lebanon

Iran has been a central player in the proxy wars of the Middle East, advancing its influence through a network of **Shia militias** and proxy forces. In **Syria**, Iran has supported **Bashar al-Assad's regime** with military advisers, financial aid, and fighters from **Hezbollah** and **Shia militias**. In **Iraq**, Iran-backed groups, such as the **Popular Mobilization Forces (PMF)**, played a crucial role in fighting ISIS but have also increased Tehran's influence over Iraq's political and security apparatus. In **Yemen**, Iran has provided weapons and training to the **Houthi rebels**, who have been fighting the **Saudi-led coalition** since 2015. Iran's support for its proxies is part of its broader strategy to create a **"Shia Crescent"** of influence stretching from **Tehran** to the **Mediterranean**.

2. Saudi Arabia

Role: Regional Rival to Iran
Primary Proxy Forces: Saudi-Led Coalition in Yemen, Sunni Militant Groups
Conflict Zones: Yemen, Syria, Iraq

Saudi Arabia has engaged in several proxy wars as part of its broader strategy to counter **Iranian influence**. The most significant of these conflicts is the war in **Yemen**, where Saudi Arabia leads a coalition of Gulf Arab states against the **Houthis**, who are aligned with Iran. Saudi Arabia's air campaign, combined with ground operations from allied Yemeni forces, has had devastating humanitarian consequences but has failed to decisively defeat the Houthis. In **Syria**, Saudi Arabia has backed **Sunni rebel groups** fighting against the Assad regime, hoping to counter Iran's growing influence in the country. Saudi Arabia's role in **Iraq** has been less direct, but it has supported Sunni factions opposed to Iranian-backed Shia militias.

3. United States

Role: Global Power and Longtime Middle East Actor

Primary Proxy Forces: Syrian Democratic Forces (SDF), Kurdish Peshmerga, Northern Alliance (Afghanistan)
Conflict Zones: Syria, Afghanistan, Iraq

The U.S. has a long history of using local forces as proxies to achieve its objectives in the Middle East. In **Syria**, the U.S. supported the **Syrian Democratic Forces (SDF)**, a Kurdish-led group that played a key role in the defeat of ISIS. However, the U.S.'s relationship with the SDF has complicated its ties with **Turkey**, which views Kurdish forces as terrorists. In **Afghanistan**, the U.S. backed the **Northern Alliance** against the **Taliban** following the **9/11** attacks. The U.S. has also supported the **Kurdish Peshmerga in Iraq**, who fought against ISIS while maintaining semi-autonomous control over Iraqi Kurdistan. U.S. reliance on proxies has allowed it to avoid large-scale military deployments, but it has also led to unintended consequences, as these groups often pursue their own agendas.

4. Russia

Role: Global Power Reasserting Influence
Primary Proxy Forces: Syrian Regime, Wagner Group, Pro-Assad Militias
Conflict Zones: Syria, Libya

Russia's involvement in Middle Eastern proxy wars has been most visible in **Syria**, where it has been a critical backer of **Bashar al-Assad**. Since 2015, Russia's military intervention, including airstrikes and logistical support, has helped turn the tide of the Syrian Civil War in Assad's favor. Russia also uses **mercenary groups** like the **Wagner Group**, which operates in **Libya**, **Syria**, and parts of **Africa**, to further its interests while maintaining plausible deniability. In **Libya**, Russia has supported **General Khalifa Haftar's Libyan National Army (LNA)** in its fight against the UN-backed government in **Tripoli**, seeking to expand its influence over Libya's resources and military bases.

5. Turkey

Role: Regional Power and NATO Member
Primary Proxy Forces: Free Syrian Army (FSA), Syrian National Army (SNA)
Conflict Zones: Syria, Libya

Turkey has been heavily involved in the Syrian conflict, where it has supported **Sunni rebel groups** against the Assad regime. Turkey's primary goal has been to prevent the establishment of a **Kurdish autonomous region** along its border, which it views as a threat to its territorial integrity due to the presence of **PKK-affiliated groups** within the **SDF**. To this end, Turkey has backed the **Free Syrian Army (FSA)** and later the **Syrian National Army (SNA)**, Sunni groups that oppose both Assad and the Kurds. Turkey also intervened in **Libya**, supporting the **Government of National Accord (GNA)** against **General Haftar's LNA**. Turkey's involvement in proxy conflicts has deepened its influence in the region but has also brought it into direct competition with other powers, such as Russia.

6. Hezbollah

Role: Iranian Proxy and Lebanese Militant Group
Primary Proxy Forces: Syrian Regime Forces, Iran-Backed Shia Militias
Conflict Zones: Syria, Lebanon, Iraq

Hezbollah, the powerful Lebanese Shia militant group and political party, is one of Iran's most important proxies. It has played a crucial role in the Syrian Civil War, fighting alongside Assad's forces to defend his regime. Hezbollah's fighters have been instrumental in major battles, and their involvement has strengthened Iran's influence in Syria. Hezbollah also operates in **Lebanon**, where it exerts significant political and military control, often positioning itself as a defender of Lebanon against Israeli and Western influence. The group has been involved in **Iraq**, supporting Iranian-backed Shia militias and opposing U.S. interests in the region.

7. Syrian Democratic Forces (SDF)

Role: U.S.-Backed Kurdish-Led Coalition
Primary Proxy Forces: Kurdish YPG, Syrian Arab Fighters
Conflict Zones: Syria

The **Syrian Democratic Forces (SDF)** emerged as one of the most effective forces in the fight against **ISIS**. Comprised largely of **Kurdish fighters** from the **YPG** but also including **Arab militias**, the SDF received substantial support from the **U.S.-led coalition** in the form of weapons, training, and air support. The SDF's success in defeating ISIS allowed it to establish control over a significant portion of northeastern Syria, creating a semi-autonomous Kurdish region. However, the SDF's ties to the PKK have complicated U.S. relations with Turkey, which views the group as a terrorist organization. Despite being a key U.S. ally, the SDF has found itself vulnerable to Turkish military incursions.

8. Houthis (Ansar Allah)

Role: Iranian-Aligned Rebel Group in Yemen
Primary Proxy Forces: Houthi Militias
Conflict Zones: Yemen

The **Houthis** are a **Zaydi Shia rebel group** in **Yemen** that has been fighting against the **Saudi-led coalition** since 2015. The group, which controls the capital, **Sana'a**, and much of northern Yemen, has received support from **Iran**, including weapons, training, and political backing. The Houthis have used **missile** and **drone attacks** against **Saudi Arabia** and **UAE**, drawing regional powers deeper into the conflict. The Yemeni civil war has turned into a proxy war between Iran and Saudi Arabia, with the Houthis playing a key role in Iran's broader strategy to challenge Saudi dominance in the Arabian Peninsula.

9. ISIS (Islamic State)

Role: Jihadist Terrorist Organization
Primary Proxy Forces: Foreign Fighters, Local Militias
Conflict Zones: Iraq, Syria, Libya

ISIS, which rose to prominence in **Iraq** and **Syria** in 2014, established a self-declared **caliphate** across large parts of both countries. While not a traditional proxy force, ISIS benefited from the power vacuums created by U.S. interventions in Iraq and Syria. The group recruited tens of thousands of foreign fighters and seized significant territory before being militarily defeated by a coalition of local and international forces, including the **SDF**, **Iraqi forces**, and U.S.-led airstrikes. However, ISIS's ideology and network of fighters remain active, particularly in parts of **Libya** and **Afghanistan**.

10. Wagner Group

Role: Russian Private Military Contractor
Primary Proxy Forces: Mercenary Fighters
Conflict Zones: Syria, Libya, Sub-Saharan Africa

The **Wagner Group**, a **Russian private military company** with ties to the Kremlin, has been involved in multiple conflicts across the Middle East and Africa. In **Syria**, Wagner fighters have supported Assad's regime, providing ground forces and acting as a proxy for Russian interests. In **Libya**, Wagner mercenaries have fought alongside **General Haftar's** LNA, attempting to secure Russian influence over the country's oil fields and strategic assets. The Wagner Group's involvement in proxy wars allows Russia to exert influence without directly committing conventional forces.

GLOSSARY OF TERMS

This glossary provides an overview of essential terms for understanding U.S. foreign policy and the complex dynamics of proxy wars in the Middle East and beyond. Each term reflects the intricate and often contentious relationships between global powers, regional actors, and local factions, shaping the landscape of modern conflict and diplomacy.

Al-Qaeda

An international jihadist organization founded by **Osama bin Laden** in the late 1980s. Initially formed to fight against Soviet forces in Afghanistan, it evolved into a global network responsible for numerous terrorist attacks, including the **September 11, 2001** attacks on the U.S. Al-Qaeda has inspired affiliate groups across the Middle East and Africa.

Arab Spring

A series of anti-government protests, uprisings, and armed rebellions that spread across much of the Arab world in the early 2010s. The movements called for political reform, democracy, and the removal of authoritarian regimes. However, the outcomes varied, with some countries experiencing civil wars (e.g., Syria and Libya) while others saw limited reforms or a return to autocratic rule.

Axis of Evil

A term coined by U.S. President **George W. Bush** in 2002 to describe governments that he believed were sponsoring terrorism and seeking weapons of mass destruction. The term originally referred to **Iran, Iraq,** and **North Korea** and became associated with the U.S.'s broader strategy in the **War on Terror**.

Ba'ath Party

A secular Arab nationalist political party that was founded in **Syria** in the 1940s. It became the ruling party in **Iraq** under **Saddam Hussein** and continues to govern **Syria** under **Bashar al-Assad**. The Ba'ath Party promoted **Arab unity, socialism,** and **secularism**.

Caliphate

A form of Islamic government led by a **caliph**, who is considered a political and religious successor to the Prophet Muhammad. In modern times, the term gained renewed attention when **ISIS** declared a caliphate across parts of Iraq and Syria in 2014, led by **Abu Bakr al-Baghdadi**.

CIA (Central Intelligence Agency)

The principal intelligence agency of the U.S. government responsible for gathering, processing, and analyzing national security information from around the world. The CIA has played a key role in many covert operations, including the **1953 coup in Iran** and various other interventions during the Cold War.

Cold War

The period of geopolitical tension between the **United States** and the **Soviet Union** (USSR) and their respective allies, which lasted from the end of **World War II** until the collapse of the Soviet Union in **1991**. The Cold War heavily influenced U.S. foreign policy in the Middle East, as the U.S. sought to contain Soviet influence and prevent the spread of communism.

Counterinsurgency

Military or political strategies aimed at defeating **insurgencies** or rebellions. These strategies often involve a combination of military force and efforts to win the support of the local population through governance, infrastructure, and development projects. The U.S. has used counterinsurgency tactics in Iraq, Afghanistan, and other regions.

Diplomatic Sanctions

A tool of foreign policy in which one country restricts or cuts off diplomatic relations with another country to punish or pressure it into changing its behavior. Sanctions may include travel bans, freezing of assets, or withdrawal of diplomatic recognition.

Drone Warfare

The use of unmanned aerial vehicles (**UAVs**) to carry out military strikes, intelligence gathering, and surveillance. The U.S. has increasingly relied on drones for targeted killings, especially in the **War on Terror**, with notable use in **Afghanistan**, **Pakistan**, **Yemen**, and **Somalia**.

Hezbollah

A Lebanese Shia militant group and political party, backed by **Iran**. Hezbollah was founded in the early 1980s to resist the Israeli occupation of southern Lebanon and has since become one of the most powerful political and military organizations in Lebanon. It also operates as an Iranian proxy in Syria and elsewhere in the region.

Insurgency

A rebellion or uprising against an established government or occupying power, often involving irregular warfare tactics like **guerrilla warfare**, sabotage, and terrorism. Insurgencies can be motivated by political, religious, or ethnic factors and are often aimed at destabilizing the existing government or occupying force.

ISIS (Islamic State of Iraq and Syria)

A jihadist militant group that emerged from al-Qaeda in Iraq and rose to prominence in 2014 when it seized large territories in **Iraq** and **Syria**. ISIS declared the creation of a **caliphate** and imposed a brutal interpretation of Islamic law. Although its territorial control has been greatly reduced, ISIS remains a potent terrorist organization.

Kurds

An ethnic group spread across parts of **Turkey, Iraq, Syria,** and **Iran**. The Kurds have long sought greater autonomy or independence, leading to conflict with the governments of these countries. In Iraq, the **Kurdish Peshmerga** played a key role in the fight against **ISIS**, and in Syria, the **Kurdish YPG** has been a major U.S. ally against ISIS.

Mujahedeen

A term referring to Islamic guerrilla fighters. The most notable mujahedeen were the Afghan rebels who fought against the Soviet invasion of Afghanistan in the 1980s, with covert support from the U.S. through **Operation Cyclone**. Some of these fighters later formed the core of groups like **al-Qaeda** and the **Taliban**.

Nation-Building

The process of constructing or restructuring political, economic, and social institutions in a post-conflict or post-intervention state. The U.S. has attempted nation-building efforts in Iraq and Afghanistan, with varying degrees of success and widespread debate about their efficacy and sustainability.

No-Fly Zone

A designated area over which aircraft, particularly military aircraft, are not allowed to fly. No-fly zones are often implemented to prevent air attacks or protect civilians during conflicts. For example, the U.S. and its allies imposed no-fly zones in northern and southern Iraq after the **Gulf War** to protect Kurdish and Shia populations.

Operation Ajax

The code name for the 1953 covert operation led by the **CIA** and **MI6** (British intelligence) to overthrow Iranian Prime Minister **Mohammad Mosaddegh**. The operation restored **Shah Mohammad Reza Pahlavi** to power and protected Western oil interests, but it also fueled anti-Western sentiment that contributed to the 1979 **Iranian Revolution**.

Operation Desert Storm

The U.S.-led military campaign during the **Gulf War** in 1991 to expel Iraqi forces from **Kuwait** after Iraq's invasion in 1990. The operation was a decisive victory for the U.S. and its coalition allies, but it left Saddam Hussein in power, setting the stage for continued tensions and the eventual 2003 invasion of Iraq.

Peshmerga

The military forces of the **Kurdistan Regional Government** in **Iraqi Kurdistan**. The Peshmerga played a key role in the fight against ISIS, particularly in northern Iraq. While they are a valuable U.S. ally, their desire for Kurdish independence has caused tensions with the Iraqi central government and neighboring countries like **Turkey**.

Proxy War

A conflict in which two or more opposing powers support

different factions or forces in a third country, without directly engaging in the fighting themselves. Proxy wars are common in the Middle East, where **Iran**, **Saudi Arabia**, the **U.S.**, **Russia**, and other powers back various local groups to advance their own strategic interests.

Regime Change

The replacement of one government regime by another, often through covert actions or military interventions. The U.S. has pursued regime change in various countries, such as **Iraq** in 2003, **Libya** in 2011, and **Iran** in 1953. However, the long-term consequences of these interventions have often been unstable governments and protracted conflicts.

Shia Crescent

A term used to describe the arc of Shia influence stretching from **Iran** through **Iraq**, **Syria**, and **Lebanon**. The term reflects the growing influence of Iran in these countries, often through proxy forces such as **Hezbollah** and various Shia militias.

Sunni-Shia Divide

The division between the two main branches of Islam, **Sunni** and **Shia**, which has historically driven conflict and political rivalry in the Middle East. The divide is particularly pronounced in proxy conflicts between **Saudi Arabia** (Sunni) and **Iran** (Shia), such as those in **Syria**, **Iraq**, **Yemen**, and **Lebanon**.

Taliban

A fundamentalist Sunni Islamic movement that rose to power in **Afghanistan** in the mid-1990s and governed the country until it was overthrown by a U.S.-led coalition in 2001 following the **September 11 attacks**. The Taliban regrouped as an insurgent force and continues to fight against the U.S.-backed Afghan government. The group regained power in

2021 following the U.S. withdrawal from Afghanistan.

Wagner Group

A **Russian private military company** with close ties to the Kremlin, often used to carry out military operations in countries where direct Russian involvement is politically sensitive. The Wagner Group has been involved in conflicts in **Syria**, **Libya**, and parts of **Africa**, often acting as a proxy force for Russia's geopolitical interests.

BIBLIOGRAPHY

Books

I. Bacevich, Andrew J. *America's War for the Greater Middle East: A Military History*. New York: Random House, 2016.

II. Brennan, John. *Undaunted: My Fight Against America's Enemies, At Home and Abroad*. New York: Celadon Books, 2020.

III. Coll, Steve. *Ghost Wars: The Secret History of the CIA, Afghanistan, and Bin Laden, from the Soviet Invasion to September 10, 2001*. New York: Penguin Books, 2004.

IV. Dreyfuss, Robert. *Devil's Game: How the United States Helped Unleash Fundamentalist Islam*. New York: Metropolitan Books, 2005.

V. Gordon, Philip H. *Losing the Long Game: The False Promise of Regime Change in the Middle East*. New York: St. Martin's Press, 2020.

VI. Kissinger, Henry. *World Order*. New York: Penguin Books, 2014.

VII. Malkasian, Carter. *The American War in Afghanistan: A History*. Oxford: Oxford University Press, 2021.

VIII. Nasr, Vali. *The Shia Revival: How Conflicts Within Islam Will Shape the Future*. New York: W. W. Norton & Company, 2007.

IX. Petraeus, David H., and Michael E. O'Hanlon. *T'*

Future of Warfare. New York: Brookings Institution Press, 2020.

X. Suskind, Ron. *The One Percent Doctrine: Deep Inside America's Pursuit of Its Enemies Since 9/11*. New York: Simon & Schuster, 2006.

Journal Articles

I. Biddle, Stephen, Jeffrey A. Friedman, and Jacob N. Shapiro. "Testing the Surge: Why Did Violence Decline in Iraq in 2007?" *International Security* 37, no. 1 (2012): 7–40.

II. Byman, Daniel. "Friends Like These: Counterinsurgency and the War on Terrorism." *International Security* 31, no. 2 (2006): 79–115.

III. Mazzetti, Mark, and Eric Schmitt. "In Tactical Shift, U.S. Refines Its Al-Qaeda Strategy." *The New York Times*, June 30, 2012.

IV. Nasr, Vali. "Iran Among the Ruins: Tehran's Advantage in a Turbulent Middle East." *Foreign Affairs* 97, no. 2 (2018): 108–118.

V. Walt, Stephen M. "Toppling Saddam: Iraq and American Foreign Policy." *World Policy Journal* 21, no. 3 (2004): 23–30.

Government Reports

I. Central Intelligence Agency. *Afghanistan: Lessons from the Soviet War*. Washington, D.C.: CIA, 1989.

II. United States Department of Defense. *The Surge: General Petraeus and the Turnaround in Iraq*. Washington, D.C.: Government Printing Office, 2009.

III. U.S. Congress. House Committee on Foreign Affairs.

Impacts of the War on Terrorism on U.S. Foreign Policy. Washington, D.C.: Government Printing Office, 2006.

IV. U.S. State Department. *Country Reports on Terrorism 2020.* Washington, D.C.: U.S. Government Printing Office, 2021.

Online Sources

I. Parsi, Trita. "How China Played Peacemaker in the Middle East." Foreign Policy, March 13, 2023. https://foreignpolicy.com

II. Riedel, Bruce. "The Cost of American Retreat from the Middle East." Brookings Institution, July 29, 2020. https://www.brookings.edu

III. Schmitt, Eric, and Helene Cooper. "The U.S. Military Mission in Syria: Oversight and Controversies." The New York Times, September 5, 2021. https://www.nytimes.com

Interviews

I. Petraeus, David H. Interview by CNN's Fareed Zakaria. *Fareed Zakaria GPS,* CNN, August 22, 2021.

II. Brennan, John. Interview with *The Atlantic,* October 10, 2016.

III. Wilkerson, Lawrence. "Reflections on Iraq: What Went Wrong." Interview with *Democracy Now,* September 15, 2015.

ABOUT THE AUTHOR

Josh Luberisse

Josh, a multifaceted entrepreneur and renowned author, has carved a niche for himself in the spheres of artificial intelligence, geopolitics, finance, and cybersecurity. With a myriad of authoritative books to his credit on these subjects, he is undeniably a luminary in the domain. Not just an author, Josh is also the charismatic host of "Disrupting Defense," a groundbreaking podcast that explores the intersection of technology and national security. Each episode unravel the intricacies of how cutting-edge innovations from Silicon Valley are not just enhancing military capabilities but are also transforming them. By tuning in you can stay at the forefront of defense innovation and discover how technology is not just supporting but leading the charge in modern military operations.

As an entrepreneur, Josh has founded several startup companies, including one specializing in AI research and another providing top-tier cybersecurity consulting services. His hands-on experience in these fields lends authenticity and depth to his writing and public speaking engagements.

Widely sought after as a speaker and consultant, Josh's contributions to the technology and defense sectors are immeasurable. His passion for knowledge and innovation is not just a professional pursuit but a personal mission to inspire and educate, leaving a lasting impact on the world.

For those seeking practical, actionable insights into the ever-evolving landscape of technology and defense, Josh's extensive collection of manuscripts and his engaging community of readers and followers offer a wealth of knowledge and inspiration.

BOOKS BY THIS AUTHOR

Surviving The Collapse: The Citizen Defender's Guide To Guerrilla Tactics And Strategic Resilience In A Lawless Society

In a world where the institutions we rely on can suddenly fail, where society's fragile fabric can unravel, and where collapse—whether through conflict, natural disaster, or systemic breakdown—becomes a reality, we face a choice: to succumb to the chaos or rise above it. Surviving the Collapse is not just a manual for surviving the worst—it's a guide to leading, thriving, and rebuilding in the face of destruction.

Surviving the Collapse is for the citizen defenders, the leaders, and the communities who refuse to be defined by the collapse of the world around them. Drawing from hard-learned lessons in history, the principles of warfare, and the indomitable human spirit, this guide offers not only the tactical and practical strategies needed to navigate life in a fractured society but also a vision of hope and empowerment. It emphasizes the strength found in resilience, unity, and leadership, inspiring readers to not only endure but to become the architects of a new, more just and resilient order.

This handbook covers essential topics such as small arms proficiency, guerrilla tactics, urban and rural defense strategies, and intelligence gathering in hostile environments. From securing resources and fortifying defenses to establishing local governance and managing psychological resilience, this guide offers clear, actionable advice for those facing a world without order. It addresses real-world scenarios where conventional systems of support no longer function, and the only option is to rely on one's training, adaptability, and community.

Whether you are already living through a societal breakdown or preparing for an uncertain future, Surviving the Collapse provides the tools and mindset to face the chaos head-on, rebuild what was lost, and create something stronger in its place. It's a call to action for those who understand that surviving isn't enough—true strength lies in the power to rebuild and thrive.

Surviving the Collapse is built on practical field-tested strategies, taking a no-nonsense approach to staying ahead of threats, maintaining operational discipline, and ensuring survival in extreme conditions. Whether defending urban spaces under siege, conducting rural survival operations, or organizing citizen defense units, this book is an indispensable resource for those who seek to lead in moments of crisis, for the protectors of communities, and for anyone who wishes to understand how to turn collapse into opportunity, this book is your guide. You are not just a survivor. You are a builder of tomorrow.

Controlling The Narrative: The Definitive Guide To Psychological Operations, Perception Management, And Information Warfare

Controlling the Narrative: The Definitive Guide to Psychological Operations, Perception Management, and Information Warfare is an essential resource designed for military professionals, strategists, policymakers, and scholars engaged in the intricate fields of psychological warfare and strategic communications. This comprehensive guide delves into the multifaceted aspects of psychological operations (PSYOP), perception management and information warfare, exploring the theories, practices, and tools that shape today's information battle-spaces.

Structured to provide a deep understanding of the historical evolution, strategic considerations, and modern applications of PSYOP, this book equips readers with the knowledge necessary to effectively execute operations that influence perceptions, decisions, and behaviors on the global stage. It covers a broad spectrum of topics, from the basic concepts of propaganda and media manipulation to sophisticated strategies involving cyber warfare, artificial intelligence, and data analytics.

Each chapter in this guide is meticulously crafted to offer detailed insights and practical advice, enriched with case studies that highlight both successful and cautionary tales from past and present operations. The book emphasizes the importance of adhering to ethical and legal standards, providing readers with a clear framework for conducting operations that respect human rights and international laws.

Controlling the Narrative also addresses the strategic imperatives for military and governmental organizations, including the need for ongoing adaptation to emerging technologies and the shifting geopolitical landscape. With its rigorous analysis and comprehensive coverage, the guide serves as an indispensable resource for those tasked with safeguarding national security and advancing military objectives through the strategic use of psychological and influence operations.

This book is not only a manual but also a call to action, urging enhanced inter-agency collaboration, investment in research and development, and the cultivation of public-private partnerships to maintain a competitive edge in the evolving arena of global information warfare. It aims to inspire a new generation of strategic thinkers who are prepared to leverage the power of information in the pursuit of security, peace, and stability.

Countdown To Extinction: Navigating The Existential Threats That Could End Humanity

Countdown to Extinction: Navigating the Existential Threats That Could End Humanity is a comprehensive and thought-provoking exploration of the critical risks that could define—or end—the future of human civilization. In a world increasingly shaped by rapid technological advancements, environmental degradation, and global interconnectedness, this book takes a deep dive into the most pressing existential threats of our time and examines how we can navigate them to secure a thriving future for all.

Spanning a wide range of topics, Countdown to Extinction begins by laying the groundwork with an introduction to the fragility of human civilization and the concept of existential risks. The book then systematically explores specific threats, including the transformative power and peril of Artificial General Intelligence (AGI), the revolutionary potential and catastrophic risks of nanotechnology, and the unseen dangers posed by high-energy particle collisions.

The narrative continues by examining the ever-present dangers of pandemics—both natural and engineered—and the ongoing threat of nuclear warfare, juxtaposed against the slow-burning crisis of climate change. It delves into cosmic hazards like asteroid impacts and supervolcanoes, the potential collapse of global ecosystems due to resource depletion, and the nightmarish scenarios involving rogue AI and cybersecurity failures.

The book also addresses emerging risks associated with synthetic biology, economic collapse, and societal breakdown, while considering the unpredictable nature of "unknown unknowns." Each chapter is meticulously researched, combining scientific analysis with ethical considerations, historical case studies, and expert insights to paint a vivid picture of the potential futures we may face.

Yet, Countdown to Extinction is not just about outlining dangers; it is equally a guide to mitigation and hope. The book offers a thorough discussion on global strategies for mitigating these risks, emphasizing technological safeguards, international cooperation, and the necessity of building societal resilience. It calls for the creation of a culture of awareness and preparedness, urging governments, businesses, and individuals to take responsibility and act decisively.

The book concludes with a powerful call to action, reflecting on the imperative of addressing these risks and the role of human ingenuity and adaptation in creating a secure and sustainable future. Through detailed analysis and an engaging narrative, Countdown to Extinction challenges readers to reconsider their assumptions, recognize the gravity of the challenges ahead, and embrace the opportunities for transformative change.

This is not just a book about survival; it is a manifesto for safeguarding humanity's future. It reminds us that while the risks are formidable, so too is our capacity to overcome them through collective action, innovation, and a deep commitment to the values that unite us all. The choices we make today will shape the course of history, and together, we can create a world that is secure, just, and sustainable for generations to come.

Waging Just Wars: The Ethical And Legal Principles Of Modern Warfare

"Waging Just Wars: The Ethical and Legal Principles of Modern Warfare" provides a comprehensive examination of the moral and legal dimensions of contemporary conflict. Authored by an expert in military ethics and international law, this book delves into the foundational principles of Just War Theory, including jus ad bellum, jus in bello, and jus post bellum.

The book explores historical precedents and modern applications, offering a detailed analysis of self-defense, humanitarian interventions, and the prevention of atrocities. It critically examines the impact of technological advancements, such as AI and autonomous weapons, on the conduct of war. Through rigorous ethical analysis and case studies, the author addresses the complexities of applying Just War principles in today's geopolitical landscape.

"Waging Just Wars" also highlights the importance of legitimate authority, right intention, and proportionality in the decision to go to war. The book discusses the ethical challenges of ensuring that military actions align with these principles and the necessity of exhausting all non-violent options before resorting to force.

Additionally, the book provides insights into the treatment of prisoners of war, the use of prohibited weapons, and the ethical considerations of modern warfare tactics. The analysis extends to post-war responsibilities, emphasizing the need for fair treatment of former enemies, reconstruction efforts, and accountability for war crimes.

This scholarly work is essential reading for national security researchers, scholars, policymakers, and ethicists. It offers a nuanced understanding of how ethical and legal standards can guide the conduct of warfare, ensuring that the use of force is both morally justified and legally compliant. With its thorough examination of Just War Theory and its application to contemporary conflicts, "Waging Just Wars" is a vital resource for anyone seeking to navigate the moral complexities of modern warfare.

Cognitive Warfare In The Age Of Unpeace: Strategies, Defenses, And The New Battlefield Of The Mind

Cognitive Warfare in the Age of Unpeace: Strategies, Defenses, and the New Battlefield of the Mind is a definitive examination of the emergent arena of cognitive warfare—a battlefield where consciousness and cognition are under siege. Rooted in the historical lineage of warfare, this seminal tome charts a course from the stratagems of yesteryear's influence operations to the digital subversions that define our current epoch.

The book is structured to provide a layered understanding of the subject. Part I lays the foundation, explaining how the age of unpeace has given rise to a new form of warfare that exists between peace and war, where the battle for influence is paramount. Part II describes the modern tools at the disposal of state and non-state actors, including AI and neurotechnological advancements, and the ways in which these tools can manipulate and coerce on a mass scale.

Through real-world case studies, Part III illustrates the practical application of cognitive strategies and the impact of such warfare on democracies, highlighting the need for robust countermeasures. In Part IV, the focus shifts to strategic insights, examining both offensive strategies for influence and subversion and the defensive strategies necessary to maintain cognitive sovereignty.

The latter sections, Parts V and VI, provide a forward-looking perspective on building societal and governmental defenses against cognitive attacks. These include fostering societal resilience through public education, developing policy and governance frameworks, and addressing the ethical dimensions of cognitive defense.

The final chapters speculate on the future trajectory of cognitive warfare, emphasizing the importance of international cooperation and the establishment of 'cognitive peace'. With its conclusion and appendices providing a roadmap and additional resources, this book stands as an essential guide for policymakers, security experts, academics and citizens alike in understanding and countering the sophisticated threat of cognitive warfare in our increasingly interconnected world.

The Art Of War In The 21St Century: Timeless Principles For Modern Military Strategy

In "The Art of War in the 21st Century," visionary author Josh brings a fresh perspective to the ancient wisdom of Sun Tzu's renowned treatise. Drawing upon his experience as an entrepreneur and his passion for strategic thinking, Josh explores the timeless principles of "The Art of War" and their applications to modern military strategy.

This book is not a mere translation or interpretation of Sun Tzu's work. Instead, it serves as a bridge between the ancient wisdom of the past and the complex challenges of the present.

Josh's unique perspective combines military strategy with insights from the world of business and innovation, offering a fresh take on how these timeless principles can be adapted and applied in the contemporary landscape.

Through engaging narratives, real-world examples, and thought-provoking analysis, Josh demonstrates how Sun Tzu's principles can guide leaders in the 21st century to navigate the complexities of modern warfare. He explores topics such as understanding the operational environment, harnessing technological advancements, fostering effective leadership, and building resilient coalitions.

"The Art of War in the 21st Century" is not solely aimed at military professionals. It is a book for visionary thinkers, entrepreneurs, and leaders from various fields who seek to enhance their strategic acumen and decision-making abilities. It serves as a guidebook for those navigating the ever-evolving landscapes of business, politics, and conflict resolution.

Josh's fresh approach to Sun Tzu's timeless wisdom makes this book an invaluable resource for those seeking innovative strategies to overcome challenges, seize opportunities, and achieve success in the modern world. The author's ability to bridge the gap between ancient principles and contemporary contexts provides readers with practical and thought-provoking insights that transcend traditional boundaries.

Whether you are a military strategist, a business leader, or an aspiring entrepreneur, "The Art of War in the 21st Century" offers a compelling exploration of strategic thinking in our rapidly changing world. Join Josh on this transformative journey and unlock the secrets of Sun Tzu's wisdom, paving the way for strategic brilliance and remarkable achievements in the 21st century.

Eyes In The Sky: A Global Perspective On The Role Of Uavs In Intelligence, Surveillance, Reconnaissance, And Security

From the simple plaything of hobbyists to the high-tech guardians of national security, the story of Unmanned Aerial Vehicles (UAVs) is a thrilling flight into the frontier of technological innovation. "Eyes in the Sky" charts this breathtaking ascent, offering readers an inside look at the machines and systems shaping the modern world, both in the air and on the ground.

Embark on a journey that spans continents, delving deep into the extraordinary uses of UAVs across military, civilian, and commercial sectors. Learn how these devices gather intelligence, conduct surveillance, and even wage war. Explore how, far from the battlefield, they monitor traffic, patrol borders, and aid humanitarian efforts.

But, like Icarus soaring too close to the sun, the story of UAVs isn't without its darker shades. In an age of cyber threats and geopolitical tension, the skies aren't always friendly. Witness how these mechanical marvels are used by criminals, terrorists, and cyber pirates, exploiting their strengths for nefarious purposes.

This comprehensive examination of UAVs wouldn't be complete without an exploration of what's being done to keep us safe. Through countermeasures and cybersecurity, witness the ongoing struggle between those who exploit technology and those who safeguard it.

From cutting-edge counter-drone technologies to the ethical hackers combating these airborne threats, this narrative unravels the complex world of UAVs, their implications for global security, and the measures in place to maintain the balance.

"Eyes in the Sky" is not just a tale of technology—it's a chronicle of change, detailing how we've reshaped the heavens to serve our needs. With unparalleled access to the latest trends and greatest minds in the field, this book is a must-read for technophiles, security enthusiasts, and anyone curious about our rapidly evolving world.

Fasten your seatbelts, dear readers. It's time to take off into a sky full of drones!

A Boydian Approach To Mastering Unconventional Warfare

A Boydian Approach to Mastering Unconventional Warfare" is a seminal work that delves deeply into the strategic principles of John Boyd, a legendary military strategist, and applies them to the complex realm of unconventional warfare. This book presents a comprehensive analysis of Boyd's key concepts, most notably the OODA Loop (Observe, Orient, Decide, Act), and explores their application in the context of irregular and asymmetric conflicts that dominate the modern geopolitical landscape.

The author meticulously explores how Boyd's principles of adaptability, speed, and fluidity in decision-making can be applied to unconventional warfare tactics such as guerrilla warfare, insurgency, counterinsurgency, and cyber warfare. The book emphasizes the importance of understanding the psychological and moral dimensions of warfare, in addition to the physical aspect, a concept Boyd championed and which remains highly relevant in today's conflict scenarios.

Through a blend of historical analysis, case studies, and contemporary examples, "A Boydian Approach to Mastering Unconventional Warfare" offers insightful strategies for dealing with non-traditional threats in a rapidly evolving global context. It addresses the challenges of combating non-state actors, the use of technology in irregular warfare, and the need for innovative and adaptive strategies in response to the unpredictable nature of modern conflicts.

This book is not only a tribute to Boyd's groundbreaking work but also an essential guide for military strategists, policymakers, and security professionals who are grappling with the complexities of contemporary warfare. It provides a nuanced understanding of how unconventional warfare strategies can be developed and executed effectively, making it a crucial addition to the field of military strategy and national security studies.

Machinery Of War: A Comprehensive Study Of The Post-9/11 Global Arms Trade

In "Machinery of War: A Comprehensive Study of the Post-9/11 Global Arms Trade," Josh offers an exhaustive exploration into the intricate world of global armaments in the aftermath of the tragic events of September 11, 2001. This seminal work probes the depths of the modern arms trade, revealing its multi-faceted nature, its key players, and its profound impact on the geopolitical landscape.

Josh delves into the roles of state actors, private military companies, and non-state entities, underlining their intertwined relationships and the ensuing effects on global security dynamics. With a balanced, objective lens, he navigates through the complexities of cyber warfare, drone technology, and the emergence of autonomous weapons systems, as well as the rise of private military and security companies.

Further, he scrutinizes the arms race in different regions, including the Middle East, Asia, Africa, and Latin America, offering a nuanced understanding of their unique circumstances and their roles in the broader arms trade. The author also addresses the significant role of regulatory efforts in the global arms trade, investigating the successes and failures of arms embargoes and international regulations. Lastly, he gazes into the future, offering predictions and identifying trends that may shape the global arms trade in years to come.

"Machinery of War" is an indispensable resource for policymakers, researchers, scholars, and anyone interested in understanding the complexities of the global arms trade in the 21st century. This in-depth study invites readers to ponder the geopolitical, ethical, and humanitarian implications of the arms trade, highlighting the urgent need for control and regulation in an increasingly interconnected world.

Private Armies, Public Wars: The Brave New World Of Private Military Companies

Private Armies, Public Wars: The Brave New World of Private Military Companies is a groundbreaking exploration of the contemporary landscape of warfare, examining the rise and impact of private military companies (PMCs) on the global stage. Written by an esteemed geopolitics expert and military history researcher, this book provides a comprehensive and thought-provoking examination of the multifaceted world of private military operations.

Drawing upon historical perspectives, legal frameworks, economic dynamics, and case studies from around the world, this book offers a nuanced and in-depth analysis of the complex relationship between states, armed conflicts, and the private entities that operate within them. It delves into the motivations, challenges, and implications of the growing presence of PMCs, shedding light on both the opportunities they present and the ethical dilemmas they raise.

Private Armies, Public Wars presents a balanced and objective assessment of the forces driving the expansion of the PMC industry. It explores the historical roots of mercenaries and traces their evolution into modern-day private military companies. The book examines the economic appeal of outsourcing military capabilities and the potential implications for state sovereignty and the monopoly on the use of force.

Through vivid case studies, the author uncovers the diverse roles that PMCs play in conflicts worldwide, from providing security and logistical support to participating in active combat. The author explores the impact of PMCs on local populations, human rights concerns, and the challenges of regulating an industry that operates beyond traditional legal frameworks.

Moreover, the book delves into emerging trends and challenges in the PMC industry, including the integration of advanced technologies such as artificial intelligence and machine learning, the use of biometric and identity verification technologies. It analyzes the potential benefits and risks associated with these technological advancements, providing valuable insights into the changing nature of warfare in the 21st century. It also addresses the growing importance of communication technologies, the role of private intelligence agencies in modern warfare and the implications of hybrid warfare and disinformation campaigns.

Private Armies, Public Wars is a critical examination of the complex interplay between states, private entities, and the pursuit of military objectives. It challenges conventional notions of warfare and offers a fresh perspective on the evolving dynamics of global conflicts. The author provides a comprehensive and well-researched analysis, drawing on a wide range of sources and expertise to present a comprehensive overview of the PMC industry.

This book is essential reading for scholars, policymakers, military professionals, and anyone interested in understanding the contemporary landscape of warfare and the evolving role of private military companies. It serves as a call to action, urging readers to engage in meaningful discussions and debates about the ethical, legal, and strategic implications of the growing influence of private actors in the world's conflicts.

The Ethical Hacker's Handbook: A Comprehensive Guide To Cybersecurity Assessment

Get ready to venture into the world of ethical hacking with your trusty guide, Josh, in this comprehensive and enlightening book, "The Ethical Hacker's Handbook: A Comprehensive Guide to Cybersecurity Assessment". Josh isn't just your typical cybersecurity guru; he's the charismatic and experienced CEO of a successful penetration testing company, and he's here to make your journey into the fascinating realm of cybersecurity as engaging as it is educational.
Dive into the deep end of ethical hacking as Josh de-mystifies complex concepts and navigates you through the murky waters of cyber threats. He'll show you how the pros get things

done, equipping you with the skills to understand and test the security of networks, systems, and applications - all without drowning in unnecessary jargon.

Whether you're a complete novice or a seasoned professional, this book is filled with sage advice, practical exercises, and genuine insider knowledge that will propel you on your journey. From breaking down the complexities of Kali Linux, to mastering the art of the spear-phishing technique, to getting intimate with the OWASP Top Ten, Josh is with you every step of the way.

Don't expect a dull textbook read, though! Josh keeps things light with witty anecdotes and real-world examples that keep the pages turning. You'll not only learn the ropes of ethical hacking, you'll understand why each knot is tied the way it is.

By the time you turn the last page of this guide, you'll be prepared to tackle the ever-evolving landscape of cybersecurity. You might not have started this journey as an ethical hacker, but with "The Ethical Hacker's Handbook: A Comprehensive Guide to Cybersecurity Assessment", you'll definitely finish as one. So, ready to dive in and surf the cyber waves with Josh? Your journey to becoming an ethical hacking pro awaits!

The Survival Guide To Maintaining Access And Evading Detection Post-Exploitation

In the intricate dance of cyber warfare, the act of gaining unauthorized access is merely the first step. The real artistry lies in staying undetected, maintaining that access, and achieving objectives without raising alarms. "The Survival Guide to Maintaining Access and Evading Detection Post-Exploitation" delves deep into this complex and ever-evolving realm of post-exploitation in cybersecurity.

From the renowned experts at Greyhat Intelligence & Investigative Solutions, this comprehensive guide reveals the hidden nuances of post-exploitation activities. Learn how threat actors secure their foothold, escalate privileges, and maneuver through networks undetected. Discover the tactics, techniques, and procedures (TTPs) that distinguish an amateur attacker from a seasoned professional.

Each chapter of the guide offers a meticulously researched look into distinct aspects of post-exploitation:

- Grasp the importance of maintaining access within compromised systems and the myriad methods employed to persist through reboots, updates, and other adversities.

- Delve into the art of evading detection, a critical skill in a world where enterprises are investing heavily in fortifying their cyber defenses.

- Explore the "live off the land" philosophy, leveraging legitimate tools and native system features for clandestine operations, sidestepping the common detection avenues.

- Navigate through advanced realms of cyber-attacks, such as tunneling, pivoting, and memory-resident malware, and understand the counter-forensic measures that elite hackers employ.

- Equip yourself with the latest strategies to defend against these surreptitious techniques. Learn how to harden systems, enhance detection capabilities, and respond effectively when breaches occur.

- Reflect on the ethical dimensions of post-exploitation and the evolving global legal landscape that shapes this domain. Plus, anticipate the future challenges and opportunities that emerging technologies bring to the post-exploitation scene.

Bolstered by real-world case studies, detailed toolkits, and a glossary of terms, this book is an essential resource for cybersecurity professionals, digital forensics experts, and IT personnel. Whether you're looking to safeguard your organization's digital assets, enhance your penetration testing skills, or understand the adversary's playbook, "The Survival Guide to Maintaining Access and Evading Detection Post-Exploitation" is the definitive compendium you need in your arsenal.

Cracking The Fortress: Bypassing Modern Authentication Mechanism

"Cracking the Fortress: Bypassing Modern Authentication Mechanism" is an essential guide for cybersecurity professionals navigating the intricate landscape of modern authentication. Written by industry expert, Josh, founder of Greyhat Intelligence & Investigative Solutions, this book delves deep into the mechanisms that protect our digital identities, from traditional passwords to cutting-edge biometrics.

Dive into the evolution of authentication, understanding the shift from rudimentary passwords to sophisticated multi-factor authentication (MFA) and biometric systems. Explore real-world case studies of major password breaches, and gain insights into the vulnerabilities that even the most advanced systems can harbor. With a special focus on red team operations and penetration testing, readers are provided with practical demonstrations, code snippets, and technical breakdowns of bypass methods.

Key features:
- Comprehensive exploration of 2FA, MFA, biometrics, and single sign-on (SSO) solutions.
- Detailed case studies of notable security breaches and their implications.
- Hands-on demonstrations and practical examples for bypassing modern authentication.
- In-depth analysis of potential flaws, vulnerabilities, and countermeasures in authentication systems.
- Future trends in authentication, including the impact of quantum computing and AI-powered mechanisms.

Perfect for cybersecurity professionals, red team operators, and penetration testers, "Cracking the Fortress" offers a blend of theoretical knowledge and practical expertise. Whether you're looking to fortify your organization's defenses or understand the attacker's perspective, this book is a must-have resource for staying ahead in the ever-evolving world of cybersecurity.

Silent Wars: Espionage, Sabotage, And The Covert Battles In Cyberspace

Silent Wars: Espionage, Sabotage, and the Covert Battles in Cyberspace delves into the shadowy world of covert cyber conflict, that unfold beyond the public eye. Scrutinizing the intricate balance between espionage and assault, the author, Josh, disentangles the convoluted web of digital warfare, where the line between intelligence-gathering and outright attack blurs.

Silent Wars navigates the intricate landscape of covert cyber operations, examining a multitude of cases that shed light on the diverse tactics and strategies employed by nations in this modern arena of intangible warfare. Through a meticulous analysis of case studies, military doctrines, and technical underpinnings, Josh unveils the striking reality that contemporary cyber operations, while seemingly groundbreaking, still embody the age-old essence of conflict waged through non-physical domains such as information space and the electromagnetic spectrum.

Silent Wars breaks down the multifaceted nature of offensive cyber operations, emphasizing the stark contrasts between various forms of cyberattacks. From the painstakingly slow and calculated infiltrations that demand unwavering discipline and patience, to the fleeting strikes designed to momentarily disrupt the adversary's tactics, Silent Wars scrutinizes the full spectrum of digital offensives.

Venturing into the clandestine strategies of prominent state actors such as the United States, Russia, China, and Iran, Josh's examination of their distinct approaches, strengths, and challenges reveals the complexities of leveraging cyber operations for strategic advantage. Silent Wars unravels the veiled intricacies of this evolving domain, exposing the concealed dynamics that shape the future of covert cyber warfare.

The Art Of Exploit Development: A Practical Guide To Writing Custom Exploits For Red Teamers

In an era where cyber threats loom large, understanding the art of exploit development is essential for any cybersecurity professional. This book is an invaluable guide for those looking to gain a deep understanding of this critical aspect of cybersecurity.

"The Art of Exploit Development: A Practical Guide to Writing

Custom Exploits for Red Teamers" delivers an exhaustive, hands-on tour through the entire exploit development process. Crafted by an experienced cybersecurity professional, this resource is not just a theoretical exploration, but a practical guide rooted in real-world applications. It balances technical depth with accessible language, ensuring it's equally beneficial for newcomers and seasoned professionals.

The book begins with a comprehensive exploration of vulnerability discovery, guiding readers through the various types of vulnerabilities, the tools and techniques for discovering them, and the strategies for testing and validating potential vulnerabilities. From there, it dives deep into the core principles of exploit development, including an exploration of memory management, stack and heap overflows, format string vulnerabilities, and more.

But this guide doesn't stop at the fundamentals. It extends into more advanced areas, discussing how to write shellcode for different platforms and architectures, obfuscate and encode shellcode, bypass modern defensive measures, and exploit vulnerabilities on various platforms. It also provides a thorough look at the use of exploit development tools and frameworks, along with a structured approach to exploit development.

"The Art of Exploit Development" also recognizes the importance of responsible cybersecurity practices. It delves into the ethical considerations of exploit development, outlines secure coding practices, runtime exploit prevention techniques, and discusses effective security testing and penetration testing.

Complete with an extensive glossary and appendices that include reference material, case studies, and further learning resources, this book is a complete package, providing a comprehensive understanding of exploit development.

With "The Art of Exploit Development," you're not just reading a book—you're enhancing your toolkit, advancing your skillset, and evolving your understanding of one of the most vital aspects of cybersecurity today.

Leave No Trace: A Red Teamer's Guide To Zero-Click Exploits

Buckle up and prepare to dive into the thrilling world of Zero-Click Exploits. This isn't your average cybersecurity guide - it's a wild ride through the dark underbelly of the digital world, where zero-click exploits reign supreme.

Join Josh, a seasoned cybersecurity professional and the mastermind behind Greyhat Intelligence & Investigative Solutions, as he spills the beans on these sneaky attacks that can compromise systems without a single click. From Fortune 500 companies to the most guarded government agencies, no one is safe from the lurking dangers of zero-click exploits.

In this witty and engaging book, Josh takes you on a journey that will make your head spin. You'll uncover the secrets behind these stealthy attacks, learning the ins and outs of their mechanics, and unraveling the vulnerabilities they exploit. With real-world examples, he'll keep you on the edge of your seat as you discover the attack vectors, attack surfaces, and the art of social engineering.

But fear not! Josh won't leave you defenseless. He arms you with an arsenal of prevention, mitigation, and defense strategies to fortify your systems against these relentless zero-click invaders. You'll learn how to harden your systems, develop incident response protocols, and become a master of patch management.

But this book isn't all serious business. Josh infuses it with his signature wit and humor, making the complex world of zero-click exploits accessible to anyone with a curious mind and a passion for cybersecurity. So get ready to laugh, learn, and level up your red teaming skills as you navigate this thrilling rollercoaster of a read.

Whether you're a seasoned cybersecurity pro or just starting your journey, "Leave No Trace" is the ultimate guide to understanding, defending against, and maybe even outsmarting the relentless zero-click exploits. It's time to take the fight to the attackers and show them who's boss!

So fasten your seatbelt, grab your favorite energy drink, and get ready to unlock the secrets of zero-click exploits. Your mission, should you choose to accept it, starts now!

Hacker Mindset: Psychological Tactics And Strategies For Mastering Social Engineering

"Hacker Mindset: Psychological Tactics and Strategies for Mastering Social Engineering" is an authoritative and comprehensive guide that delves deep into the psychology of cyber attackers and equips cybersecurity professionals with the knowledge and tools to defend against social engineering attacks. This essential resource offers a unique blend of psychological insights and practical cybersecurity strategies, making it an invaluable asset for red teamers, ethical hackers, and security professionals seeking to enhance their skills and protect critical systems and assets. With a focus on understanding the hacker mindset, this book provides a thorough exploration of the techniques and methodologies used by social engineers to exploit human vulnerabilities.

Gain a deep understanding of the psychological principles behind social engineering, including authority, scarcity, social proof, reciprocity, consistency, and emotional manipulation. Learn how attackers leverage these principles to deceive and manipulate their targets. Discover the latest tools and techniques for conducting advanced reconnaissance, vulnerability scanning, and exploitation, covering essential frameworks and software, such as Metasploit, Cobalt Strike, and OSINT tools like Maltego and Shodan. Explore the unique social engineering threats faced by various sectors, including healthcare, finance, government, and military, and learn how to implement targeted defenses and countermeasures to mitigate these risks effectively.

Understand how AI, machine learning, and other advanced technologies are transforming the field of cybersecurity and how to integrate these technologies into your defensive strategies to enhance threat detection, analysis, and response. Discover the importance of realistic training scenarios and continuous education in preparing cybersecurity professionals for real-world threats. Learn how to design and conduct effective red team/blue team exercises and capture-the-flag competitions. Navigate the complex legal and ethical landscape of offensive cybersecurity operations with guidance on adhering to international laws, military ethics, and best practices to ensure your actions are justified, lawful, and morally sound. Benefit from detailed case studies and real-world examples that illustrate the practical application of social engineering tactics and defensive strategies, providing valuable lessons and highlighting best practices for safeguarding against cyber threats.

"Hacker Mindset: Psychological Tactics and Strategies for Mastering Social Engineering" is designed to not only enhance your technical skills but also to foster a deeper understanding of the human element in cybersecurity. Whether you are a seasoned cybersecurity professional or new to the field, this book provides the essential knowledge and strategies needed to effectively defend against the growing threat of social engineering attacks. Equip yourself with the insights and tools necessary to stay one step ahead of cyber adversaries and protect your organization's critical assets.

The Quant Trader's Handbook: A Complete Guide To Algorithmic Trading Strategies And Techniques

In "The Quant Trader's Handbook," Josh masterfully navigates the intricate world of algorithmic trading, shedding light on its various complexities and revealing the secrets that drive the success of some of the most prominent quantitative hedge funds and traders. Through a blend of captivating storytelling and rigorous analysis, this guide offers readers an unparalleled opportunity to delve into the mechanics of quantitative trading, exploring the strategies, technologies, and practices that have transformed the financial landscape.

As modern markets continue to be shaped by the silent precision of algorithms, it becomes essential for traders and investors to understand the underlying mechanics that drive these systems. This book promises to immerse its readers in the rich tapestry of the algorithmic trading realm, stretching from its nascent beginnings in the 1970s to the AI-integrated strategies of the 21st century.

Inside, you'll embark on a chronological journey starting with the pioneering days of electronic stock markets and culminating in the sophisticated high-frequency trading systems of today. Alongside this, Josh takes you through the ins and outs of popular quantitative trading strategies, illustrated with intuitive pseudocode examples, like the Moving Average Crossover and the Pair Trading Strategy, ensuring even those new to the domain can grasp the nuances.

But this isn't just a book about code and numbers. The Quant Trader's Handbook paints the bigger picture. With detailed network diagrams, you'll gain insights into the architectural complexity and beauty of modern trading systems, understanding how various components seamlessly intertwine to make real-time decisions in the blink of an eye.

As you embark on this journey with Josh, you'll discover the foundational concepts of algorithmic trading, unravel the mysteries of quantitative analysis and modeling, and gain valuable insights into the inner workings of execution and order management. From the depths of data mining techniques to the heights of infrastructure and technology, each chapter is meticulously crafted to provide a thorough understanding of the various aspects that contribute to a successful algorithmic trading business.

In addition to its wealth of practical knowledge, "The Quant Trader's Handbook" also delves into the regulatory and compliance considerations that are essential for navigating today's financial markets. With a keen eye for detail and a remarkable ability to contextualize even the most technical topics, Josh brings to life the fascinating stories of industry giants like Renaissance Technologies, DE Shaw, and Two Sigma, painting a vivid picture of the rise of quantitative finance.

Whether you're an aspiring quant looking to make your mark in the world of finance, an investor trying to demystify the black box of algorithmic trading, or merely a curious soul eager to understand how bits and bytes are silently shaping the financial world, "The Quant Trader's Handbook" is an indispensable resource that will captivate, inform, and inspire you. Join Josh as he unravels the secrets of the world's most successful traders and embark on a journey that may just change the way you see the markets forever.

Sun Tzu In The Boardroom: Strategic Thinking In Economics And Management

In "Sun Tzu in the Boardroom," Josh, an esteemed entrepreneur and the innovative mind behind VC capital firm Other People's Capital and defense military contractor Fac Bellum Industries, casts a refreshing and enlightening gaze into the myriad ways ancient military strategies carve pathways to triumph in today's dynamic business terrains. Drawing from a well of timeless wisdom, the book molds the unyielding philosophies of Sun Tzu into a pragmatic guide tailored for the contemporary leader, entrepreneur, and strategist embedded in the enthralling world of economics and management.

Josh's unique vantage point, sculpted by his ventures that intertwine the worlds of venture capital and defense, beckons readers into a compelling journey through the seamless integration of military sagacity and business acumen. Inspired significantly by the entrepreneurial journeys and philosophies of Palmer Luckey, founder of Anduril Industries, and Peter Thiel of Palantir Technologies, Josh elucidates the inextricable ties binding strategic thought in ancient battlefields to decision-making amid the volatility of modern markets.

"Sun Tzu in the Boardroom" takes you on an exploratory odyssey, amalgamating profound ancient Chinese military strategies with the robust, high-stakes world of contemporary business. Through rich, expansive content that spans topics from leadership, competitive advantage, and ethical considerations to organizational culture and beyond, Josh deciphers and applies Sun Tzu's doctrines, delivering them through a lens focused sharply on the economic and managerial landscapes of today.

Whether diving into the subtle art of negotiation, peeling back layers on the ethical dimensions of strategic decisions, or meandering through the strategic corridors of marketing warfare, "Sun Tzu in the Boardroom" assures a compendium of wisdom that is as pragmatic as it is reflective, offering not just a lens to view the world of business, but a compass to navigate its multifaceted terrains.

This tome is not merely a guide; it is an invitation. An invitation to comprehend, to reflect, and to deploy the ageless wisdom of Sun Tzu into the boardrooms, marketplaces, and beyond. Here, Josh weaves a narrative that is both timeless and urgently contemporary, an invaluable asset for anyone looking to harness the strategic sagacity of the past to navigate, conquer, and thrive amid the complex challenges of the modern business world.

Embark on a journey through time, strategy, and business, and discover how the ancient can inform the present, shaping strategies, decisions, and pathways to success amid the ever-shifting sands of the economic and business environment.

The Future Of Money: How Central Bank Digital Currencies Will Reshape The Global Financial System

The global financial landscape is on the brink of a monumental shift. Central Bank Digital Currencies (CBDCs) promise to revolutionize the way we think about money, transactions, and economic policy. But what does this mean for the future of finance, and how will it affect you?

Authored by a leading expert in finance and technology, 'The Future of Money: How Central Bank Digital Currencies Will Reshape The Global Financial System' provides an in-depth exploration of CBDCs and their potential to transform the global economy. Drawing on extensive research and expert analysis, this book delves into the mechanics of CBDCs, their implementation by central banks, and the profound impacts they will have on international trade, financial inclusion, and monetary policy.

CBDCs aren't just a new form of money; they are a total overhaul of our financial infrastructure, promising to make transactions faster, cheaper, and more accessible for people everywhere—from bustling urban centers to remote rural communities. But how will these digital currencies affect global trade, privacy, or even the sovereignty of nations? And what can we do to prepare for this imminent financial transformation?

"The Future of Money" breaks down complex financial and technical concepts into clear, engaging language, making it accessible to both finance professionals and casual readers interested in the future of technology and money. Drawing on comprehensive research, expert interviews, and case studies, the book explores the potential of CBDCs to democratize financial services and outlines the challenges and opportunities that lie ahead.

Whether you're a policy maker, an investor, or simply curious about the future of digital currencies, this book provides everything you need to know about the upcoming shifts in global finance. Prepare to discover:

How CBDCs work, and their potential impact on global

economic dynamics.
The technological infrastructure behind digital currencies.
The potential risks and rewards of a digitally dominated financial future.
The benefits and challenges of integrating CBDCs into existing financial systems
Strategic insights for businesses, governments, and individuals to navigate the new financial landscape.

With a focus on both the opportunities and challenges presented by CBDCs, "The Future of Money" is an essential resource for financial professionals, policymakers, and anyone interested in the future of finance. Luberisse's authoritative and accessible style makes complex concepts understandable, providing readers with the knowledge they need to navigate the digital transformation of global finance.

Prepare to be enlightened and empowered as you explore the cutting-edge of digital finance. Discover how CBDCs could democratize financial services, enhance efficiency, and ensure stability in the global financial system. Whether you're a seasoned finance expert or simply curious about the future of money, this book offers a comprehensive blueprint for understanding and embracing the financial revolution ahead.

BOOKS IN THIS SERIES

National Security

From Roman Speculatores To The Nsa: Evolution Of Espionage And Its Impact On Statecraft And Civil Liberties

"From Roman Speculatores to the NSA: Evolution of Espionage and Its Impact on Statecraft and Civil Liberties" is a thrilling journey from the shadows of ancient espionage to the high-tech spy networks of today. It's a must-read for anyone captivated by the enigmatic world of spies, as depicted in iconic fiction like James Bond and John le Carré, but eager to peel back the curtain on the real-life drama of intelligence work.

Dive into the clandestine operations that shaped history, from the cunning Speculatores of Rome to the cutting-edge surveillance of the NSA. This book doesn't just recount tales of daring exploits and shadowy figures; it delves deep into the moral and ethical mazes navigated by spies throughout history. As you traverse through time, you'll discover the intricate dance of espionage and statecraft, and how it has continuously morphed to adapt to technological advancements and shifting geopolitical landscapes.

"From Roman Speculatores to the NSA" doesn't shy away from the dark side of espionage. It confronts the ethical quagmires, the personal sacrifices of those living double lives, and the impact of clandestine operations on individual freedoms. It's a thought-provoking exploration of how intelligence work, often glamorized in popular culture, grapples with issues like torture, privacy invasion, and the thin line between security and liberty.

Perfect for fans of spy fiction seeking to understand the real-life complexities behind the glamour and action, this book is a fascinating guide through the evolution of espionage. It's an eye-opening read that reveals the high stakes and hard choices inherent in a world where knowledge is power, and secrecy is a necessary shield in the game of nations. Prepare to have your perceptions challenged and your understanding of the spy world transformed.

The narrative is enriched with case studies and real-world examples, making it a valuable resource for understanding the complexities and challenges of modern intelligence work. The book also addresses the legal frameworks and oversight mechanisms that govern espionage activities, providing a comprehensive overview of the contemporary intelligence landscape.

For professionals and scholars in the fields of international relations, security studies, political science, and history, "From Roman Speculatores to the NSA" offers a scholarly yet accessible analysis. It invites readers to critically engage with the strategic, ethical, and legal aspects of espionage and consider its future trajectory in an increasingly interconnected and digital world. This book is a thought-provoking contribution to the discourse on espionage and national security, offering a well-researched and balanced perspective on a subject that continues to be relevant in the field of international affairs

A Comprehensive Framework For Adapting National Intelligence For Domestic Law Enforcement

"A Comprehensive Framework for Adapting National Intelligence for Domestic Law Enforcement" is a groundbreaking book that delves into the intricate process of integrating sophisticated national intelligence methodologies into domestic law enforcement practices. Authored by a seasoned expert in the field of private intelligence, this book emerges as a critical resource for military leaders, policymakers, members of the intelligence community, and law enforcement personnel.

This insightful work begins by exploring the historical evolution of intelligence sharing, offering a thorough analysis of past and present strategies. It then seamlessly transitions into discussing the current challenges and opportunities faced in integrating national intelligence into domestic law enforcement. The book provides an in-depth examination of legal and ethical frameworks, ensuring that the proposed methods adhere to the highest standards of civil liberties and legal compliance.

Central to the book is the development of a comprehensive framework that bridges the gap between national intelligence operations and local law enforcement requirements. This framework not only addresses operational aspects but also focuses on the technological advancements, such as AI and big data analytics, reshaping intelligence gathering and analysis.

The author brings to light the importance of cross-sector collaboration, suggesting innovative ways to enhance cooperation between various sectors – government, private, and non-profit – in intelligence activities. Case studies of successful intelligence collaboration, both domestic and international, are meticulously analyzed, offering practical insights and lessons learned.

Moreover, the book addresses the training and skill development necessary for effectively adapting national intelligence practices in a domestic context. It emphasizes the need for continuous professional development and the cultivation of a learning culture within law enforcement agencies.

"A Comprehensive Framework for Adapting National Intelligence for Domestic Law Enforcement" concludes with strategic recommendations for policy and practice, advocating for a progressive approach towards intelligence integration. This book is an invaluable asset for anyone involved in or interested in the intersection of national security, intelligence, and domestic law enforcement, providing a comprehensive guide to navigating this complex and evolving landscape.

Surviving The Collapse: The Citizen Defender's Guide To Guerrilla Tactics And Strategic Resilience In A Lawless Society

In a world where the institutions we rely on can suddenly fail, where society's fragile fabric can unravel, and where collapse—whether through conflict, natural disaster, or systemic breakdown—becomes a reality, we face a choice: to succumb to the chaos or rise above it. Surviving the Collapse is not just a manual for surviving the worst—it's a guide to leading, thriving, and rebuilding in the face of destruction.

Surviving the Collapse is for the citizen defenders, the leaders, and the communities who refuse to be defined by the collapse of the world around them. Drawing from hard-learned lessons in history, the principles of warfare, and the indomitable human spirit, this guide offers not only the tactical and practical strategies needed to navigate life in a fractured society but also a vision of hope and empowerment. It emphasizes the strength found in resilience, unity, and leadership, inspiring readers to not only endure but to become the architects of a new, more just and resilient order.

This handbook covers essential topics such as small arms proficiency, guerrilla tactics, urban and rural defense strategies, and intelligence gathering in hostile environments. From securing resources and fortifying defenses to establishing local governance and managing psychological resilience, this guide offers clear, actionable advice for those facing a world without order. It addresses real-world scenarios where conventional systems of support no longer function, and the only option is to rely on one's training, adaptability, and community.

Whether you are already living through a societal breakdown or preparing for an uncertain future, Surviving the Collapse provides the tools and mindset to face the chaos head-on, rebuild what was lost, and create something stronger in its place. It's a call to action for those who understand that surviving isn't enough—true strength lies in the power to rebuild and thrive.

Surviving the Collapse is built on practical field-tested strategies, taking a no-nonsense approach to staying ahead of threats, maintaining operational discipline, and ensuring survival in extreme conditions. Whether defending urban spaces under siege, conducting rural survival operations, or organizing citizen defense units, this book is an indispensable resource for those who seek to lead in moments of crisis, for the protectors of communities, and for anyone who wishes to understand how to turn collapse into opportunity, this book is your guide. You are not just a survivor. You are a builder of tomorrow.

Cognitive Warfare In The Age Of Unpeace: Strategies, Defenses, And The New Battlefield Of The Mind

Cognitive Warfare in the Age of Unpeace: Strategies, Defenses, and the New Battlefield of the Mind is a definitive examination of the emergent arena of cognitive warfare-a battlefield where consciousness and cognition are under siege. Rooted in the historical lineage of warfare, this seminal tome charts a course from the stratagems of yesteryear's influence operations to the digital subversions that define our current epoch.

The book is structured to provide a layered understanding of the subject. Part I lays the foundation, explaining how the age of unpeace has given rise to a new form of warfare that exists between peace and war, where the battle for influence is paramount. Part II describes the modern tools at the disposal of state and non-state actors, including AI and neurotechnological advancements, and the ways in which these tools can manipulate and coerce on a mass scale.

Through real-world case studies, Part III illustrates the practical application of cognitive strategies and the impact of such warfare on democracies, highlighting the need for robust countermeasures. In Part IV, the focus shifts to strategic insights, examining both offensive strategies for influence and subversion and the defensive strategies necessary to maintain cognitive sovereignty.

The latter sections, Parts V and VI, provide a forward-looking perspective on building societal and governmental defenses against cognitive attacks. These include fostering societal resilience through public education, developing policy and governance frameworks, and addressing the ethical dimensions of cognitive defense.

The final chapters speculate on the future trajectory of cognitive warfare, emphasizing the importance of international cooperation and the establishment of 'cognitive peace'. With its conclusion and appendices providing a roadmap and additional resources, this book stands as an essential guide for policymakers, security experts, academics and citizens alike in understanding and countering the sophisticated threat of cognitive warfare in our increasingly interconnected world.

Controlling The Narrative: The Definitive Guide To Psychological Operations, Perception Management, And Information Warfare

Controlling the Narrative: The Definitive Guide to Psychological Operations, Perception Management, and Information Warfare is an essential resource designed for military professionals, strategists, policymakers, and scholars engaged in the intricate fields of psychological warfare and strategic communications. This comprehensive guide delves into the multifaceted aspects of psychological operations (PSYOP), perception management and information warfare, exploring the theories, practices, and tools that shape today's information battle-spaces.

Structured to provide a deep understanding of the historical evolution, strategic considerations, and modern applications of PSYOP, this book equips readers with the knowledge necessary to effectively execute operations that influence perceptions, decisions, and behaviors on the global stage. It covers a broad spectrum of topics, from the basic concepts of propaganda and media manipulation to sophisticated strategies involving cyber warfare, artificial intelligence, and data analytics.

Each chapter in this guide is meticulously crafted to offer detailed insights and practical advice, enriched with case studies that highlight both successful and cautionary tales from past and present operations. The book emphasizes the importance of adhering to ethical and legal standards, providing readers with a clear framework for conducting operations that respect human rights and international laws.

Controlling the Narrative also addresses the strategic imperatives for military and governmental organizations, including the need for ongoing adaptation to emerging technologies and the shifting geopolitical landscape. With its rigorous analysis and comprehensive coverage, the guide serves as an indispensable resource for those tasked with safeguarding national security and advancing military objectives through the strategic use of psychological and influence operations.

This book is not only a manual but also a call to action, urging enhanced inter-agency collaboration, investment in research and development, and the cultivation of public-private partnerships to maintain a competitive edge in the evolving arena of global information warfare. It aims to inspire a new generation of strategic thinkers who are prepared to leverage the power of information in the pursuit of security, peace, and stability.

Made in the USA
Columbia, SC
30 March 2025